The Best Bread Ever

The Best Bread Ever

Great Homemade

Bread Using Your

Food Processor

Charles van Over

with Priscilla Martel

Foreword by Jacques Pépin

BROADWAY BOOKS / NEW YORK

BROADWAY

Broadway Books titles may be purchased for business or promotional use or for special sales. For information, please write to: Special Markets Department, Bantam Doubleday Dell Publishing Group, Inc., 1540 Broadway, New York, NY 10036.

BROADWAY BOOKS and its logo, a letter B bisected on the diagonal, are trademarks of Broadway Books, a division of Bantam Doubleday Dell Publishing Group, Inc.

Library of Congress Cataloging-in-Publication Data

van Over, Charles.
The best bread ever: great homemade breads using your food processor /
Charles van Over; foreword by Jacques Pépin. — 1st ed.
p.   cm.
Includes bibliographical references and index.
ISBN 0-7679-0032-4 (hc)
1. Bread.   2. Food processor cookery.   I. Title.
TX769.V36   1997
641.8′15—dc21   97-16360
                                                                      CIP

FIRST EDITION

Designed by Richard Oriolo
Color photographs by Beatriz Da Costa
Black-and-white photographs © 1997 by M. T. Beecher

97 98 99 00 01 10 9 8 7 6 5 4 3 2 1

To my love, Priscilla,
and my son, David,
and to all the children who have tasted and
loved my bread.

Contents

....

Foreword

....

by Jacques Pépin

When I think of Charlie van Over, I think of bread. I associate Charlie with the wonderful smell of dough rising or of bread baking at his home or at Restaurant du Village in Chester, Connecticut, where he officiated, sometimes behind the stove and sometimes in the dining room, for more than ten years with his companion, Priscilla Martel, herself an executive chef and a superlative baker.

Fifteen years ago, bread wasn't as fashionable as it is today, except at du Village, where bread always took center stage. The success of the restaurant was due in no small part to the warm, crunchy, chewy, and nutty baguettes that accompanied every meal. Patrons looked forward to Charlie's bread, and he never disappointed them.

Whereas most people who investigate one subject, such as the making of bread, cheese, or wine—three basic and essential components of good living—often devise a formula that satisfies them and stop pursuing the process, Charlie was never completely happy with his bread. Retaining his enthusiasm and excitement, he continued his pursuit of the elusive extraordinary baguette. His endless experimentation was indeed fortunate for me and Charlie's other friends who, as the beneficiaries of his many attempts, happily consumed the results of minute adjustments and endless variations. Charlie's search for the perfect loaf of bread has consumed him for more than two decades, and you now hold the results of his quest in your hands.

Not one to sneer at new technology, Charlie has succeeded in bringing the ancient art of the old baker to the modern kitchen. His bread-baking techniques are compatible with the demands and constraints of contemporary life. While using modern technology, Charlie has retained the essence of good bread making. The comforting smell of a fermenting starter or rising dough along with the sensual pleasure of shaping a loaf of bread by hand remains, but Charlie's process is more accurate and easier to follow.

As a cooking teacher, a Cartesian Frenchman, and a pragmatic American, I try to take professional recipes and adapt them to fit the lives and levels of skill of home cooks. Charlie does the same thing with his bread, not an easy task, since bread has always mystified home bakers because its seeming simplicity hides its extremely complex nature.

Using a food processor, Charlie has succeeded in developing a foolproof method for baking extraordinary bread at home. His method is based on the theory that the processor mixes the dough in specific ways that uniquely develop the gluten in the flour. The mixing time must be precisely 45 seconds and, once mixed, the dough's temperature must range between 75°F and 80°F—no more, no less. Achieving the required temperature is a question of balancing the temperature of the flour and the temperature of the water, so when they are combined and mixed for 45 seconds, the dough has reached the magic 75°F to 80°F range.

Throughout my life, bread has been a central part of my everyday meals. To me, a meal without bread is like a cold, rainy day—sad, boring, and unfulfilled. Charlie's obsession of the past twenty years, the creation of the best bread ever, will gratify a lot of people, please a lot of bellies, and make for many sunny meals. Get your ingredients and equipment together, and follow Charlie's remarkable method. You will never be without good bread again.

Acknowledgments

For me, making bread is child's play. Writing this book was another thing all together. Having taken on a life of its own, this book owes a great deal of thanks to all of those who have contributed to its birth. So my thanks go to:

Priscilla Martel whose heart and hands are on every page. Our lives together are very much entwined in creating this book. Thanks for always picking up the pieces and knowing when your Tom Sawyer needs help painting the fence.

Harriet Bell, my editor at Broadway Books, who showed up at my door one day having sniffed the bread from Manhattan. Every author should have a Harriet if they want their bread to rise. To her assistant, Daisy Alpert, and the rest of the team at Broadway, who always seemed to be there when I needed help.

Many thanks to those who helped this book take shape: Jane Mollman and Janice Race, who continually reminded me that it's all in the details; Thérèse Shere for her superb index; Rose Brodeur, who helped burn the midnight oil to pull the book together; Carole Pierce for her calm judgment and humor; and Bob for his inexhaustible wit.

A great team of photographers, Beatriz Da Costa, Midge Beecher, and Joel Baldwin, whose work speaks for itself. It was great working with all of you.

I owe a special thanks to my friend and boules partner, Jacques Pépin who really supported me and understood what I am trying to do. Thank you for your terrific introduction. And to Gloria, who first suggested I mix dough in the food processor.

To food-writing friends who have continued to be interested in what's in my oven: Mark Bittman and Linda Giuca, whose articles on my bread-making techniques keep bringing my ideas into the home kitchen of thousands of their readers; Bryan Miller, for casting a critical eye when needed; and Jane Segal, who suggested I write a bread book. I was unresponsive at first, but her idea was the germ that got me going.

Jane and Morley Safer for their friendship and encouragement along the way, not to mention long afternoons of serious research on the boules piste.

For their technical help, I am indebted to:

The late Pierre Franey, who suggested that the steel blade might work just as well as the plastic dough blade.

Maggie Glezer, my bread guru who writes for the *Bread Baker's Guild of America Journal*, for her wonderful insights into all aspects of bread making and her exhaustive knowledge of flour.

Frank and Brinna Sands of King Arthur Flour for guidance on the flour section and for their insights into what interests today's home baker.

Howard Kaplan, neighbor, friend and smitten bread maker who worked on sourdoughs with great diligence.

The following people all contributed to developing and testing recipes, which sometimes meant just sampling the bread: Ray Frosti, Norma Galehouse, Norma Johnson, Doug Rodgers, Mary Sheridan, and Gloria Zimmerman. And to the home team whose enthusiasm for good bread, food, and wine is a constant source of inspiration: Darrol and Dee, Marty and Jim, Brigette, Michel and the kids, Peter and Jan, Catherine and Fred, Laura Lee and Michael, Charlie and Joanne.

To the manufacturers of high-speed mixers for allowing me to test their equipment: Braun, Cuisinart, KitchenAid, Krups, and Stephan. And to the folks at SAF Instant, especially Bill Weekley, for his insights into working with yeast.

To the support of my two partners in Village Breads where it all got started, Paul Zazzaro and Greg Cook.

This book would not have been possible without the knowledge learned through the sweat and toil of the many artisan bakers who have been patiently and tirelessly making dough over the years. And so I thank my professional colleagues, those I have read about and those who have personally shared their secrets and enthusiasm with me over the years. May my work add a little help to what we do. To those who taste our bread, may we always give you the very best.

Introduction

Twenty-five years ago, I decided that I would learn to make bread. More precisely, I decided to conquer the baguette, those legendary long, crackling loaves found throughout France. When I began, I struggled to tame a shaggy mass of flour, water, salt, and yeast on the table in front of me into a smooth ball of dough. Sometimes, the mixture would be too wet. The dough would cement my fingers together and end up on my nose and the backs of the kitchen chairs. Or, it would be too dry, and lumps of dough as tough as licorice would resist my kneading even when beaten with a rolling pin.

The summer I set out to learn to make bread was unbearably hot and humid, and this imperfect environment became the ideal laboratory for everything that could go wrong during bread baking. I read that the secret to French bread was to let it rise twice. But in the heat, the dough would shoot up like the mercury on the porch thermometer, only to collapse out of sheer exhaustion before it reached the oven. The result was sad, sunken loaves instead of plump, straight ones. I tossed ice cubes and water into the oven to create steam as they do in the bakeries of France, but too much steam made the bread pale, and its lumpy texture resembled oatmeal, not the burnished, crackling loaves of my imagination. And, more often than I care to remember, the loaves looked like dumbbells when baked.

I persevered, however, determined to make the perfect baguette. And, with time and practice, the shaggy mass became a silken ball. I learned to mix a sticky dough in an oversize bowl and then knead more flour in by hand right on my kitchen table until the consistency of the dough was neither too soft nor too firm. Once I figured out to apply firm, even pressure to coax a baguette into shape, my loaves became uniformly round and smooth.

That summer I learned two important bread-baking lessons. First, in order to make great bread, you must start with dough made from the best quality flour, kneaded for the necessary amount of time so it is springy and smooth to the touch. Second, the dough needs sufficient time to sit, rise, and develop a complex flavor.

When we opened a restaurant and could no longer mix enough dough by hand for the amount of bread we needed to serve our customers, we squeezed a commercial mixer next to the dishwasher in the kitchen of our apartment above the restaurant. For sixty guests, we needed at least forty long loaves, and sometimes as many as fifty if certain bread gobblers had made reservations. I'd get up in the middle of the night to mix a few batches of dough in the mixer, and then bring it downstairs to the restaurant kitchen to bake later in the morning. Each batch of dough took 15 minutes to mix and, thankfully, my family of sound sleepers was deaf to its clackety clump and low drone.

Sometimes I mixed too much dough to be baked before we opened for lunch, so I'd cover the trays of skinny loaves with plastic and stash them somewhere in our compact kitchen to be baked later that afternoon. I noticed that those loaves would be different than those baked right after mixing. They were slightly heavier and chewier, with a more pronounced wheat flavor.

When the demands of our customers outgrew our ability to mix and bake bread on the premises, we opened a commercial bakery to supply thousands of baguettes each day to our restaurant and to other happy customers. We kneaded more than 200 pounds of dough at a time in a spiral mixer the size of a hot tub and baked them in an oven I could walk into without crouching. The bread was golden and crunchy, its crumb fluffy and tender. And yet, I was never completely satisfied with its quality, not to mention the challenges of running a large operation.

Bread had become such an integral part of my life that after we sold our restaurant and bakery, I continued to make bread at home. Always a tinkerer, I continued to experiment with bread, sometimes using an electric mixer, sometimes kneading by hand, and experimenting with longer and longer rising times to develop richer flavor and better texture.

Then one day something happened that I can only describe as pure serendipity. We were invited to a party at Jacques Pépin's house for Carl Sontheimer, founder of Cuisinart, the company that first introduced the food processor to American home cooks. Naturally, I offered to bring the bread. As a nod to the guest of honor, Gloria, Jacques' wife, suggested that I mix the dough in the Cuisinart. My first thought was, "There goes my wonderful bread." It was like being told to bring a TV dinner to a potluck supper in honor of Charles de Gaulle. I thought that mixing the dough in the food processor was a gimmick that would destroy the delicate taste and chewiness of my signature loaves.

The bread turned out far better than I ever imagined it would. The smooth, pliable dough had the feel of flour and water lovingly kneaded by hand. The bread tasted wheaty and rich with uneven air bubbles that show a country bread has character.

In the eight years since, I have perfected the food processor technique. I make bread every day in my home kitchen and I only mix dough in the food processor. The food processor mixes dough in a fraction of the time needed for traditional methods of bread mixing, and the flour stays in the bowl of the machine so I can clean up and be off to play tennis before most home bakers have proofed their yeast.

Once you try the food processor method, I guarantee it will become your preferred method for making everything from multigrain rolls to crusty baguettes to serve with a platter of ripe cheese. You won't need to scour the supermarket for the kind of tangy rye bread that makes pastrami sandwiches memorable. You won't have to keep baker's hours or become a professional to make great bread at home. On the contrary. On your very first try, you'll have a kitchen filled with the earthy smell of flour and yeast and a batch of flavorful, crusty bread.

Ingredients

The beauty of bread making is in the simplicity of its ingredients: flour, salt, yeast, and water. The baker's art lies in mastering how to maintain a delicate balance between these basics to make flavorful bread. Starting with the four most important fundamentals of bread dough, this section will guide you through the sometimes confusing world of the baker's pantry.

Flour

The purity of bread springs from the ground up, the fertile ground from which wheat grows. Flour is the foundation of bread making and, in all likelihood, the flour you use will come off the supermarket shelf. Despite what you have heard or read about it, the flour on the shelves of supermarkets can help you bake bread that is considerably better than the bread you'll find a few aisles away.

What matters in bread making is the protein content of the flour. Different levels of protein determine the uses for that particular flour. More protein is not necessarily better. To keep it simple, remember that, in most cases, the higher the protein, the more gluten it will produce. Gluten is the substance that enables bread to rise.

When the protein in flour comes in contact with water, a strong elastic bond called gluten is formed. As you knead bread dough, the gluten transforms what was a sticky mass of flour and water into a smooth elastic ball. When dough is left to sit, it ferments, releasing carbon dioxide gas. The gluten acts like a skin, trapping the gas, which causes bread dough to expand and rise.

Different strains of wheat have different protein and starch contents; the higher the protein content of the flour, the more gluten-forming ability the flour has. What is referred to as "hard" wheat has a higher protein content than "soft" wheat. Bread flour is made up of strains of hard wheat with a high protein content and the ability to develop a sturdy elastic structure for breads that will rise to great heights. To obtain a light spongy structure, on the other hand, cake flour is made up of soft wheat flours with the lowest protein content, just enough to hold the cake together. Cake flour, due to its low protein content, is never used to make bread dough. I use bread flour for my bread baking because its high protein content results in big air holes and a chewy crust.

For centuries, millers turned hard wheat berries into flour by grinding the wheat between massive mill stones. This is what is referred to as "stone-ground" whole wheat flour. In stone-ground flour, the hull or bran of the wheat berry and the rich, nutty wheat germ is left intact. When I am making a large loaf of peasant bread with a thick, chewy crust, I use stone-ground flour for it makes a heartier bread with the full taste of sweet oils in the wheat germ. For a lighter baguette, I don't use stone-ground flour because it makes a loaf that's too heavy for my taste. If you can't find stone-ground flour, add a few tablespoons of raw wheat germ and bran to your bread dough to enrich the flavor of the flour.

Flour is often bleached and bromated, two chemical processes that are used to lighten its color and artificially and immediately oxidize it. After several weeks, all flour gets bleached naturally when it comes into contact with oxygen in the air. The addition of chemicals like benzoyl peroxide, chlorine dioxide and potassium bromate, speeds the process but destroys nutrients, leaving the flour with a residual chemical taste. Look for flour that is labeled "unbleached and unbromated." I've tested bread made with bleached flour side by side with bread made with unbleached flour. The bleached flour produced a bread with a peculiar chemical smell and little of the true wheat taste. (Selling flour treated with potassium bromate is banned in Canada, Japan, and Europe because it has been determined that potassium bromate is carcinogenic.)

Here is a list of the different flours that I use in my bread making:

Bread Flour For most of the recipes in this book, I recommend bread flour. It is readily available and has a high protein content, ensuring breads that will rise to great heights. Bread flour is milled from hard wheat with a protein content between 11.5 percent and 14 percent. When dough is mixed in the food processor, bread flour produces a dough with a good gluten structure and pleasant texture. I prefer King Arthur Special Bread Flour for its consistent quality, high protein content, and lack of chemical additives, but I have used other national brands, such as Hecker's, Gold Medal, and Pillsbury, with good results.

All-Purpose Flour The protein content of all-purpose flour ranges from 8 percent to nearly 12 percent. All-purpose flour is designed for the widest range of everyday uses. Each flour mill has its own formula designed to suit its customers' taste. I have used a higher protein all-purpose flour, such as King Arthur's, for bread making with good results. If you use all-purpose flour instead of bread flour in The Best Bread Ever recipe (page 50), you will get a lighter loaf with a more tender crumb than bread made with a flour with a higher protein content. I use all-purpose flour for pizza dough because I like the crisp crust and tender crumb it produces.

Whole Wheat Flour In the milling process, the whole wheat berry is ground and the bran coating and wheat germ are sifted and separated off to make white flour. Whole wheat flour on the other hand, contains the entire wheat berry with its bran and germ intact. The protein content of whole wheat flour is generally high, between 11 percent and 14 percent. This means that whole wheat flour makes a chewy, springy bread. But the bits of bran, the hard hull of the wheat berry, can actually cut through the sturdy gluten. As a result, you don't get the same rise out of most breads made with a large percentage of whole wheat flour. The red hull of the winter wheat berry gives whole wheat flour its color and a somewhat bitter flavor. I like to blend it with white bread flour to soften its bitter taste and get greater loaf volume. Stone-ground whole wheat can be coarser than ordinary roller-milled whole wheat. Store whole wheat flour in a cool place, preferably under refrigeration, or in the freezer and use within a couple of months because the vitamin E and the volatile oils in the kernel are prone to rancidity.

A newer variety of whole wheat called "whole white wheat" is a specialty flour made from a strain of wheat with a pale hull and bran layer with a lighter taste and none of the bitterness of whole wheat flour, which can be used in any recipe that calls for whole wheat flour or bread flour. King Arthur Flour markets this flour in grocery stores and by mail order. I like to use it for the Country Wheat Crown (page 183), because it gives a subtler and less bitter taste to the loaf.

Graham Flour In the 1830s, Reverend Sylvester Graham put his name to a type of coarse whole wheat flour and one of America's favorite snack cookies, the graham cracker. It is slightly coarser than regular whole wheat flour. I use it to add a bit more color and texture to certain loaves, such as the Crunchy Wheat Rolls (page 77). Regular whole wheat flour can be substituted in any recipe in which graham flour is used.

Durum Flour Finely ground durum wheat makes a golden, high-protein flour used in Italian semolina breads and pasta. What is referred to as semolina is merely a coarse grind of durum wheat used primarily for making pasta. It is best used in place of cornmeal sprinkled on the baking sheet to prevent dough from sticking.

Pastry Flour This type of flour is milled from soft wheat and has a low protein content that is slightly higher than that of cake flour. It is used in Danish pastry doughs and piecrusts. It has enough gluten-forming strength to give cookies and piecrusts resilience, but not so much as to toughen the dough excessively. I use pastry flour in Basic Brioche Dough (page 133), Danish Pastry Dough (page 159), and other delicate doughs enriched with butter or eggs, although all-purpose flour will work just as well.

High-Gluten Flour The protein content of high-gluten flour is at least 13.7 percent. When blended with rye and other flours that have less gluten-forming protein or with heavy, whole grains, high-gluten flour ensures that the bread will rise and have a pleasing texture. It is used in bagel dough to make the characteristic dense bread with a chewy crust. It is generally available only through commercial bakery distributors or specialty mail-order catalogs. Since high-gluten flour is difficult to obtain, bread flour can be substituted in any recipe that calls for high-gluten flour.

Rye Flour There is little of the gluten-forming protein in the rye grain and what protein it has is of poor quality. Customarily, it is blended with at least 30 percent wheat flour to produce a bread with a springy texture. Rye ferments readily, which makes it a good medium for a sourdough starter.

Rye, a grain that thrives in the damp, cool climates of Northern Europe, comes in number of ways—flour, meal, or chops. Like wheat flour, rye is milled and the bran and germ are removed to make what is known as rye flour. Most of the rye flour available in supermarkets is what is called medium rye flour, a light tan-colored flour, though "cream rye" and "dark rye" are also available. Rye meal, like whole wheat flour, is made from the entire rye berry with its hull coating and germ intact. Rye meal is sold according to the grind—fine, medium, or coarse. What is known as pumpernickel flour is actually a coarse-ground rye meal available in health-food stores and in mail-order catalogs.

For most rye breads, I prefer a medium rye meal because I like the solid texture it gives the finished bread dough. Hodgson Mill's stone-ground rye flour (technically a "meal") is widely distributed and a good choice. Each recipe that uses rye specifies the type to use, either "stone-ground rye flour" when a coarse product is recommended or "rye flour" when a refined flour is preferred. If you cannot find coarse rye meal, use whatever rye flour is available. Expect your bread to be lighter if you use a rye flour as opposed to a rye meal. If you use a finer grind rye flour, you'll notice that it absorbs more water and makes a lighter bread. This is something to get used to when working with rye bread dough.

A wide variety of organic and regional flours is available and I encourage you to try them and experiment. Do as French bakers do: Create your own blend. In each recipe, I have specified which flour to use based on the flour I prefer for a specific result.

If you are interested in trying the flours available to commercial bakers, check the Yellow Pages for bakery supply companies in your area. Many have cash-and-carry stores open to the public where flours and other ingredients are sold in bulk.

Be prepared to add more or less water when you experiment with different types of flour since flours have different absorbency rates, varying from grain to grain and from season to season. The blend or brand of flour you use on a regular basis may vary depending on the moisture in the air the day you make your bread or the growing conditions of the wheat during that particular year. When experimenting with a new type of flour, be prepared to add more water or a bit more flour to a dough to accommodate the variations.

Salt

Salt serves three purposes in bread baking: It flavors the dough, enhancing the natural taste of the leavened flour; it contributes to the color of the crust; and it keeps the yeast from growing too quickly, giving the dough a chance to develop its flavor during a long rising period.

Too much salt will turn the bread's crust red, or the bread may have difficulty rising and the resulting loaves may be dense and gummy. Omit the salt and the loaves will inflate like zeppelins and brown improperly.

In professional bread baking, the amount of salt used is 2 percent of the weight of the flour called for in the recipe, and all of the recipes in this book follow this principle. When adding a starter, the percentage of salt increases slightly to account for the increased flour in the starter itself. Enriched doughs usually contain a bit less salt to sweeten the taste of the finished bread.

I prefer fine sea salt in my bread making, although I often use kosher or pickling salt interchangeably. These are natural salts with a pure, clean taste. Regular table salt may be used, but it does have a harsh chemical taste.

Coarse sea salt is ideal for sprinkling on a bagel before baking, or on the surface of rosemary focaccia, but it is too rough to dissolve in bread dough.

If you have mixed a dough and then realize that you forgot to add the salt, dissolve the salt in a tablespoon of warm water and add the water to the dough. Process the dough for 5 to 10 seconds longer to blend well.

Yeast

Yeast is a naturally occurring fungus that grows on everything from table grapes to wild grass. There is even yeast in flour itself. When mixed with flour and water, yeast enzymes allow its cells to extract oxygen from starch and sugars in the flour to produce alcohol and carbon dioxide gas. When these gases are released, the miracle of bread rising takes place as gas bubbles are caught in the elastic web of bread dough. Before commercial yeast was developed, natural yeast captured in small batches of dough was the only way to make bread dough rise.

There are three types of yeast commercially available today—instant, active dry, and compressed cake yeast. I only use instant yeast in my bread making. It is a convenient and concentrated dry yeast that is activated when it comes in contact with the moisture in the bread dough. Instant yeast does not need to be dissolved in water and proofed before being added to bread dough. It is mixed with the dry ingredients before the liquid is added.

The brand of instant yeast I use is SAF Instant. Originally available only to commercial bakers, SAF Instant is now sold in specialty stores and some supermarkets. It comes in individual foil packets and 4-ounce bags. (The foil packets hold 2¼ teaspoons of yeast, the same amount found in packets of active dry yeast.)The King Arthur Flour Company sells instant yeast in economical 1-pound bags under the label "European Yeast." If you bake a lot of bread, buy this large bag; it costs less than smaller sizes and keeps for up to a year if tightly sealed in the freezer. If you cannot find instant yeast where you live, contact one of the mail-order sources, page 259.

Fleischmann's and Red Star are two of the most widely recognized brands of yeast sold in supermarkets nationally. Both companies sell instant yeast in individual foil packets, in 4-ounce jars, and in bulk 1-pound bags available at club stores. Yeast with the words "for use in bread machines" or "instant" are suitable as long as you use the amounts called for in these recipes.

Store instant yeast in a tightly sealed jar in the refrigerator. Always use a dry spoon to measure the yeast. Moisture in the yeast can activate it and shorten its shelf life.

Wetting instant yeast before adding it to bread dough gives it a little boost. I moisten instant yeast before I add it to sweet doughs because the quantity of fats and sugars tends to keep yeast from dissolving easily. Some breads with a high percentage of rye flours, like Pumpernickel Bread, get a better rise when I dissolve the instant yeast before adding it to the dry ingredients.

I use a long, slow rise to develop the flavor in my bread and instant yeast gives excellent results. Since instant yeast is concentrated, the amounts of yeast called for in these recipes might seem small to those of you who have used active dry or compressed yeast in other bread recipes. But there is just the right amount of yeast in these recipes to ensure that the breads rise slowly to get the most taste. Use the amount of yeast recommended in these recipes, no more, no less. Too much yeast in dough will affect the speed of the dough fermentation.

If you cannot find instant yeast and you want to try these recipes, I recommend that you use the following conversions:

If the recipe calls for:	Substitute:	Or:
INSTANT YEAST	ACTIVE DRY YEAST	COMPRESSED YEAST
	(1 PACKET = 2^1/$_4$ TEASPOONS)	(1 CUBE = .60 OUNCES)
^{1}/$_2$ TEASPOON	^{3}/$_4$ TEASPOON	^{1}/$_4$ CUBE
^{3}/$_4$ TEASPOON	1 TEASPOON	^{1}/$_3$ CUBE
1 TEASPOON	1^1/$_4$ TEASPOONS	^{1}/$_2$ CUBE
1^1/$_4$ TEASPOONS	2 TEASPOONS	^{3}/$_4$ CUBE
2 TEASPOONS	2^1/$_2$ TEASPOONS	1 CUBE

With this mixing method, you can actually add the active dry yeast or the compressed yeast directly into the dry ingredients as specified in the recipe. But if you feel more comfortable, moisten active dry or compressed yeast with a tablespoon of water, then add it to the dry ingredients.

Water

Water moistens the flour, enabling the yeast and enzymes in the dough to activate and begin the process of fermentation. Water also helps to regulate the temperature of the dough; it is easy to adjust the temperature of water going into the mix right at the tap.

Overly chlorinated water can affect the taste of the bread and interfere with the activity of the yeast. Water with a high mineral content is said to affect the elasticity of the dough.

I am fortunate to have well water where I live, so I have never had to be concerned about the quality of the water I use for my baking. If you are uncertain about your water, find an inexpensive source of bottled spring water.

Other important ingredients:

Buttermilk

Cultured sour buttermilk gives a pleasing tang to bread and it helps a sour rye starter quickly develop its characteristic taste. It comes in a convenient powdered form, so it may be kept indefinitely at room temperature although regular liquid buttermilk may be used in its place. You may need to reduce the amount of liquid called for in a recipe proportionately when substituting liquid buttermilk.

Cornmeal

When sprinkled on a baking sheet or a peel, cornmeal keeps bread from sticking and gives a crunchy texture to the underside of pizzas and hearth-baked breads. Use yellow or white cornmeal, preferably coarsely ground, although fine cornmeal will also work. Cornmeal is sometimes combined with flour to give a golden color and crunchy texture to the loaves, as in the Anise-Scented Moroccan Bread (page 62).

Dried Fruits, Nuts, Seeds, and Candied Fruit

Raisins, currants, figs, dates, tart cherries, pineapple, blueberries, and mango are some of the dried fruits I've kneaded into basic bread doughs with success. Grandma's Cherry Babka (page 147) is delicious when an assortment of dried fruit is added to the dough.

When kneaded into bread dough, dried fruits and nuts tend to burst through the surface of the loaf once it is formed. To keep fruit-and-nut-studded loaves from burning, reduce the oven temperature by 50°F before placing the loaves in the oven, and then bake the bread for the full amount of time indicated in each recipe or longer if the bread is not browning. For the same reason, dried fruit or nuts are not suitable for sprinkling on the outside of a loaf before baking. Seeds such as sesame, poppy, fennel, anise, and nigella can be pressed onto the dough and baked without concern.

Milk

Many enriched breads owe their tender crumb to milk. Whole milk is preferable, but 1 percent and skim milk are so popular that I have used them all interchangeably with good results. Nonfat dry milk powder is used in a few breads to add some richness.

Oat Flakes, Oatmeal, and Steel-Cut Oats

There are many varieties of oatmeal and rolled oats available. Coarse rolled oats, also known as oat flakes or steel-cut oats, give taste and texture to breads such as Coarse Oatmeal Bread (page 71) and Crunchy Wheat Rolls (page 77). When sprinkled on the surface of a loaf before baking, the oats cook into a decorative detail on the crust. Steel-cut oats are the coarsest. If you want more of the oat texture to remain in a loaf, use a brand like Mc-Cann's Irish Oatmeal. If you use oatmeal or quick-cooking oatmeal, the texture of the bread will be softer.

Olive Oil

When I want to perfume the surface of a bread or pizza with the rich taste of olive oil, I use a fruity, extra virgin olive oil from the first pressing of the olive. A deep green color, extra virgin olive oil has a pronounced flavor that enhances Focaccia (page 107) and Savory Carrot and Leek Bread (page 83). A good quality olive oil is a fine substitute. In general, I am against the use of any oil in bread dough, including the use of oil to grease the bowl in which it ferments. Oil destroys the taste and texture of bread.

Rice Flour

I use rice flour interchangeably with wheat flour to dust rolls and loaves of bread before placing them in the oven. The tiny rice granules form a coating on the crust of the bread, making it more crunchy. To keep dough from sticking to the peel, I also use rice flour in place of cornmeal or wheat flour. Rice flour in bread dough gives a moistness to the finished bread, which I find especially appealing in the Thai Jasmine Rice Rolls (page 79).

Sweeteners

Many commercial breads are loaded with sugar and other sweeteners that feed yeast and promote an accelerated rise. I use sugar, honey, and barley malt only to enhance the flavor and appearance of certain breads.

Unsalted Butter

I only use unsalted sweet cream butter in my baking. Salt is used in butter to extend its shelf life. The salt masks the true flavor of the butter, so you cannot tell how fresh it is.

Vital Wheat Gluten

This is added to rye bread dough to compensate for the lack of gluten in the rye grain. It is extracted from wheat and sold in health food stores and specialty food mail-order catalogs.

Equipment

My bread-making equipment—peels, oven brushes, linen-lined baskets, curved black iron bread pans for baguettes—fills two closets and lines the walls and shelves of my kitchen. While many tools are essential—a good sharp knife for slashing a baguette before baking—others are not, but do make bread baking easier. You can always form a loaf by hand, plop it on a tray, and bake it.

For the avid baker, the acquisition of equipment is part of the fun. In truth, you need only a few essential items beyond those found in most home kitchens to make The Best Bread Ever—a food processor, an instant-read thermometer, and a baking stone.

Baking Pans

Almost every bread in this book can be rolled and baked directly on a baking stone, but there are some exceptions. For a Classic Pullman Loaf (page 127), a large-faced white sandwich bread, I use a large metal bread pan about

6 × 12 inches. Pain de Mie (page 129), a French slicing bread for canapés, is baked in a special rectangular loaf pan with a lid. (If you don't have one, place a greased baking sheet on top of a metal loaf pan.) I use this type of pan to make perfect square bread from many doughs; Basic Brioche Dough (page 133), The Best Bread Ever (page 50), and Coarse Oatmeal Bread (page 71) are excellent when baked in this type of pan. Just be certain to grease the pan and lid generously. To use this pan, fill it half full. Slide the lid over the dough and let the bread proof. In the oven, the bread rises, touching all four sides of the pan. When baked and unmolded, the loaf is surrealistically square with a buttery golden crust.

Metal baguette pans, either perforated or formed from curved steel, were designed to be used in commercial convection ovens without baking stones. These pans are sold to the home baker. If you use such pans along with a baking stone, you may need to reduce your oven temperature. The metal in the pans conducts heat readily and can make the crust blacken at the higher temperatures I recommend when using the baking stone. If you are making baguettes in a home convection oven, try baking them in the convection mode without a pizza stone. You may have better results.

Sweet doughs have their own special baking pans, many of which have evolved to highlight the best features of these breads. A brioche mold is known by its sloped, fluted sides, which increase the surface of delicate buttery crust on the baked bread. Kugelhopf molds are ceramic or tin and sport a ridged design with a center spoke. When baked, the loaf has a hollow in the center that may be filled with rum-soaked fruits and whipped cream. A tube pan may be used in its place. Baked in thimble-shaped cups, rum babas are a balance between a sturdy crust and the rum syrup sealed inside, but delicious baba dough may also be baked in a tube pan.

Baking Sheets

You'll need a couple of heavy-gauge baking sheets on which to proof formed loaves and bake some breads. Any will do, but look for the largest your oven can hold, made from heavy-gauge aluminum. I use a commercial type called a half sheet tray. It measures about 12 × 18 inches. (Twice its size, a full sheet tray fits inside commercial ovens.) Some of these trays come Teflon-coated, great for sweet doughs because the Teflon helps keep doughs from sticking.

A cookie sheet, a flat tray often with only one rim, is great for sliding the bread in and out of the oven. You can also use the back side of a baking sheet. (What is called a jelly roll pan will also work when the pan is flipped on its back side.)

Baking Stone

Top-quality commercial bread is baked in hot, brick-lined hearth ovens. The mass of stone in a hearth oven provides "thermal inertia," the ability to retain heat at a constant temperature, thus baking more evenly. This is rarely the case in most home ovens, where the temperature can drop as much as 75°F when baking a batch of bread before the oven recovers its heat. With the popularity of home baking and pizza making, porous terra-cotta stones and quarry tile are inexpensive and readily available for the home bread maker. Look for the largest pizza stone or baking stone that will fit inside your oven.

Bowls

I ferment bread dough in clear plastic containers so I can see the activity of the dough as it rises. Glass or ceramic bowls work well as long as they have a generous capacity. Since metal is an excellent conductor of heat, use metal bowls for mixing liquids that may need to be chilled or heated before being added to the dough. That same characteristic makes metal bowls inferior for storing dough as it ferments, the period when dough benefits from a constant, unwavering temperature. Tall, clear, plastic buckets such as those sold in restaurant supply stores are ideal for mixing starter. You can see the yeast come alive through the sides of the container.

Bread Baskets and Molds

For years, European bakers have formed loaves and let them rise in wooden or wicker baskets. Known as *banneton,* these wicker or reed baskets come in all shapes and sizes—long ovals, rounds, stubby ovals. There are two basic types, a cloth-lined wicker basket, or a sturdier unlined style made of thick coiled reeds. The cloth basket produces loaves with smooth crusts; the reed baskets leave impressions on the dough that appear on the surface of the baked bread. When using a banneton, heavily flour the inside of the basket and the loaf being placed in it. The flour keeps the dough from sticking and leaves a beautiful coating on the bread when baked. Breads rise in the bannetons, then are turned out onto a baker's peel or tray to be placed directly on the hearth.

If you don't have a banneton, line a small open basket with a towel. Flour it heavily and use it when a banneton is suggested.

Bread Knife

The best way to cut bread is with a long serrated bread knife, using a back and forth sawing motion.

Canvas

Sometimes, elongated breads are left to rise in the folds of a floured canvas known as a *couche* or bed. A coarse piece of linen is dusted with flour, then folded in ridges to accommodate the bread dough. The sides of the folded cloth hold up the bread while it rises. This soft couche makes a warm environment for the bread and keeps out any air that might dry the crust as it rises. A piece of canvas or a kitchen towel may be used for this purpose.

Cooling Rack

To preserve the beautiful, crisp crust on fresh bread, cool hot loaves on a wire cooling rack before serving. Slide pizza and focaccia onto the rack to sit for a few minutes before slicing so that steam escaping from the crust doesn't make them soggy.

Dough Scrapers

Metal and plastic commercial dough scrapers are handy for scraping dough out of a bowl, for dividing dough into pieces, and for general baking cleanup. Many bakers keep them in a breast pocket, always ready for any kitchen task that comes up. The rounded plastic scrapers help you clean every last speck of dough from the processor.

Dustpan and Bench Brush

I have a set of these to use only for my bread making. I use the clean brush to dust flour from the table where I work and to brush off the baking stone in the oven. (Cornmeal and flour fall from the loaves as the bread bakes. After a few batches of bread, the cornmeal begins to burn, smoking in the oven and leaving an unpleasant coating on the bottom of breads baked later.)

The Food Processor

The cornerstone for mixing The Best Bread Ever, the food processor is actually a high-speed cutting mixer, called a VCM (Vertical Cutter Mixer), and has been used in industry for decades. Everything from commercial sausage to face creams is made in these mega food processors. The high-speed cutting and blending action of the home food processor blade makes chopping ingredients and incorporating liquids a snap.

In the early 1970s, the first food processors were introduced in the United States by Carl Sontheimer, who founded Cuisinart. The original Cuisinart machine is the prototype on which many competing brands are based. All home models feature clear plastic bowls with tight-fitting lids and motors that run only when the bowl is covered and locked in place, a safety feature that is essential and universal because of the machine's speed and sharp blades. Some include different bowls, cutting tools, or slicing blades, but all operate on the same principle.

Some food processors come with a plastic dough blade and a metal cutting blade. The plastic dough blade attempts to mimic a mixing method similar to machine mixing and kneading, thereby creating less drag and strain on the machine. Many manufacturers recommend the plastic dough blade for mixing breads. I, however, have found that the metal cutting blade works best, despite manufacturers' recommendations.

While many companies have tried their hand at making and marketing food processors, only three major brands are widely available today. (A fourth machine from Krups just reached the market. See page 33.) If the machine that you own is not listed here, read these descriptions, because many machines will share common features. Familiarize yourself with the instruction book provided with the machine you own to find its bowl capacity and motor speed. To mix bread dough, the bowl of the machine should have, at the minimum, a capacity of 11 cups. Anything smaller is a mini processor designed for chopping and blending small quantities of ingredients.

If you are uncertain about how your machine will perform in mixing bread dough, test it with The Best Bread Ever recipe (page 50). If you encounter difficulties with your machine, read the section on Troubleshooting Your Food Processor (page 20) and chances are good that your problems will be addressed.

I have tested the recipes in this book using the three processors discussed below. All are reliable and will make top-quality bread dough. Their only differences lie in their bowl capacities and ease of use. I have not listed model numbers because manufacturers upgrade machines so frequently.

Braun When it comes to ease of use and motor power, the Braun is the David of the food processors. Light in weight—I can pick it up with one hand—the Braun can beat the Goliath of restaurant models manufactured by Robot Coupe in France. Of all of the processors I have used, the Braun is the only machine that has never stalled on me.

The Braun machine includes additional attachments that convert it from processor to mixer and blender. The capacity of the bowl is 11 cups. Its thin, sharp blades sit close to the base of the bowl and the entire blade shaft is kept in place when the lid is securely attached to the bowl. Like the KitchenAid food processor, these features help prevent dough from creeping underneath the blades and shaft as it is mixed. Long and narrow, the blades sweep through the dough with ease. The lid must be fitted on top of the bowl with some precision, and a tiny hole in the top collects dough and can be cleaned regularly with a skewer or toothpick if you misplace the tool provided for this purpose.

A push button and variable speed controls sit on top of the machine. You select the speed; I recommend number 3. The pulse feature times the motor to turn on and off every few seconds, although it can also be manually operated.

Despite its light weight, the Braun can easily process as much as 1 kilo or 2.2 pounds of flour at a time. This machine can handle any recipe in this book with ease. Another advantage is that the "base temperature" for the Braun processor, discussed on page 33, is 150°F. This means that even in hot weather you will not need to chill the water when mixing dough.

Cuisinart The grandfather of American home food processors, Cuisinart has made many models since its first machine was introduced. The weight of the Cuisinart suggests the rugged solidity of these machines. Look for a model with an 11-cup to a 20-cup capacity. The largest 20-cup model barely shakes when mixing even the thickest dough.

In the Cuisinart, a short, chunky shaft holds two wide blades with extremely sharp serrated edges. The blades sit deep in the bowl, wedged onto a metal drive shaft. Two or three flat buttons are depressed for "on," "off," and "pulse" control. The larger models come with a special lid designed for dough; a small opening in the center of the lid makes it easy to add flour, water, or other ingredients with the machine running.

Both the 11- and 14-cup models can handle all of the recipes in this book, although the smaller machine may tend to slow down and stall with heavier doughs.

KitchenAid KitchenAid markets two sleek compact machines, each with an 11-cup capacity. The metal blade is assembled so that the shaft reaches up and touches the lid, a feature that keeps the blade in place while the machine is mixing. A flat key pad on the face of the machine has three buttons, "on," "off," and "pulse," which are easy to use and clean.

The KitchenAid food processor is a relatively small machine, best for using with recipes that call for 1 pound (500 grams) of flour. For better results, divide larger recipes and mix the dough in two batches. Or, if the machine slows down during the mix, remove half of the dough and process it in two batches.

Using Your Food Processor The capability of food processors to mix bread dough varies among brands, sizes, and even between the same models. Get to know how your machine works by trying it on The Best Bread Ever (page 50). Test the limit of its capacity. If the machine seems sluggish or stalls, reduce the amount of dough being mixed. It is always easier to mix the dough in two small batches than to divide one larger batch halfway through the mixing process should the machine stall.

In general, when mixing dough in the food processor, it is better to begin with less liquid and mix a dry dough. The dough comes together in a ball and the blade is free to turn. A wetter dough may stick to the sides of the bowl and cause the blades to stop. If the dough is too wet, you may need to remove it from the bowl to add more flour. Most of the recipes in this book include the step of reserving a small amount of the liquid in the recipe when you begin to mix the dough, adding more as you continue.

When mixing bread dough in a food processor, it is always wise to keep one hand on the machine. Some processors tend to shake and crab-crawl across the counter when mixing any bread dough, especially those enriched with butter and eggs.

Troubleshooting Your Food Processor Although the doughs are mixed for a mere 45 seconds, those 45 seconds can seem like an eternity when things start going wrong. These are the most common problems that arise when mixing dough in the food processor and how to solve them. After a few experiences of mixing, you'll develop a feel for working with your food processor and will be well on your way to making great bread.

1. The dough has come together in a ball but the processor is slowing down and is about to stall.

If the machine starts to slow down and you are close to the end of the mixing, keep the machine running and add the remaining water or a few tablespoons of additional water. The water will land on the bottom of the bowl, slicken its surface, and loosen the dough enough to finish the mixing.

2. The dough looks fine and seems to be mixing easily but the processor stalls.

If the processor stalls or slows to a crawl, pulse the machine on and off to see if you can get it going again. In some models, holding down the pulse mechanism will give a surge of power and make it easier for the processor to continue to blend. If this does not help, remove all the ingredients and process the dough in two smaller batches. If the machine stalls completely, let it rest for 10 minutes or consult the owner's manual. The stall mechanism is a safety device designed so that you do not burn out the machine's motor.

It is also possible that your machine cannot handle the amount of flour called for in a particular recipe. Often, the smaller machines perform the initial mix with ease but can't last the full 45 seconds, especially on a batch of dough with more than 1 pound of flour. If your machine becomes sluggish, remove half of the dough and process the dough in two batches. Divide larger recipes in half if your machine cannot handle them. With the 45-second mix, you'll still finish mixing in a fraction of the time needed for conventional mixing.

3. *The dough is very wet and not forming into a ball. The processor is slowing down and having trouble mixing it.*

Food processors tend to work better with a dryer mix. If you are having this problem with The Best Bread Ever, Pizza Dough, or any dough in the basic bread section, sprinkle some flour through the feed tube as you are mixing the dough. If you see that a dough is not coming together in the bowl, stop the machine. Scrape the dough into a ball in the bowl of the machine and sprinkle it with more flour. This might tighten the dough and make it easier for the machine to handle. If that doesn't work, remove the dough and process it in two batches.

If you are mixing a sweet dough, which tends to be wet and sticky, and encounter the same problem, remove the dough from the machine and process it in two batches.

4. *The dough always seems to be too wet to turn in the machine.*

It is possible that your dough may be wet and sticky if you measure the ingredients with cups instead of weighing the ingredients with a scale. If this is a recurring problem, use a few tablespoons less water at the beginning of the mixing process.

5. *The dough blade is stuck on the shaft.*

When the dough works its way up under the shaft, it sometimes seems impossible to remove the blade. This wedge of dough acts like glue and the blade adheres to the processor shaft. If you can't get the blade out, remove all the dough you can, and then pour cold water into the bowl of the machine. Process for a few seconds, then remove the blade.

6. The food processor cover is stuck on the bowl, creating a seal.

As a precaution, rub vegetable oil along the inside rim of the processor cover where it comes in contact with the bowl.

7. Dough sticks to the food processor and you can't get it off.

Cold water dissolves bread dough, while hot water sets it like cement. Always wash your processor bowl, blades, and tools in cold or tepid water. Once the dough is mixed and set aside to ferment, I place my processor bowl in a sink full of cold or tepid water. After 10 minutes, all the dough is dissolved, making final cleanup a snap.

Instant-Read Thermometers

The instant-read thermometer has taken much of the guesswork out of baking. With my food processor technique, it is used at every stage of bread making—to measure the temperature of flour and water, to ensure that the bread dough is the ideal temperature after mixing, and to see if the bread dough reaches the proper temperature after retardation. I even use it to measure the temperature of finished bread so as not to be fooled by a loaf with a golden crust but a still soggy interior.

The instant-read thermometer has a long heat-sensitive probe or stem that is inserted deeply into ingredients or baked loaves of bread. After 5 to 20 seconds, the temperature registers on a small dial at one end.

At under fifteen dollars, the inexpensive pocket dial models are easy to carry and accurate because they can be recalibrated. Quality models have a tiny nut on the back side of the dial which can be turned with pliers if the thermometer needs adjusting. To determine whether your thermometer needs to be recalibrated, insert it in a pot of boiling water. If it does not register 212°F, the temperature of boiling water at sea level, use pliers to turn the nut until the needle on the dial reads 212°F.

Instant-read thermometers are sold in hardware stores, gourmet shops, and restaurant supply stores, and through mail-order catalogs that feature kitchen tools. Taylor, Cooper, and Polder are manufacturers of pocket dial and digital models.

Don't use an instant-read thermometer to measure the temperature inside your oven; it will melt. Instead, use a standard oven thermometer designed to withstand its high heat.

Measuring Cups and Spoons

Measure liquids in clear measuring cups with a 4-cup capacity. Measure flour and dry ingredients in graduated metal or plastic cups or spoons that can be filled and leveled off.

Oven

My experimentation with home ovens ranges from a battered electric stove now retired to my garage to a commercial-style gas range designed for the home cook. Each oven has its own personality. As long as your oven is calibrated and provides consistent temperature, it will bake good bread. If you feel that you cannot control the temperature in your oven, ask your electric or gas company to come in to calibrate it properly.

Using fire bricks combined with a baking stone, you can convert a home oven into a hearth oven. Fire bricks are available in hardware stores and where masonry supplies are sold. Often creamy in color, these flat rectangles withstand the heat of a roaring wood fire; masons use fire bricks to line chimneys and fireplaces.

Line one of the lower shelves in your oven with six fire bricks. Place a terra-cotta baking stone on top of the fire bricks. Lean another row of three or four fireplace bricks against each side of your oven on top of the stone. This produces an oven lined on three sides with brick.

The fire bricks provide the mass of stone needed to preserve and radiate heat. The baking stone furnishes a smooth surface on which to bake bread and pizzas. A home oven with fire bricks and a baking stone preheated to 500°F for about 45 to 60 minutes will produce a dry, even heat imitating that of a commercial hearth oven. (This hearth oven roasts chicken to perfection; the skin browns while the interior is moist and basted with natural juices.)

The Source Guide (page 259) lists some suppliers of oven stones.

Parchment Paper

Restaurant supply stores sell this silicone-coated paper, as do mail-order sources and some supermarkets. It is useful for placing under sweet dough that might have a leaky filling.

Pastry Brushes

To spread cornstarch glaze on rye bread or egg wash on brioche, I use bristle pastry brushes. A new bristle paintbrush reserved exclusively for this purpose would be ideal if you cannot find pastry brushes, which are sold in houseware stores and through mail-order supply sources.

Peel

The baker's peel is a flat wooden or metal shovel used to slide bread and pizza in and out of the oven. It is indispensable, though a flat cookie sheet can serve the same purpose. I have a thick wooden peel as well as a thin metal peel; the metal peel is perfect for pizza.

Plastic Wrap

I use sheets of thick, clear plastic purchased at the hardware store to cover my bread dough as it ferments and proofs. The thick plastic doesn't stick as easily to the surface of the loaves as regular plastic wrap. If using regular plastic wrap, dust the loaves with flour before draping the plastic over the bread. Cover the loaves loosely for the same reason.

Razor Blades

Single-edged razor blades, called *lame,* are a must for making functional and decorative slashes in the tops of the bread dough before it is baked. The French have devised a holder for double-edged blades that holds them firmly in a curved shape for incising loaves. It is available through mail-order catalogs. A serrated knife is a good substitute. I also use a pair of stainless steel scissors for cutting dough, especially for rolls or the decorative *epi* shape (page 42).

Rolling Pin

When rolling Danish Pastry Dough or even pizza dough to make Pissaladière (page 110), I use a heavy wooden rolling pin. I like the type made from a solid piece of wood. In a pinch, a full bottle of wine will do the job.

Scales

An accurate scale with tare capabilities is useful. (The tare feature discounts the weight of the container in which you are weighing ingredients.) Electronic models convert from ounces to grams at the push of a button.

Sifter and Strainer

When I need to dust a loaf of bread finely with flour, I use a hand-held sifter or strainer. It has a delicate metal mesh and lets just enough flour through to coat the bread evenly before baking. You can use your hands to sprinkle the loaves, but the sifter does a neater job.

Spatulas

These protect your fingers from the ferocious processor blades and help get every last bit of dough from the bowl.

Spray Bottles

Available in hardware stores, these are good for spraying loaves when they come out of the oven. That extra spray will put a shine on the surface of a loaf that hasn't been dusted with flour. Also use the spray bottle to inject steam at the beginning of your bake.

Timer

I use a portable digital timer to time the baking of my bread. To time the 45-second mix, I use the second hand on my wristwatch or a stopwatch. You could set a minute timer, but I feel I have more control when I am keeping an eye on my watch and checking the dough at the same time.

Water Pan

Steam in the oven during the early stages of baking produces a bread with a thin crust. To create steam in a home oven, place a small pan for water in the bottom of the oven. A small cast-iron pan is a good choice. It retains heat and the water poured into it turns readily to steam. An old pie pan or rimmed baking sheet will also do. I have thrown water directly onto the bottom of my oven, but the bottom tends to warp, and the water can cause damage or put out your pilot light.

Work Surface

I work on an old pine table. The texture of wood makes the ideal surface for rolling dough. Wood does not react to the temperature in the kitchen, keeping a constant heat. To some extent, Formica counters share this property.

You can roll bread on any surface, though cold surfaces like stainless steel may make rolling the dough more difficult.

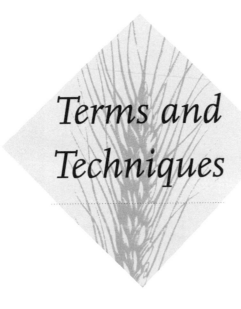

Terms and Techniques

From Flour into Dough

The beauty of bread making is that it is both intuitive and scientific. A sense of the temperature in the air and a feel for the dough contribute to one's ability to make good bread. The experienced baker relies on instinct and practice; the novice relies on a formula.

No matter how much or how little bread-baking experience you have, this chapter shows you how to handle the ingredients at every stage and turn them into The Best Bread Ever. Many of these techniques are adapted from the commercial bakery. Others are unique to my food processor mixing method. Here is where I guide you through the essential steps of making a great bread dough.

Measuring
dry ingredients
using an
electronic
scale

Understanding the Recipes

When I mix bread dough, I measure all ingredients using a scale. I use the metric system because it seems so logical to me. In this book, all of the bread recipes are presented with three systems of measurement—by weight in grams, by weight in ounces, and by volume. I've done this because, despite my urging, some of you aren't going out to buy a scale, and others think they have to speak French in order to understand the metric system. Conventional measuring spoons are used for ingredients such as yeast that are simply too light to weigh in small quantities without a scientific scale.

Stick with One System of Measurements Each recipe is really two different recipes, one formulated in grams and one formulated in ounces represented by weight and volume. Each recipe is designed to fit the average capacity of all food processors—1 to 1½ pounds of flour.

To simplify the measurements, I have chosen not to convert grams to ounces or the reverse. Instead, each recipe includes three different sets of measurements. Most recipes are written for 500 grams of flour or 16 ounces (1 pound) of flour. Since 500 grams equals about 17.6 ounces and 16 ounces equals about 454 grams, each recipe yields a slightly different amount of dough.

You must stick to one set of measurements within each recipe. If you are weighing ingredients using an ounce scale, stick to the ounce measurements in the middle column. If you only use cups, stay with the volume measurements in the right-hand column.

Proper Measuring Ensures the Best Results

For accuracy, commercial bakers weigh all ingredients, including the water. Five hundred grams of flour always weighs 500 grams, but 1 cup of flour can weigh from 3¼ to 5½ ounces depending on how it is measured, which will affect the outcome of your bread. The weight of different flours varies, depending on the blend of wheat or even the weather on the day you measure.

Flatten the dough into an oval

Sprinkle the dough with the ingredients

Fold the dough over onto itself

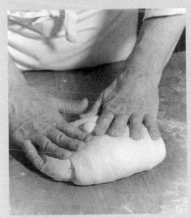

Push down to seal

Repeat these movements, folding from the right side of the dough

Kneading by Hand

I use a simple fold-and-push movement to hand-knead nuts, seeds, and other ingredients into finished bread dough and to make any adjustments should a dough feel softer near the bottom of the bowl or uneven when I remove it from the food processor.

On a lightly floured table, flatten the dough into an oval measuring about 8 to 10 inches across the widest part. Sprinkle the dough with the ingredients to be kneaded in. Fold the dough over onto itself, then push down on it to seal. Repeat these movements, folding from the right side of the piece of dough. Before long, you'll find yourself getting into a rhythm, with the dough practically jumping into place with each kneading motion. With some doughs, I use just one hand to knead; others require two. If a dough is particularly firm, I hit it with a rolling pin to soften and relax the gluten as it forms. When kneading in other ingredients to one of the basic doughs, or to a dough made with high-gluten flour, I often let the dough rest for 5 or 10 minutes before proceeding, to relax the gluten and soften the dough, making it easier to handle.

Humidity and temperature also affect the weight of flour. And different people may scoop flour into a cup with a light or heavy touch. I urge you to buy an inexpensive scale for measuring flour.

Despite my pleas, many people insist on using cups. If you do, all flour should be measured using the scoop and scrape method. Stir the flour with a spoon to lighten it slightly, then dip a measuring cup into the flour. Use a knife to level off the flour in the cup. Don't shake or tap the cup. This will compact the flour and result in more weight in the measure. Use this same technique to measure sugar and other dry ingredients.

When using tablespoons or teaspoons, follow the same procedure. Dip the spoon into the ingredient to be measured, then level it off with a knife. Measure liquids using clear liquid measuring cups.

Mixing the Dough

Mixing bread dough, whether by hand or by machine, is critical for developing the gluten in the flour. A good gluten web is needed to make a strong dough in which the structure is capable of containing the carbon dioxide gases released from the active yeast. Experienced bakers look for a stretchy dough with a smooth, homogenous texture. The dough should be soft and just come away from the sides of the bowl; it should be moist but not sticky. Break off a piece and pull it between your two hands. A dough with proper gluten development should stretch a few inches and form a transparent film before breaking apart.

Mechanical Mixing of Bread Dough For years the standing mixer has relieved the home and commercial baker of the time-consuming effort of kneading, but the quality of the bread has suffered. By their very nature, most mixers tend to oxidize the dough, resulting in pale bread that becomes stale very quickly.

It can take 8 to 10 minutes to knead dough in a home mixer, even longer in a commercial bakery where a batch of dough weighs hundreds of pounds. With each rotation of the metal paddle, dough is exposed to an enormous amount of air. The oxygen in the air leaches out some of the color, flavor, and nutrients in the dough. In many cases, machine mixing actually puts air into the dough resulting in featherlight, bland bread.

Artisanal bakers of traditional breads have long been aware of the problems with mechanical mixing. Professor Raymond Calvel, a world-renowned professor of baking, believes that quality bread requires a shorter and faster mixing time than traditionally used, and has devised a method called "autolyse" to counter the oxidizing effects of machine mixing. Here's how it works: flour, water, salt, and yeast are mixed just long enough for the dough to come together, and then the dough rests for 20 minutes. During this resting period, the flour softens as it absorbs water. Imperceptibly, fermentation begins and the yeast releases gas, causing the dough to expand. The stretchy gluten strands in the dough relax and it becomes so soft that, after resting, the dough requires less kneading than if it had been mixed all at once. The result is bread with a creamy color and the full flavor of wheat. Today many fine artisan bakers use this technique with excellent results.

Mixing Bread Dough in the Food Processor

Mixing dough in the food processor

When I began to mix bread dough in the food processor, there was no consensus on how to use the machine for this purpose. Some said that the processor mixed too quickly and violently, resulting in overheated dough. Friction built up during the mixing caused the dough to heat rapidly. Some books suggested using ice water to counterbalance the heating effect of the high-speed mixer. Yet even dry ice won't keep dough cool if you mix it in the processor for as long as some books recommend.

When I experimented with my food processor method, I deliberately kept the mixing time as short as possible, just long enough to develop the gluten in the flour but not so long as to overheat the dough. The result is that all of the dough recipes in this book are mixed in just 45 seconds.

The finished dough

What mixing method could be shorter or faster? What I did not anticipate was that dough mixed properly in the food processor bakes into bread with more of a wheaty color, more flavor, and a longer shelf life than bread mixed by any other method. I have my friend and colleague, Maggie Glezer, to thank for suggesting one explanation for why bread dough mixed in the processor seems so much more golden and flavorful than breads I have mixed conventionally. When it is mixed in the food processor, less oxygen is introduced into the dough for three reasons: The mixing time is brief, the metal blades do not aerate the dough, and the enclosed space limits the dough's contact with air.

As with Professor Calvel's autolyse technique, mixing bread dough in a food processor makes bread with superior color, taste, and keeping qualities. In fact, I believe that this method produces a basic bread dough that rivals dough produced by any other method.

Temperature, Time, and Taste Mixing dough in the processor takes only 45 seconds. Developing this dough into great bread takes time. Bakers use several techniques to balance temperature and time to produce bread with the most taste.

The Base Temperature

The professional baker works with what is called the base temperature to ensure that the bread dough reaches the ideal range of 75°F to 80°F. By maintaining this temperature range, the yeast is alive, but not so active as to cause dough to expand too quickly. There are several variables that regulate the final temperature of the dough: the temperature of the ingredients, the temperature and humidity in the bakery, and the friction created by the action of the mixer. I have adapted the concept of the base temperature in bread mixing for use at home when mixing dough in a food processor. And don't worry, I have done all the math for you.

Using a food processor and a 45-second mixing period, I have determined that the individual temperatures of the flour, other dry ingredients, and liquid in bread dough before mixing must add up to a base temperature that ranges between 130°F and 150°F, depending on the model of food processor being used. This is the magic number to calculate when using every recipe in this book.

Here's how the base temperature works. Using an instant-read thermometer, I take the temperature of the flour used in the initial mixing of the dough. I subtract that temperature from the base temperature of 130°F. I then know what temperature the water must be before I start mixing the dough. For example, if the temperature of the flour is 70°F, then the temperature of water must be 60°F to equal the base temperature of 130°F, if using a Cuisinart or KitchenAid. If using a Braun food processor and the temperature of the flour is 70°F, the temperature of the water must be 80°F to give the base temperature of 150°F. The temperature of the water is easily adjusted at the tap by adding either warm or cold water until the required temperature is reached.

Because of the type of motor unique to the Braun food processor, I have found that it performs best at a base temperature of 150°F. Use the Braun processor set to speed 3 for the best results. Adjust your recipes accordingly if you own a Braun machine with a direct-drive motor. (Krups has just released a small, 11-cup processor with a direct-drive motor like the Braun. In preliminary tests, the Krups food processor performs best at a base temperature of 150°F.) All other home food processors I have tested have a base temperature of 130°F. Most of the food processors sold during the last fifteen years have a motor similar to those of the Cuisinart and the KitchenAid. If you have a food processor not listed in this book, use these recipes with a base temperature of 130°F.

Fermentation Equals Flavor: Time Equals Taste

Fermentation is the process that takes place when dough sits, covered, at room temperature for 1½ to 3 hours. In many other bread books, this would be called the first rising. The professional baker calls this stage fermentation because the yeast is feeding on the sugars in the flour and fermenting the dough. The dough rises because the gluten structure developed in the mixing process captures the alcohol and carbon dioxide gases released by the yeast in billowing bubbles in the dough. If you've ever uncovered a big bucket of dough that has been sitting for an hour or two, you've smelled the alcohol that has built up as the dough has fermented.

Like wine and cheese, with which bread marries so well, bread dough develops its taste through fermentation. Dough that has had a long fermentation will produce a more flavorful bread, with a chewy crumb and irregular and billowing air pockets. Professionals know that fermentation equals flavor, or that time equals taste.

In most of the bread recipes in this book, I recommend a long, cool fermentation. Unlike recipes in other bread books, my recipes don't tell you to look for the warmest spot in the kitchen in which to let your bread ferment. Instead, find a draft-free area that has a constant temperature ranging between 70°F and 72°F. If the dough is too warm at the outset, the yeast cells may ferment too quickly and the bread will rise too rapidly.

For most doughs in this book, I recommend a minimum 1½- to 3-hour initial fermentation. Breads with a high percentage of rye flour, and some sweet doughs, are exceptions. The lack of gluten in rye flour makes it a dough that lends itself to a short fermentation. Likewise, the sugar, honey, or other enhancements in some sweet doughs make them more active. The yeast cells can burn out before the end of a long fermentation period.

If you've ever baked bread, you know that most recipes have a step that says, "Allow the dough to double in bulk." This is often not the case with dough mixed in the food processor using instant yeast. The dough may rise very little during the fermentation process and begin rising noticeably only after the loaves are formed and put through their final proof.

Retardation

Retardation describes the stage when dough is put in a cool place to inhibit, or retard, the yeast activity, yet leave it with enough strength for the final proofing stage after the loaves are formed. At home this usually means in the refrigerator between 37°F and 45°F for 2 to 36 hours before forming, proofing, and baking. The cool temperature slows down the yeast activity and gives the dough maximum opportunity to develop its flavor. (Commercial bakeries have special retarders designed for this purpose.) Many sweet doughs like brioche are fermented and then retarded overnight to develop flavor.

Retardation also gives you control, allowing you to coordinate the time when you want to bake your bread. If I have mixed several batches of dough, I can retard the dough at several stages. If I have too much bread to bake at once, I won't have room in the oven. Retarding the dough lets me stagger my baking accordingly.

Once you've mixed The Best Bread Ever recipe once or twice, try "A Lesson in Fermentation" (page 56) to discover the difference in appearance, taste, and texture between loaves made from the same dough, but fermented and allowed to rise for different amounts of time.

Forming the Loaves

Once you've made the bread dough and allowed it to ferment, the fun begins. You will want to portion it and form it into the myriad of shapes that make up the bread repertoire of the world. The Best Bread Ever (page 50) may be rolled into any of the shapes described below, and I have used it as a guideline in determining how many loaves or rolls of each shape may be made with each batch.

Use the directions that follow to learn how to form the bread shapes used throughout this book. With some recipes, tradition dictates that a certain dough be formed in a certain way: Ciabatta (page 116) takes its name from its shape, that of a well-worn slipper. But in most cases, the choice of shape is your own.

Once the dough has been divided, let it rest before forming it. This gives the gluten a moment to soften and relax, making it easier to roll into the desired shape. Treat finished bread dough gently, rolling and shaping in a way that ensures that some of the air bubbles remain intact. These gas bubbles give the bread an interesting texture when baked. Smaller shapes will be ready to bake more quickly than larger shapes, and will bake at higher temperatures.

Round Loaf The simplest shape is the round loaf. Its shape permits long keeping, and its crusty surface protects the moist interior crumb. In rural Europe, communal ovens were lit once every week or two. Big round loaves had to last until the next bake. The Best Bread Ever recipe (page 50) makes one classic round loaf that weighs about 1½ pounds when baked. There are two ways to form a round loaf.

The Rolling Method

Place the fermented bread dough on an unfloured work surface, so the dough grabs the dry surface when rolled. Lightly cup both of your hands around the dough. Scoop the palms of your hands under the loaf a few times. As the dough stretches, tension develops on the surface of the loaf. While gently pressing down on the piece of dough, use a circular motion to roll it along on the table, allowing the dough to catch and drag. (The tension helps to form a taut ball.) Continue rolling until the dough becomes a tight ball under your hands.

The Pinch Method

Place the fermented dough on a lightly floured work surface and sprinkle a little flour on top. With the palms of your hands, lightly flatten the dough. Fold its edges into the center and pinch them together to form a taut ball. By pulling on the edges of the dough, you stretch the elastic skin of the dough, forming what feels like a tight balloon. Seal the edges carefully or they may burst open during baking.

Place this round shape directly on a flour- or cornmeal-coated baking sheet, or in a floured cloth-lined basket or banneton with the seam side up. Cover and proof the loaf for 45 minutes to 1 hour at room temperature, 70°F to 72°F. Slash, then bake the round shape at 425°F for about 45 to 50 minutes.

Baguette: The Classic French Loaf The baguette is based on a log shape, which you then roll out to 12 or more inches, depending on the size of your oven and baking stone. One batch of The Best Bread Ever (page 50) makes three baguettes.

On a lightly floured work surface, divide the dough in thirds. Lightly cup your hands around one piece of dough. Using a circular motion, roll the

To form a baguette

Flatten the dough into a crude rectangle

The rectangle should measure about 4 x 5 inches

Fold the long side toward you about 2/3 of the way and press the folded edge to seal the dough

Turn the bread and fold the other edge toward you, sealing the edges

dough along the surface of the table until you have a ball. Repeat with the remaining dough. Let rest 15 minutes. Gently pat the dough down to an even thickness of 1 inch. (Do not attempt to deflate every air bubble.) Use the heels and palms of your hands to flatten the dough into a crude rectangle measuring about 4 × 5 inches. Fold the long side toward you a little over ⅔ of the way. Using the heel of your hand or your fingertips, gently press the folded edge to seal the dough. Pick up the dough and turn it 180 degrees. Bring the long edge of the dough toward you, folding it about ⅔ of the way. Seal the edges.

Fold the log in half lengthwise and press your thumbs on the inside of the fold

To make a compact cylinder easy to roll into a baguette shape, use both hands to fold the log in half lengthwise. This time, as you fold, press your thumbs gently inside the fold to create tension on the surface of the log. Using your fingertips, press the edges together to seal the dough into a taut cylinder. This will produce a visible seam running the length of the dough.

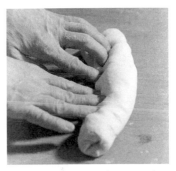

Press the edges together to seal the dough

Place both hands on the center of the log with your fingers spread apart. Cup your hands slightly, and using light uniform pressure, gently roll the dough back and forth into a long snake. The dough will gradually begin to lengthen. Don't pull on it; you might tear the loaf. Roll the dough to a length that will fit your oven, about 12 to 14 inches with a diameter of about 2½ inches. Cover and proof about 35 to 40 minutes at room temperature, 70°F to 72°F. Slash, then bake baguettes at 450°F for 20 to 25 minutes.

Using both hands, gently roll the dough back and forth

Ficelle Ficelle means "string" in French. It is a skinny long loaf with a very high ratio of crust. The Best Bread Ever (page 50) makes four ficelles. Form them in the same manner as baguettes, rolling them to a length of at least 12 inches with a 2-inch diameter. Cover and proof ficelles about 35 minutes at room temperature, 70°F to 72°F. Slash, then bake ficelles at 450°F for about 16 to 18 minutes.

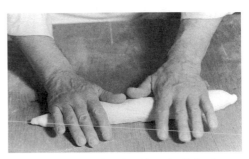

The dough will gradually begin to lengthen

To form football loaves

Press the dough into a crude rectangle

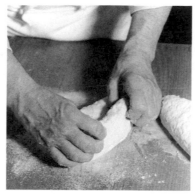
Fold the long side toward you

Seal the edge with your fingertips

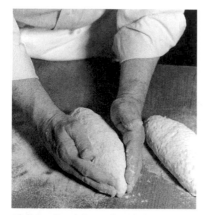
Roll the dough into a log shape and taper the ends into blunt points

Finished football loaves

Football The football is a very Italian shape, so instead of round loaves, shape the dough into a football and, *ecco*, you've gone Italian. I like to form certain breads, such as the Seeded Deli Rye (page 221) and the Walnut Bread (page 185), into plump oblong loaves. This is a good slicing loaf. Most of the bread recipes in this book can be formed into one or two football-shaped loaves. Round the ends of the loaf or make them slightly pointed as described below. The Best Bread Ever (page 50) makes one large football-shaped loaf.

Press the fermented dough out into a rectangle measuring about 10 inches across. Fold the long side toward you a little over ⅔ of the way. Gently seal the folded edge with your fingertips. Pick up the dough and turn it 180 degrees. Fold over the other long edge of the dough about ⅔ of the way, and seal with the palm of your hand.

Roll the dough into a log shape about 10 inches long. Taper the ends of the dough into blunt points; press your right hand on the right end of the dough and roll it until it begins to form a cone shape. Repeat with your left hand on the left side of the bread. Sprinkle a baking sheet with cornmeal. Transfer the loaf to the baking sheet. Cover and proof about 45 minutes to 1 hour at room temperature, 70°F to 72°F. Slash, then bake football loaves at 450°F for about 35 to 40 minutes.

To form a roll by pinching

Press on the center of the dough with your fingertips

Gather the edges together to form a tight ball

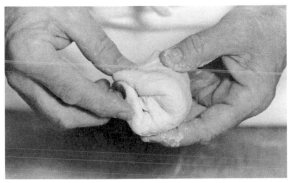

Seal the edges of the ball

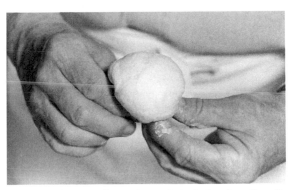

Pinch the edges together underneath the ball to form the roll

Petits Pains, Panini, or Rolls Small round breads and rolls may be formed in one of two ways, by pinching or by hand rolling. Experienced bakers roll two at a time under cupped hands on an unfloured surface. Any of these small roll shapes may be lengthened to make stubby baguettes or thick finger breads. The Best Bread Ever (page 50) makes about twelve dinner rolls or six sandwich rolls.

To Form by Pinching

Scrape the fermented dough onto a lightly floured work surface and divide it into six or twelve uniform pieces, depending on how many rolls you would like to make. Place one piece of dough in the palm of one hand. With the fingers of your other hand, press on the center of the dough, then gather the edges of the dough together to form a tight ball. Seal the edges carefully or the roll may pop open during baking. Place the formed roll, pinched side down, on a flour- or cornmeal-coated baking sheet.

To form a roll by hand rolling

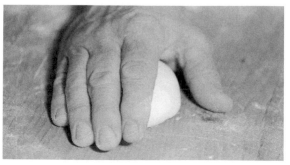
Cup your hand over a piece of dough

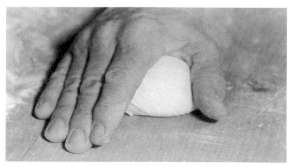
Press down on the dough

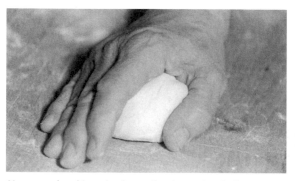
Move your hand in a circular motion to create a ball

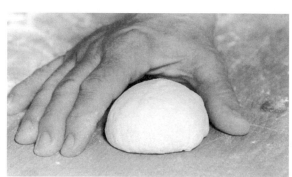
A finished roll

To Form by Hand Rolling

Scrape the fermented dough onto an unfloured work surface. Cup your hand over a piece of the rested dough. Using minimum pressure, press down on the dough and move your hand in a circular motion. As you roll, the dough will stick to the surface just enough to create tension. Use your thumbs to control it. Once the dough feels as if it has formed a uniform ball, lessen the pressure. Roll a few more times, then transfer it to a flour- or cornmeal-dusted baking sheet. Cover and proof for about 35 to 40 minutes at room temperature, 70°F to 72°F. Bake small rolls at 450°F for about 20 to 25 minutes.

To Form a Small Oval Bread

Form each piece of dough into a roll, then roll it back and forth in one direction until it lengthens slightly. Cover and proof for 35 to 45 minutes at room temperature, 70°F to 72°F. Bake small rolls at 450°F for about 20 to 25 minutes.

To form a crown loaf

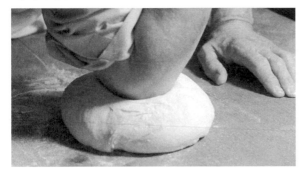

Press your elbow into the middle of the loaf

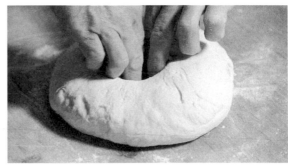

Press your fingers into the indention until a hole is formed

Use your hands to widen the hole

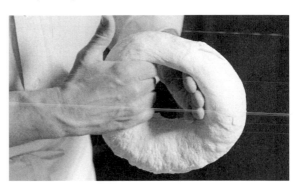

Slide your hands into the hole until the hole is 6 inches in diameter

Couronne: The Crown The center hole in a crown loaf is both decorative and utilitarian. It bakes up into a bread that looks attractive and has a higher percentage of crust. Use one batch of The Best Bread Ever (page 50) to make one *couronne*.

Place the fermented bread dough on an unfloured work surface so it can grab the dry surface when rolled. Lightly cup both of your hands around the dough. Scoop the palms of your hands under the loaf a few times. As the dough stretches, tension will develop on the surface of the loaf. While gently pressing down on the piece of dough, use a circular motion to roll it along on the table, allowing it to catch and drag. Continue rolling until the tension helps the dough form a tight ball under your hands. Lightly dust the round shape with flour. Roll up your sleeve and press your elbow right into the middle of the loaf. Rub and press until your elbow hits the work surface. Press your fingers into the indentation in the dough until a hole is formed in the center of the dough. Pick up the dough, and turn it between your two hands to stretch and enlarge the hole in the loaf. Slide your hands into the hole in the dough and rotate the dough around them until the hole becomes approximately 6 inches in diameter. Place the dough, seam side down, on a floured baking sheet. Cover and proof the loaf for 45 minutes to an hour at room temperature, 70°F to 72°F. Slash the loaf, then bake it at 425°F for about 40 to 45 minutes.

Using scissors to form the epi

Epis: Shafts of Wheat The *epi* is a loaf formed to resemble a shaft of wheat. It is a deceptively simple bread to shape. Serve epi instead of dinner rolls and let each guest tear off one of the crusty knobs of bread. It makes a light loaf with larger holes than individual rolls that have been hand formed using the same dough. The Best Bread Ever (page 50) makes two loaves.

Divide and form each piece of the fermented dough into a baguette (page 36).

Proof, covered, at room temperature, 70°F to 72°F, for 30 to 45 minutes. Just before baking, transfer the loaves to a cornmeal-dusted baking sheet or peel. Dust the top of each loaf with flour. Starting at one end of the loaf, hold a pair of scissors at a 45-degree angle over the top of the loaf and cut about 2 inches into the dough. Lift this piece of dough and twist and turn it over to one side. Make another cut about 2 inches farther down the loaf. Lift this piece of dough and twist and turn it over to the opposite side. Continue cutting and twisting each piece, in opposite directions, for the entire length of the loaf. Dust the loaf with flour and bake immediately at 450°F for about 25 to 30 minutes.

Preheating the Oven

About an hour before you plan to bake, you must put your baking stone in the oven and preheat. With the weight of the baking stone, a home oven needs time for the heat to build up and penetrate the stone. If you use a single baking stone in your oven, it may be hot enough in as little as 30 minutes, but when I load my oven with two layers of baking stones and line it with fireplace brick, I allow an hour to guarantee correct heat.

The Final Proof—Gauging When to Put the Bread in the Oven

Once bread dough has been formed, it must be left to take its final shape. This stage, called proofing, is the period when the loaf develops its final texture. During the proofing period, dough must be kept covered so that it does not dry out and form a skin. Such a skin would prevent the loaf from expanding properly during baking, and could result in a misshapen loaf.

A cloth towel, a sheet of heavy plastic, or a sheet of plastic wrap placed over the shaped dough provides a moist environment during proofing to keep the dough supple. Often I'll slide a baking sheet of proofing loaves into a clean plastic trash liner to make a snug, humid home for them. Just be certain to sprinkle the loaves with a light dusting of flour so that the dough doesn't stick to the plastic!

To catch bread at just the right moment for baking, you want the dough to be visibly expanded with some yeast activity left in the loaf. When you touch a loaf that is fully proofed, the dough will be noticeably softer than when it was rolled, yet it will still spring back slowly when pressed with a finger. Bread that is overproofed will not spring back when touched, which means it may collapse when placed in the oven. (Bread that has overproofed may be reserved and kneaded into another batch of bread.)

If your kitchen is cold, let loaves proof a bit longer than recommended in the recipes. In hot humid weather, the dough may proof in 20 minutes instead of 45. Larger loaves need to proof longer than smaller loaves. In hot and humid climates, retard the formed loaves, covered, in the refrigerator at 37°F to 45°F for a few hours or longer if the dough is proofing faster than you have time to bake it.

Most doughs benefit from a period of retardation but will need to warm up to an internal temperature of at least 60°F to 62°F before being placed in the oven. Use an instant-read thermometer to check whether a loaf that has been retarded is ready for baking.

A baguette is usually given a short proof so that there is enough energy left in the dough to make the loaves expand in the oven and burst with a handsome *grigne,* a French word to describe the crusty openings in a slashed, baked loaf.

Decorative Slashing of Bread

Moments before a loaf is placed in the oven, bakers cut the top of the dough with a sharp knife or razor to make an escape hatch for the gases released during fermentation. When the intense oven heat hits the loaf, a last burst of activity from the yeast causes the loaf to expand, rising from the hearth, swelling its sides in what is called a moment of "oven spring." Like a balloon about to pop, the dough inflates, literally bursting at the seams. The cuts allow the loaf to expand uniformly.

To score a loaf, use a single-edged razor or a sharp knife. Make swift, smooth strokes, holding the blade almost parallel to the loaf. For a baguette or long thin loaf, position the blade at the center of the furthest tip and slash the loaf diagonally toward you, making a cut that is 1/3 of the length of the loaf. For the second slash, position the blade at the midway point of the first slash and 1/4 inch below it. Slash diagonally toward you, making a cut that is 1/3 the length of the loaf. For the third slash, position the blade at the midway point of the second slash and 1/4 inch below it. The slashes will be 3 to 4 inches long, depending on the length of the loaf.

Scoring the baguette with a lame

A baguette has about three diagonal slashes placed parallel to one another. A ficelle can hold about four or five slashes. A round loaf may be slashed in a tic-tac-toe pattern with two horizontal and two vertical slashes, or it may be slashed a number of times in each direction to produce a quilted pattern. A football loaf may be slashed right down the middle to allow the bread to burst open from within the dough. The slash marks are a baker's individual signature.

The angle with which you hold the blade will affect the shape of the finished loaf. A slash placed on the edge of a loaf, angled to the right, allows the dough to burst up and out. A deep slash straight down the middle of the loaf causes it to burst open almost in two. On a fat oval loaf, two parallel slashes angled toward the center will cause a strip of dough to rise and brown in the center. Large round loaves give you a chance to express your creativity; experiment and create your own design of slashes, which will become your signature on the breads you bake.

Dense rye breads that don't rise significantly after they are placed in the oven, like the Swedish Wheat Berry Loaf (page 218), are not slashed at all but are docked: You poke a skewer or the handle of a wooden spoon about ¼ inch into the dough in a few places.

Steaming the Oven

Just before the bread goes in to bake, the oven is given a burst of steam, which protects the loaf from the intense heat and gives it a chance to expand to its full volume. Steam reactivates the yeast, increasing the production of carbon dioxide gas to promote expansion. The result is what is called "oven spring." Sometimes you can see your loaves rise up off the surface of the baking stone, acquiring a curved bottom. Bakers will often steam the oven at the end of the bake to help gelatinize the starches on the crust, giving it in an attractive shiny appearance.

You create steam in a home oven by throwing water in a pan in the bottom of the oven or by spraying the oven with water from a plastic spray bottle, the type used to mist plants. I keep an old baking sheet or flat cast-iron pan like one made by Le Creuset in the bottom of my oven at all times. Just before the bread goes in, I throw about 1 cup of hot water into the tray to create the steam. I repeat this after 2 or 3 minutes as often as three times, depending on the bread I am making. If you use a spray bottle, about six to eight good blasts of water should steam the oven each time.

Be careful when you toss water into a hot oven. A hot gush of steam can burn your hands. While you may throw water directly on the oven floor, over time the bottom may warp, rust, and eventually develop holes. In an electric oven, the water can burn out the heating element or the lights in the oven if it touches either. Don't throw water on the baking stones as this will cool them off and lower your oven temperature.

Baking Bread

Bread is done when it reaches an internal temperature of 205°F to 210°F. Determine this by inserting an instant-read thermometer into the center of the bread. If you don't want to make a hole in the center of your loaf, use the old-fashioned thump test. When thumped on the bottom, a fully cooked loaf will make a hollow, resonating sound.

If you find that your oven is browning bread before it is thoroughly cooked inside, bake at a lower initial temperature than suggested in these recipes. Preheat your oven as recommended in the recipe but reduce the baking heat by 50°F just before putting in the bread. For larger loaves, which take longer to bake, you may find that your particular oven requires lower cooking temperatures.

Bread's Flavorful Shell

The crust on bread is its flavorful shell. It seals in the moisture so that the interior crumb remains tender. The texture of the crust makes a delightful contrast to the creamy, chewy interior of the loaf. But crust also flavors the bread in a paradoxical way.

When I bake a Peasant Wheat Loaf (page 191), I leave it in the oven until the crust is a deep mahogany color, almost burnt in places, because the crust contains what are referred to as "flavor precursors." The dark brown bits actually inject flavor into the crumb of the bread. A pale loaf never has the flavor of a dark, evenly burnished one. This rule has no exceptions.

Cooling Bread

Contrary to what many think, bread tastes best when allowed to cool. I wait at least two hours before eating or serving fresh baked bread. Believe it or not, bread made in the food processor tastes even better the next day, though it tastes pretty darn good the first. Move finished breads to wire cooling racks to keep air circulating around them, so they cool rapidly and the crust retains its crunch. If left on a counter or baking sheet, the bread will become soft on the bottom.

Cutting Bread

The best tool for slicing bread is a long, serrated knife. A back-and-forth sawing motion cuts uniform slices. Even the most inexpensive steak knife from the hardware store will do a decent job if it is serrated. The kind of knife sold to cut frozen food is another good choice.

When you are cutting a crusty loaf of bread, crumbs fly everywhere and end up in, around, and under every appliance in your kitchen. Set your cutting board inside a shallow tray to contain these crumbs, and save the morsels for toasted bread crumbs.

Cutting a large round loaf is somewhat like cutting a watermelon. First slice the bread in half right through the top center. This will be the most difficult cut. Then, stand the bread flat on one cut side and slice neat pieces from one end. I like to quarter a large round loaf and wrap it in four pieces to be eaten as needed. Smaller loaves are cut in half and stored, cut

Slicing a baguette

side down, near my toaster. (A French superstition says that storing bread cut side down will bring bad luck. I disagree. It keeps the first slice and the interior moist.) I often use an electric meat slicer for cutting even slices for toast or croutons. Krups and Chef's Choice make excellent home models.

Storing Bread

Unlike other breads, those made from dough mixed using the food processor method have long keeping properties. You will be amazed when you discover that the bread you made two days ago is still fresh. Store all bread in a paper bag or covered with a cloth towel at room temperature. I rarely refrigerate bread, preferring to freeze it as soon as possible. Freezing is the best way to store fresh loaves of your favorite bread if you plan on serving them later in the week or are building inventory for a special party.

To store bread in the freezer, place the loaves in a plastic bag. Use a large clean trash can liner to store several loaves together. It saves space and wastes less plastic. Or, wrap each loaf in plastic wrap. When stored this way, breads will stay fresh in the freezer for up to one month.

Often I'll slice a sandwich loaf, then freeze it in a plastic bag. When I want a slice for toast, I remove what I need and thaw it in the toaster. I keep sliced bread for bruschetta on hand the same way.

Doughs made with butter and eggs will keep overnight, covered, at room temperature, but are best if tightly wrapped in plastic and frozen until ready to be served.

Reviving Stored Breads If you should have leftover bread, The Best Bread Ever can easily be stored at room temperature for a couple of days. What is important is that you revive the bread properly.

To revive rolls, baguettes, and thin loaves that have been stored at room temperature for a day or two, preheat the oven to 375°F to 400°F. Place the bread directly on the oven rack and heat for 6 to 8 minutes. This will restore the crust and moisten the crumb.

Long-fermented rustic breads, like Country Wheat Crown (page 183), often need little reviving.

To restore frozen baguettes, rolls, or ciabatta-type bread, remove the wrapping. Let the bread come to room temperature for 10 to 15 minutes while preheating the oven to 375°F to 400°F. Place the bread directly on the oven rack and heat it for 6 to 8 minutes.

To revive larger loaves of frozen bread, unwrap the loaves and let them come to room temperature for 30 minutes. Preheat the oven to 375°F. Place the bread directly on the rack in the oven and bake for 15 to 20 minutes, until the crust is crisp and the interior fluffy.

To revive frozen sweet breads like brioche, challah, or stollen, unwrap the loaves and let them come to room temperature for 10 to 15 minutes while preheating the oven to 350°F. Place the bread directly on the oven rack and heat for 15 to 20 minutes. The crust should be crisp and the center moist.

Sharing a Gift of Bread

While some people search for that special bottle of wine or flowers to take to a host, my calling card is always a basket of bread with a note on how to serve it.

If you are giving baguettes, ficelles, or rolls, the note should read:

1. Preheat oven to 375°F to 400°F. Place the bread directly on the oven rack and heat for 6 to 8 minutes. The crust should be crisp and the interior moist and fluffy.

2. If you freeze this bread, thaw it at room temperature for 10 minutes before reheating. (Frozen bread may take a few minutes longer in the oven.)

For larger gift loaves, the note might say:

1. Preheat oven to 350°F to 375°F. Place unwrapped bread directly on the oven rack for about 15 minutes. The crust should be crisp and the interior moist and fluffy.

2. Thaw frozen bread at room temperature for 30 minutes before slicing and serving or thaw and reheat it at 375°F for 15 to 20 minutes.

The Best Bread Ever
(page 50)

Walnut Bread with Mixed Green Salad
(page 185)

Pumpernickel Bread
(page 224)

From top: Pizza Margherita (page 98), *Focaccia* (page 107),
and Provençal Pizza (page 101)

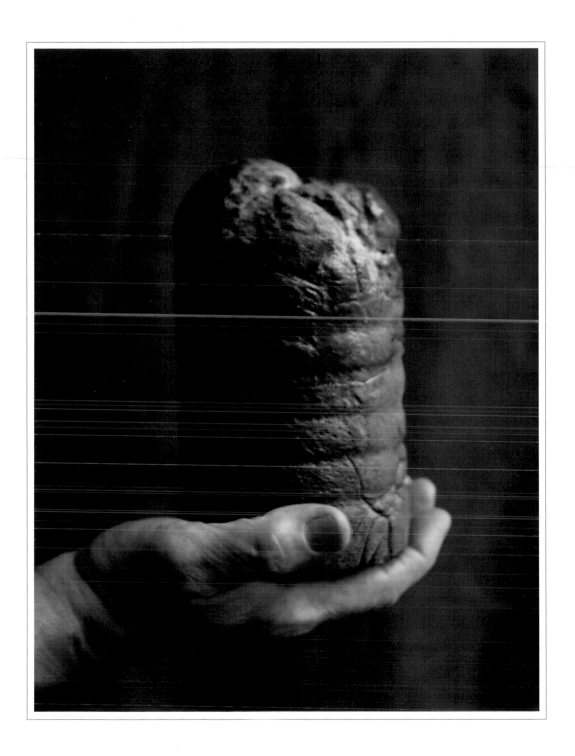

Brioche Mousseline
(page 137)

Danish Twists
(page 162)

Sesame Bagel with Smoked Salmon and Crème Fraîche
(page 251)

Grilled Vegetable Sandwich
(page 255)

The Best Bread Ever

This is the most important chapter in this book, a step-by-step guide to mixing dough in the food processor. Read this chapter carefully, try the basic recipe, and then put up your feet and let this unassuming dough develop. Bread with character, a golden crumb, irregular texture, and a rich taste and aroma is within your grasp using the methods outlined in this chapter.

If you have always thought that baking bread was too time-consuming or if you are terrorized by the thought of a kitchen dredged in flour, read on. In just 45 seconds, you can mix a batch of dough and have crusty bread on the table the very first time you bake. If you feel awkward rolling dough into the classic long French loaf shape detailed in the basic recipe, form it into a simple round loaf or dinner rolls instead for delicious results.

Once you feel comfortable with the mixing method, experiment to see how a longer fermentation changes the taste and appearance of your bread. If you prefer a fluffy crumb, use the mix and rest mixing method described in this chapter. If you're the creative type who likes to put your initials or signature on every thing you own, follow the guidelines for customizing bread. Try a mixture of different types of flour and some whole grains, or knead in nuts, seeds, or raisins to make a bread that is uniquely your own.

Should you want to convert your favorite recipes to kneading in the food processor, turn the page to learn the trick. You need never go beyond this chapter to bring the appetizing smells fresh of bread and the pleasure of creating something with your own hands back into your kitchen.

The Best Bread Ever

Dough that is too dry

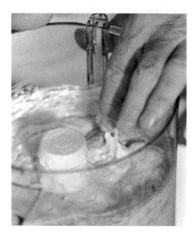

Dough that is too moist

Each step in this recipe is designed to make you feel at ease mixing dough in the food processor. If you've made bread by hand before, then you're accustomed to adding water to the flour as it mixes if the dough feels too firm or flour if the dough feels sticky. When mixing dough in the food processor, you will achieve the same results by holding back a few tablespoons of the water at the beginning of the mixing, adding it if the dough appears to be crumbly or if it is not coming together into a ball in the bowl. Depending on the brand and type of flour you are using, you may not need to add all of the water called for in the recipe. Set out all of your ingredients and have extra flour and a small amount of cool water handy should you need to make adjustments.

The first few times you mix this dough, stop the machine and feel the dough. If it feels very soft and clings to your fingers, add a few tablespoons more flour then resume mixing the dough for the time remaining. Once you have mixed this dough a few times, you'll probably end up throwing the entire amount of water in at the beginning.

Unlike many bread doughs you may be familiar with, this dough does not always double in bulk. In fact, it may seem down-right sleepy as it quietly ferments. Once the dough is formed into loaves, it becomes more active. The loaves will puff and swell.

The beauty of this dough is its versatility. Use it to make baguettes or hearty peasant rolls. *Make this dough with bread flour as I do or with all-purpose flour for a lighter texture. Once you become adept with this recipe, experiment by adding different blends of flours.*

The Lesson in Fermentation (page 56) explains how you can store unbaked loaves in the refrigerator to be baked when you have the time to do so.

This recipe makes three long baguettes or the dough can be divided and formed into any of the shapes described in the section on forming bread (pages 35–42).

If you are making baguettes in a home convection oven, try baking them in the convection mode without a pizza stone. You may get better results.

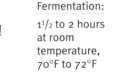

Three 14-inch loaves

Fermentation:
1¹/₂ to 2 hours at room temperature, 70°F to 72°F

Proofing:
35 to 40 minutes at room temperature

Unbleached bread flour	500 grams	1 pound	3¹/₃ to 4 cups
Fine sea salt	10 grams	2 teaspoons	2 teaspoons
Instant yeast	1 teaspoon	1 teaspoon	1 teaspoon
Water	315 grams	10 ounces	1¹/₄ cups
Cornmeal for the baking sheet			

1. Place the flour, salt, and yeast in a food processor fitted with the metal blade. Using an instant-read thermometer, adjust the water temperature so that the combined temperatures of the water and the flour give a base temperature of 130°F if using a Cuisinart or KitchenAid or 150°F if using a

Pour the water through the feed tube

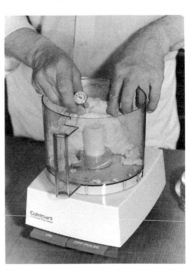

Process the dough for a total of 45 seconds

The temperature of the dough should be between 75°F and 80°F

Braun. (See page 33 for other models.) With the machine running, pour all but 2 tablespoons of the water through the feed tube. Process for 20 seconds, adding the remaining water if the dough seems crumbly and dry and does not come together into a ball during this time. Continue mixing the dough another 25 seconds, for a total of 45 seconds.

2. Stop the machine and take the temperature of the dough with an instant-read thermometer, which should read between 75°F and 80°F. If the temperature is lower than 75°F, process the dough for an additional 5 seconds. If the temperature of the dough is still lower than 75°F, then process the dough for 5 seconds, up to twice more, until it reaches the desired temperature. If the temperature is higher than 80°F, remove the thermometer, scrape the dough from the food processor into an ungreased bowl, and refrigerate for 5 to 10 minutes. Check the temperature of the dough after 5 minutes; the dough should be 80°F or cooler by that time.

3. Remove the dough from the processor and place it in a large ungreased bowl. Cover the bowl with plastic wrap and allow the dough to ferment for 1½ to 2 hours at room temperature, about 70°F to 72°F. It will increase in volume somewhat, but don't be concerned by how much.

4. Turn the dough onto a lightly floured work surface. With a dough scraper or kitchen knife, divide the dough into 3 equal pieces and shape them into rough balls. Cover them with a sheet of plastic wrap and let rest for 15 to 20 minutes.

5. In preparation for the final proofing, spread a sheet of canvas or a heavy linen cloth on a counter or tabletop and sprinkle it lightly with flour. (If using a baguette pan, spray it with vegetable cooking spray.)

6. Sift a fine coating of flour on the work surface. Place one ball of dough on the surface and gently pat it down to an even thickness of 1 inch. Do not attempt to deflate every air bubble. Using the heels and palms of your hands, flatten the dough into a crude rectangle measuring about 4 × 5 inches and 1 inch thick. Fold the long side farthest from you a little over ⅔ of the way toward you. Using the heel of your hand, gently press the folded edge to seal the dough. Pick up the dough and turn it 180 degrees. Fold over the other long edge of the dough about ⅔ of the way, and seal with the palm of your hand.

7. To make a compact cylinder easy to roll into a baguette shape, use both hands to fold the log in half lengthwise. This time, as you fold, press your thumbs gently inside the fold to create tension on the surface of the log. Using your fingertips, press the edges together to seal the dough into a taut cylinder. This will produce a visible seam running the length of the dough.

8. To roll the dough into a baguette shape, place both hands on the center of the log with your fingers spread apart. Using light uniform pressure, gently roll the dough back and forth into a long snake. Taking care not to stretch the dough, move your hands from the center of the dough to the ends as the loaf begins to lengthen to about 14 inches. If the dough resists rolling, let it rest for 5 minutes before continuing. Repeat steps 6 through 8 with the remaining dough.

9. Using both hands, gently transfer each baguette, seam side up, to the lightly floured cloth. Fold the fabric up to form channels in which each loaf will rise. (Place the baguettes close together so that they rise and don't spread out.) Sprinkle the loaves with flour and cover them loosely with plastic wrap or a kitchen towel. Let the baguettes proof for 30 to 45 minutes, until the dough increases by half its size. It should feel soft but still spring back slightly when poked with your finger.

Proofing the baguettes in a couche

10. One hour before baking, put the oven rack on the second shelf from the bottom of the oven and place the baking stone on the rack. Place a small pan for water on the oven floor. Preheat the oven to 475°F.

11. Uncover the loaves. Place them seam side down on a peel or on the back of a baking sheet that has been lightly sprinkled with cornmeal. Or place the loaves in greased and lightly floured baguette pans. Sprinkle each loaf lightly with flour, and slash the tops several times diagonally with a razor blade.

12. Carefully pour about 1 cup of warm water into the pan on the oven floor. Slide the baguettes from the peel or the back of the baking sheet onto the baking stone in the oven. Or, place the baguette pan directly on the baking stone. Reduce the heat to 450°F.

Store the bread in a paper bag or loosely covered with a towel at room temperature. The bread will remain fresh for up to two days at room temperature when covered with a towel.

13. Bake the loaves for 2 minutes. Open the oven and quickly pour another cup of water into the pan on the oven floor. Continue baking for 20 to 22 minutes until the crust is golden brown. Tap the bottom of the loaves; a hollow sound means they're done. Or, insert an instant-read thermometer into the bread, and if the internal temperature is 205°F to 210°F, the bread is done.

14. Remove the bread from the oven and immediately place the loaves on a wire rack to cool completely before storing.

For Lighter, Fluffier Bread

When I want a light-textured baguette with a fluffy crumb, I use a slightly different mixing method. Once the dough has come together into a visible ball of dough in the bowl of the food processor (after about 20 seconds of mixing), I stop the machine and let the dough rest in the processor bowl for about 5 to 10 minutes.

As the dough rests, the gluten relaxes and the dough begins to ferment. It softens perceptibly during this brief pause in the mixing. Then I complete the mixing for the remaining 25 seconds and proceed with the recipe.

I often use this method when making Semolina Bread (page 60) or Crunchy Wheat Rolls (page 77).

The Best Bread Ever Dough Makes Classic Bread

Like any classic, it is always good and never goes out of style. By adding simple ingredients to the basic dough, you can create as many variations as your imagination allows, changing the bread to make it your own or adapting it to the type of food you are serving.

Here are some of my favorite additions. Add chopped fresh or dried herbs and spices directly to the flour before mixing the dough in the food processor. Scrape the mixed dough onto a lightly floured work surface and knead in chopped nuts, vegetables, or diced fruits by hand.

Herb Bread—1/2 cup chopped fresh parsley, chives, marjoram, tarragon, or any combination

Lemon Pepper Bread—2 tablespoons coarse black pepper and 1 tablespoon grated lemon zest

Eight Steps to Making the Best Bread Ever

1. Use the food processor fitted with the metal blade to mix and knead dough.

2. Be precise in measuring all ingredients. A scale is best. If you are measuring by volume, be consistent in your measuring.

3. Use instant yeast for ease of handling and superb results.

4. The temperature of the water is neither lukewarm nor ice cold. The water temperature must be calculated based on the temperature of the flour being used. Use the "base temperature," the magic number for mixing dough in the food processor.

5. Mix the dough for 45 seconds. This short mixing time is designed not to overmix the dough.

6. Careful measurement of the finished dough temperature ensures excellent results. An instant-read thermometer is one of the baker's better friends. Use it at every stage of bread making.

7. Time equals taste or fermentation equals flavor. Learn to understand the desirability of a lengthy, cool rise to produce the most flavorful breads.

8. Bake at the recommended oven temperatures and steam the oven to create crackling crust on breads.

Sun-dried Tomato and Basil Bread—$^1/_2$ cup fresh basil leaves, tightly packed, then shredded, and $^1/_4$ cup sun-dried tomatoes cut into thin strips
Simple Olive Bread—$^1/_2$ cup each pitted black olives such as kalamata or niçoise and $^1/_2$ cup pitted green olives
Nut and Fruit Loaf—$^1/_2$ cup chopped roasted almonds and $^1/_2$ cup dried cherries, $^1/_2$ cup raisins, $^1/_2$ cup dried cranberries, or $^1/_2$ cup dry currants
Summer Vegetable Bread—$^1/_2$ cup grated carrots, $^1/_2$ cup grated zucchini, and $^1/_4$ cup chopped celery leaves
Autumn Harvest Loaf—$^1/_2$ cup diced fresh pears, $^1/_2$ cup diced fresh apples, and $^1/_2$ cup chopped toasted walnuts

A Lesson in Fermentation

4 baguettes
and one 10-
inch round loaf

BREAD 1
Fermentation:

1¹/₂ to 2 hours
at room
temperature,
70°F to 72°F

Proofing:

30 to 45
minutes at
room
temperature

BREAD 2
Fermentation:

1¹/₂ to 2 hours
at room
temperature,
70°F to 72°F

Retardation:

3 to 4 hours
in the
refrigerator,
37°F to 45°F

Proofing:

1¹/₂ to 2 hours
at room
temperature

From The Best Bread Ever dough you can make three breads with distinctly different tastes and textures. Use the power of retardation, slowing down the action of the yeast by placing the dough in the refrigerator, to develop flavor in each loaf.

Time is one of the most powerful tools the baker can employ to create flavor and texture in a loaf of bread. As bread dough ferments and the yeast begins to react to the nourishment in the flour, the ingredients develop complexities that change the way a finished loaf of bread will look and taste. A baguette that has been fermented for 3 hours will have a fluffy crumb and a rich, full taste. A baguette made with the same dough that has fermented overnight under the chill of refrigeration will have a more compact crumb with a deeper color and chewier texture. That same dough left to ferment even longer and baked into a plump, round shape will develop a thicker crumb and denser, darker crust.

To discover the effects of a long rise on the appearance, taste, and texture of bread, try the following experiment. No one would ever suspect that these three breads came from the same batch of dough. Use the lessons learned in this experiment to develop the maximum flavor in all the breads you make.

Retardation lets you control when you will bake your bread. If you mix a batch of dough and find that you don't have time to bake it, place it in the refrigerator and bake it later. Note that chilled bread dough is firm and needs to warm up before it can be easily handled.

2 recipes The Best Bread Ever dough	Cornmeal for the baking sheet

1. Combine the two batches of dough in a large, ungreased bowl. Cover the bowl with plastic wrap and let the dough ferment at room temperature, 70°F to 72°F, for 1¹/₂ to 2 hours.

2. Remove ¹/₃ of the dough and divide it into 2 pieces. Form the dough into 2 baguettes, proof, and bake the loaves as directed in The Best Bread Ever recipe. Cool the loaves and store them.

3. Cover the remaining dough and retard it in the refrigerator for 3 to 4 hours.

4. Take the bowl of dough from the refrigerator and remove half of the dough.

Place it on a lightly floured work surface. Cover the remaining dough and retard it in the refrigerator for 8 to 12 additional hours.

5. With a kitchen knife or dough scraper, divide the dough on the work surface into 2 pieces. Cover the dough with plastic wrap and let it rest for 15 to 20 minutes until it warms slightly and is easy to handle. Form the dough into 2 baguettes as directed in The Best Bread Ever recipe.

6. Proof the baguettes for about 1½ to 2 hours, until the dough is soft and visibly doubled in bulk. Because the dough will be cool from the refrigerator, allow the formed loaves sufficient time to come to room temperature. The dough will be ready to bake when an instant-read thermometer shows it has reached an internal temperature of 60°F to 62°F. Bake the bread as directed in The Best Bread Ever recipe. Cool and store the loaves.

BREAD 3
Fermentation:
1½ to 2 hours at room temperature, 70°F to 72°F

Retardation:
12 to 16 hours in the refrigerator, 37°F to 45°F

Proofing:
1½ to 2 hours at room temperature

7. Remove the last piece of dough from the refrigerator, scrape it onto a lightly floured work surface and form it into a round shape (page 35). Place the formed loaf on a floured baking sheet or in a floured banneton, cover the loaf, and let it proof at room temperature for about 1½ to 2 hours, until it visibly doubles in bulk. The dough will be ready to bake when an instant-read thermometer shows it has reached an internal temperature of 60°F to 62°F.

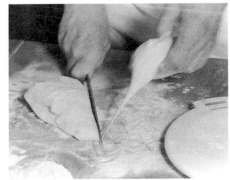

Dividing the dough

8. One hour before baking, place a small pan for water on the floor of the oven, put the oven rack on the second shelf from the bottom of the oven, and place the baking stone on the rack. Preheat the oven to 475°F. Transfer the bread onto a peel or onto the back of a baking sheet heavily coated with cornmeal.

9. Carefully pour about 1 cup of hot water into the pan on the floor of the oven. Slide the loaf from the peel or baking sheet directly onto the baking stone and turn the heat down to 450°F.

10. Bake the loaf for 2 minutes. Create steam by adding another cup of water to the pan on the floor of the oven. Continue baking for 40 to 45 minutes, until the crust is a dark brown. Or, the bread will be finished when it reaches an internal temperature of 205°F to 210°F on an instant-read thermometer. Cool the bread on a wire rack before cutting.

Converting Your Favorite Bread Recipe to The Best Bread Ever Method

Mixing any yeast bread dough using the food-processor method described in this book is easy, and will probably improve the bread. If you have a favorite bread dough recipe, especially one that uses a large percentage of wheat flour, use The Best Bread Ever recipe as a template to guide you on how much yeast, salt, and water to use in your recipe. If you are converting a recipe with starter, use the Country Baguettes with Starter (page 180) as your guide.

Figure out the weight of all of the dry ingredients in the recipe. If the flours total about 500 grams or 1 pound, you're in luck, and you won't have to make many changes. (The large Cuisinart and the Braun processor can handle up to 750 grams or 1½ pounds of flour with ease.) If the recipe is larger, reduce the amount of dry ingredients so that the dough will fit in your machine, or divide the recipe in two. For 500 grams or 1 pound of flour, use 1 teaspoon of instant yeast. If your recipe calls for a starter, reduce the yeast to ¾ teaspoon for 500 grams of flour.

Different flours absorb different amounts of water. If you are converting a wheat flour recipe to The Best Bread Ever method, try using the same amount of water specified in The Best Bread Ever or the Country Baguette with Starter. Most bread doughs in this book are 60 percent to 65 percent liquid. The Best Bread Ever dough is 63 percent. This means that the weight of the liquid in the recipe is between 60 percent and 65 percent of the weight of the flour. If you take the weight of the flour in your recipe and multiply it by 63 percent, you will come up with the quantity of water to use in your recipe to come up with a bread dough that is about the same consistency as The Best Bread Ever dough.

Or, note the amount of liquid called for in your favorite recipe, including any that is used to dissolve yeast. Measure that amount of liquid and adjust its temperature according to base temperature for your machine.

When adjusting the temperature of your ingredients, if the recipe calls for less than 2 eggs, don't be concerned about the temperature of the eggs. If it calls for more than 2 eggs, add the eggs to the liquid and adjust the temperature according to the method outlined in The Best Bread Ever recipe.

Mix the dough according to The Best Bread Ever recipe or the Country Baguette with Starter recipe, holding back some of the water to see how the dough comes together in the bowl of the food processor. Mix the dough for 20 seconds and, with the machine running, add more water or flour if needed. Then process for the remaining 25 seconds.

Ferment the dough for at least 1½ hours, or the time recommended in your recipe. Your recipe may call this the "first rise." Form and proof the dough.

Breads, Rolls, and Bagels

The breads in this chapter would make any baker proud, from a rich Italian semolina loaf formed into a chunky half moon to the kind of bread served in Morocco to eat with olives and a crisp salad.

If you have admired the beautiful breads adorned with designs in dough, use the recipes and tips in this chapter to make them with your own hands. Learn how to make a bagel as good as those sold on the streets of New York right in your own kitchen. Or try an untraditional rice bread flavored with lemongrass. Make a meal from a slice of bread starring bits of ham and cheese or a spongy square loaf stuffed with savory vegetables. From earthy rolls from the heartland to substantial loaves that brim with cooked oatmeal, this chapter offers many varieties of breads that are easy to make and wonderful to serve.

Semolina Bread

Two 8-inch
curved loaves

Fermentation:

2 to 2½ hours
at room
temperature,
70°F to 72°F

Proofing:

1 to 1½ hours
at room
temperature

If the golden color or the nutty fragrance of toasted sesame seeds doesn't whet your appetite, then the delicate open crumb and chewiness of this semolina bread will. The food processor does a yeoman's job developing the gluten in the durum wheat, the same resilient grain used to make pasta in Italy. Durum flour has a high protein content, making for a springy, elastic dough. It absorbs water and you may find yourself wanting to add more water while processing the dough, which should be moist and somewhat sticky when mixing is completed. For a fluffier crumb, blend this dough using the mix and rest method described on page 54.

This dough is shaped into small, oblong loaves, and then each is cut to form a mezzaluna, half-moon in Italian. This gives the bread more surface, hence more seed-coated crust.

Durum wheat flour	350 grams	11 ounces	2¼ to 2⅔ cups
Unbleached bread flour	150 grams	5 ounces	about 1 to 1¼ cups
Fine sea salt	10 grams	2 teaspoons	2 teaspoons
Instant yeast	¾ teaspoon	¾ teaspoon	¾ teaspoon
Water	315 grams	10 ounces	1¼ cups
Sesame seeds	60 grams	2 ounces	¼ cup
Cornmeal for the baking sheet			

1. Place the flours, salt, and yeast in a food processor fitted with the metal blade. Using an instant-read thermometer, adjust the water temperature so that the combined temperatures of the water and the flour give a base temperature of 130°F if using a Cuisinart or KitchenAid or 150°F if using a Braun. (See page 33 for other models.) With the machine running, pour all but 2 tablespoons of the water through the feed tube. Process for 20 seconds, adding the remaining water if the dough seems dry and does not come together into a ball during this time.

2. Stop the machine and let the dough rest in the processor bowl for 5 minutes. It will soften noticeably as it rests. Then process for 25 seconds longer, for a total of 45 seconds.

3. Stop the machine and take the temperature of the dough with an instant-read thermometer, which should read between 75°F and 80°F. If the temperature is lower than 75°F, process the dough for an additional 5 seconds. If the temperature of the dough is still lower than 75°F, process the dough for an additional 5 seconds, up to twice more, until it reaches the desired temperature. If the temperature is higher than 80°F, remove the thermometer, scrape the dough from the food processor into an ungreased bowl and refrigerate for 5 to 10 minutes. Check the temperature after 5 minutes; the dough should be 80°F or cooler by that time.

4. Remove the dough from the processor and place it in a large ungreased bowl. Cover the bowl with plastic wrap and ferment the dough for 2 to 2½ hours at room temperature, 70°F to 72°F. It will be active and will noticeably double in volume.

5. Turn the dough onto a lightly floured work surface. Divide it in half and shape into 2 crude balls, taking care not to deflate all the air bubbles. Cover the dough with a sheet of plastic wrap and let it rest for 15 to 20 minutes.

6. Sprinkle a baking sheet with cornmeal. Uncover the dough, then sift a fine coating of flour on each piece on the work surface. Form each ball into a blunt football shape (page 38). Brush each loaf lightly with water, then sprinkle with the sesame seeds. (Be generous, as many of the seeds fall off as the bread rises.) Place the formed loaves on the baking sheet, spaced 4 inches apart so they don't stick together while rising and baking. Loosely cover with plastic wrap. Allow the bread proof for 1 to 1½ hours at room temperature, until the loaves puff and increase by half their size. The dough should feel softer but still spring back slightly when poked with your finger.

7. One hour before baking, put the oven rack on the second shelf from the bottom of the oven and place the baking stone on the rack. Place a small pan for water on the floor of the oven. Preheat the oven to 450°F.

8. To make the mezzaluna shape, use a sharp knife to cut nine 2-inch-

Stored at room
temperature
and covered
with a kitchen
towel, this
bread will stay
fresh for two to
three days. For
longer storage,
wrap the bread
in plastic wrap
and freeze for
up to three
weeks.

thick "teeth" about 2 inches deep along one edge of each loaf. Gently curve each loaf so that the cuts open slightly.

9. Pour about 1 cup of warm water into the pan on the floor of the oven. Place the baking sheet on the stone in the oven. Bake the loaves for 2 minutes. Open the oven and quickly pour another cup of water into the pan. Continue baking for 20 to 25 minutes, until the crust is a rich golden brown. Insert an instant-read thermometer into a loaf, and if the internal temperature is 205°F to 210°F, the bread is done.

10. Remove the bread from the oven and immediately place the loaves on a wire rack to cool.

Anise-Scented Moroccan Bread

Two 7-inch
round loaves

Proofing:

1 to 1½ hours
at room
temperature,
70°F to 72°F

One of my favorite memories of a trip to Morocco is of a small bakery I visited in a walled market in Marrakech. Narrow planks were covered with flat, round loaves balanced on pots above the stone floor. The baker shoved the boards deep into a small waist-high wall opening. It was difficult to imagine the size of the oven but the planks went in full and came out empty in a flash. Almost as quickly, the fragrant anise-scented loaves placed in the oven earlier were removed and transferred to baskets for immediate delivery to shops and restaurants in the quarter.

I was determined to re-create that memorable bread at home. Flour and cornmeal gives these loaves a heavy texture and adds some crackle to the dense crust. Because the dough is mixed, rested, then mixed again, it bakes into a loaf with a lighter crumb than you would imagine from such a dense dough. And, since it is formed into loaves right after mixing and then fermented, it is ready to bake in a very short time.

Serve this bread with a cumin-flavored lamb stew or roast chicken.

Unbleached bread flour	500 grams	1 pound	3¹/₃ to 4 cups
Cornmeal	85 grams	3 ounces	¹/₂ cup
Aniseeds	2 tablespoons	2 tablespoons	2 tablespoons
Fine sea salt	10 grams	2 teaspoons	2 teaspoons
Instant yeast	1 teaspoon	1 teaspoon	1 teaspoon
Olive oil	1 tablespoon	1 tablespoon	1 tablespoon
Honey	1 teaspoon	1 teaspoon	1 teaspoon
Water	330 grams	10¹/₂ ounces	1¹/₄ cups plus 1 tablespoon

Cornmeal for the baking sheet

1. Place the flour, cornmeal, 1 tablespoon of the aniseeds, the salt, and yeast in a food processor fitted with the metal blade. Add the olive oil and honey to the water. Using an instant-read thermometer, adjust the temperature of the liquids so that the combined temperatures of the flour and liquids give a base temperature of 130°F if using a Cuisinart or KitchenAid or 150°F if using a Braun. (See page 33 for other models.) With the machine running, pour all but 2 tablespoons of the liquid through the feed tube. Process for 20 seconds. With the machine running, add the remaining liquid if the dough seems too dry and is not coming together in a ball.

2. Stop the machine and let the dough rest in the processor bowl for 5 minutes. It will soften noticeably as it rests. Then process the dough for 25 seconds longer, for a total of 45 seconds.

3. Stop the machine and take the temperature of the dough with an instant-read thermometer, which should read between 75°F and 80°F. If the temperature is lower than 75°F, process the dough for an additional 5 seconds, up to twice more, until it reaches the desired temperature. If the temperature is higher than 80°F, remove the thermometer, scrape the dough from the food processor into an ungreased bowl, and refrigerate it for 5 to 10 minutes. Check the temperature after 5 minutes; the dough should be 80°F or cooler by that time.

4. Scrape the dough from the food processor onto a lightly floured work surface. It will be soft and sticky. Divide the dough into 2 pieces. Flat-

Store the bread in a paper bag at room temperature for two or three days. For longer storage, wrap the loaves in plastic and store in the freezer.

ten each piece of dough to a thickness of about 1 inch. Fold over the edges and gather each piece of dough into a small ball, then roll each into a round shape (page 35).

5. Transfer the loaves to a baking sheet sprinkled with cornmeal, spacing the loaves about 4 inches apart so they do not stick together when baking. With the palms of your hands, press on the edges of each dough round, flattening them slightly to about 7 inches in diameter. (Leave a slight rise in the center of each loaf.) Lightly dust the loaves with flour and cover the bread loosely with plastic wrap. Let the dough proof for 1 to 1½ hours at room temperature, 70°F to 72°F.

6. One hour before baking, put the oven rack on the second shelf from the bottom of the oven and place the baking stone on the rack. Put a small pan for water on the floor of the oven. Preheat the oven to 475°F.

7. Uncover the dough, spray the loaves with water, and sprinkle them lightly with the remaining aniseeds. Using a fork, lightly pierce the surface of each loaf about ¼ inch deep to make a decorative pattern. A cross pattern is traditional; space the intersecting horizontal and vertical marks every ½ inch to form the pattern. Immediately place the bread in the oven and turn the heat down to 450°F.

8. Bake the loaves for 10 to 15 minutes. Remove the baking sheet from the oven and carefully transfer each loaf directly to the baking stone. Reduce the oven temperature to 400°F and bake the bread 20 to 25 minutes longer, until the crust is golden brown. Insert an instant-read thermometer into the bread, and if the internal temperature is 205°F to 210°F, it is done.

9. Remove the bread from the oven and immediately spray each loaf with water. (Two sprays per loaf will help develop a shiny crust.) Place the bread on a wire rack to cool.

Decorative Breads

One of the great joys of bread making is working with a supple dough and transforming it into a majestic loaf. When you mix dough in the food processor, you get superior bread dough and more time to devote to making these loaves a thing of beauty. While The Best Bread Ever can be formed into many shapes and baked in many pans, it can also be embellished with a simple decorating dough to make a very special loaf.

The humblest round loaf, or, in fact, any loaf of bread that has been fully proofed, can be decorated with this easy decorating dough. Before the bread is placed in the oven, cut small pieces of decorating dough and roll them into strips to be placed on the surface of the loaf. Lightly flour the decorating dough and roll it with a rolling pin to make flat shapes. When the surface of the loaf is moistened with water, the decorating dough stays in place and bakes into a dark contrasting crust on the finished loaf.

Decorating Dough

2 pounds
dough

Chilling:

6 hours in the
refrigerator,
37°F to 45°F

This recipe is adapted for the food processor from an excellent professional book called Special and Decorative Breads. *The dough has no yeast, which allows it to retain its shape when baked. The eggs, sweetener, and butter in this recipe ensure that the dough turns a deep mahogany color in the oven.*

One batch of this dough weighs 2 pounds, enough to heavily embellish four or more presentation loaves with decorative script. Stored tightly wrapped in the freezer, it will keep for up to one month. Use this dough to decorate any bread with a good oven spring such as The Best Bread Ever (page 50), Country Wheat Crown (page 183), or the Presentation Loaf (page 68).

Unbleached all-purpose flour	500 grams	16 ounces	3$^{1}/_{3}$ to 4 cups
Fine sea salt	10 grams	2 teaspoons	2 teaspoons
Unsalted butter	140 grams	5 ounces	$^{1}/_{2}$ cup plus 2 tablespoons
Water	125 grams	4 ounces	$^{1}/_{2}$ cup
Light corn syrup	3 tablespoons	3 tablespoons	3 tablespoons
Large egg yolks	2	2	2

1. Place the flour, salt, and butter in the bowl of the food processor fitted with a metal blade. Combine the water, corn syrup, and egg yolks in a small bowl. Whisk to blend. With the food processor running, add the egg mixture and process for 30 seconds. Remove the cover and check the dough for consistency. Add additional water if the dough seems too dry and is not coming together in a ball. Process for another 15 seconds to blend.

2. Scrape the dough from the processor bowl onto a lightly floured work surface. Hand-knead for about 30 seconds to bring it together into a ball. The dough will be firm but pliable. Wrap it tightly in plastic wrap and place it in the refrigerator for at least 6 hours before using. The dough keeps in the refrigerator for three days or may be frozen for several weeks. The night before you need to use the frozen dough, transfer it to the refrigerator to thaw. It will be ready to use within 12 hours.

To Use Decorating Dough

1. Plan the design on paper before starting. Simple lettering, decorative scrolls, lacy script, and cut-out leaf shapes are all ideal.

2. Have a shaped and fully proofed loaf ready to decorate. Use a dry pastry brush to dust off any loose flour that may be clinging to it. Lightly mist the surface of the loaf with water from a plastic spray bottle.

Dust excess flour off the loaf

3. With a dough scraper or kitchen knife, cut off a small piece of decorating dough about 3 inches in diameter. Wrap the remaining dough and set aside. On a lightly floured work surface, roll the dough into a narrow strip if you are going to use it for lettering the surface of the bread. Determine how much decorating dough you will need by measuring the strip of dough over your planned design. Work in small batches. Since decorating dough tends to dry out quickly, keep it tightly wrapped in plastic when not using.

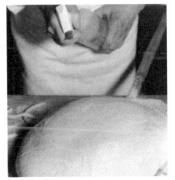

Moisten the top of the loaf using a spray bottle

4. Place the decorating dough on the surface of the loaf in the design you have chosen. You can apply flat pieces of dough first, then use decorative script on top, as in the photo at right. Be careful not to layer the decorating dough too thickly. As the bread rises in the oven, the decorating dough will shift, and too much weight may alter the bread's ability to rise. Keep the main part of your design centered on top of the loaf. Pieces that trail down the sides may be distorted by the way the loaf rises.

Place the decorating dough on the loaf in the design you have chosen

5. Once the design is in place, wet the surface of the design with a pastry brush or an artist's paintbrush, keeping water off the undecorated sections of the loaf. Dust the loaf with a fine sifting of flour, trying to put as little flour on the decorations as possible. The undecorated surface of the bread should look as it has received a fine dusting of snow. (If you have written on top of the loaf, be certain to get flour in the spaces between the letters.) Once the loaf is well dusted, remove any flour that has landed on the decorations with an artist's paintbrush dipped in water. The letters and designs will darken as the loaf bakes and form a dark contrast to the floured top of the loaf.

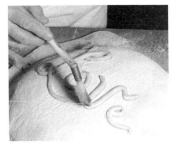

Brush excess flour off the design before baking

6. Score the loaf with 4 or 5 slashes, each about 3 inches long, placed low along the sides so that as they open, the top of the loaf will rise and be level. Bake the decorated loaf according to the recipe.

Presentation Loaf

One 16-inch loaf

Fermentation:

2¹/₂ to 3 hours at room temperature, 70°F to 72°F

Retardation:

12 to 14 hours in the refrigerator, 37°F to 45°F

Proofing:

3 to 5 hours at room temperature

When a close friend or family member has something special to celebrate, I make a presentation loaf inscribed with a message or decorated with grapes, shafts of wheat, swirls of dough, or a name written with the dough.

To make this loaf, mix two or more batches of the The Best Bread Ever (page 50) or King of Bread dough (page 191) and shape it into the biggest free-form round loaf that will fit into your oven. A long fermentation at room temperature and a long retardation in the refrigerator will give the bread a tangy taste. For the best results, form the loaf after the dough has fermented. Then place it in a banneton or large basket lined with a clean cloth heavily dusted with flour. The dough retards in the basket and is inverted onto a peel or baking sheet and baked.

With a loaf this size, it may take 3 or more hours for the dough to proof fully and come to the right temperature for baking after it has spent 12 hours in the refrigerator. Work carefully to slide this giant loaf onto the baking stone, and be certain to coat your peel heavily with cornmeal before transferring the loaf from the banneton. It can stick to the peel and be impossible to slide onto the baking stone. It also requires a good amount of time to bake. Adjust the heat in your oven if the loaf seems to be browning quickly.

Bake this loaf until the crust develops a blistered, dark surface, almost black in places. Those slightly charred bits of crumb actually flavor the loaf, perfuming it with a nutty taste from the toasted grains in the flour. When the decorating dough bakes, it darkens and makes a decorative contrast to the flour-dusted loaf.

This recipe will make one loaf approximately 16 inches in diameter, weighing more than 3 pounds when baked. One friend has kept the loaf we made for her wedding on a high shelf in her kitchen for five years. This loaf may outlast some marriages, but it is best when eaten within a week.

2 recipes of The Best Bread Ever (page 50) or the King of Bread dough (page 191)

½ recipe Decorating Dough (page 66), about 1 pound

Cornmeal for the peel or baking sheet

1. Combine the two recipes of dough in a large ungreased bowl. Cover and let rise at room temperature, 70°F to 72°F, for 2½ to 3 hours.

2. After the dough has fermented, place it in the refrigerator for 12 to 14 hours.

3. Remove the dough from the refrigerator, scrape it out onto a lightly floured work surface, and form it into a large round shape (page 35). Place the dough seam side up in a well-floured cloth-lined basket or banneton. If you do not have a basket, place the dough seam side down on a generously floured baking sheet.

4. Let the formed dough come to room temperature and proof for as long as it takes, from 4 to 5 hours at 70°F to 72°F. The dough is ready to be decorated and baked when it reaches an internal temperature of 60°F to 62°F. It will be soft and about doubled in bulk. The dough will still spring back slowly when pressed with your finger.

5. One hour before baking, put the oven rack on the second shelf from the bottom of the oven and place the baking stone on the rack. Place a small pan for water on the bottom of the oven and preheat to 500°F.

6. When the bread has risen to almost double in bulk, transfer the loaf onto a peel or the back of a baking sheet heavily coated with cornmeal. (If the dough has proofed on a baking sheet, you will not be moving it.) Decorate and score the loaf (page 67).

7. Pour about 1 cup of warm water into the pan in the oven. Slide the bread directly onto the baking stone. Bake about 3 or 4 minutes, then create steam by adding another cup of water to the pan on the oven floor. Reduce the heat to 450°F and bake the loaf for 30 minutes. Rotate the loaf so that it browns evenly and continue baking it for another 40 to 45 minutes, long enough so that the crust darkens and is deep brown, almost blackened in places. Insert an instant-read thermometer into the bread, and if the internal temperature is 205°F to 210°F, it is done.

8. Cool this loaf on a wire rack completely before serving or storing. It will stay fresh at room temperature, covered with a kitchen towel, for up to a week.

Cereal Breads

When you want a loaf of solid country bread with the full-bodied taste of whole grains, try one of the next two recipes. Before wheat was widely culti-vated, the earliest breads were made from whole grains and cereals softened by cooking with water into a crude porridge. Like those distant cousins, these are rugged loaves best served with hearty stews and comforting bowls of steaming soup.

In these recipes, wheat flour is blended with a moist porridge made from cooked oatmeal or cooked rye flakes. The wheat flour gives these breads the ability to rise into chewy loaves and the cooked grains give them a moist, even crumb. If you have high-gluten flour, use it when making these breads to produce a dough with the most spring.

The food processor mixes these sticky doughs in a snap, but you may need to add more flour near the end of the mixing. It is impossible to gauge the wetness of the cereal; the longer it sits after cooking, the drier it will be-come, as more of the water is absorbed into the flakes. If your processor struggles to mix one batch of The Best Bread Ever dough (page 50), divide each of the following recipes in half and mix in smaller batches.

Coarse Oatmeal Bread

The cooked oatmeal in this recipe is made using a combination of coarse, steel-cut oats and regular oatmeal. Steel-cut oats such as McCann's Irish Oatmeal gives this dough a nubbly texture. If you cannot find steel-cut oats, substitute regular oatmeal. Even quick-cooking oats will work, giving this dough a more uniform crumb.

Once you've made the cooked oatmeal, this bread dough is easy to mix. It ferments readily into a springy dough, easy to shape into two hearty loaves.

The addition of chopped walnuts or hazelnuts changes the character of the loaf, deepening the color of its crumb and enhancing the dough with the sweet taste of nuts. With or without nuts, this bread makes excellent toast and is a delicious sandwich bread. Enjoy it with a wedge of sharp Cheddar, pickled onions, and piccalilli (a relish of pickled vegetables).

Two 10-inch loaves

Fermentation: 2¹/₂ to 3 hours at room temperature, 70° to 72°F

Proofing: 1 hour at room temperature

FOR THE OATMEAL:

Steel-cut oats	85 grams	3 ounces	¹/₂ cup
Oatmeal, uncooked	60 grams	2 ounces	³/₄ cup
Water	250 grams	8 ounces	1 cup

FOR THE BREAD:

Unbleached bread flour	500 grams	1 pound	3¹/₃ to 4 cups
Fine sea salt	15 grams	2³/₄ tablespoons	2³/₄ tablespoons
Instant yeast	1¹/₂ teaspoons	1¹/₂ teaspoons	1¹/₂ teaspoons
Water	300 grams	9¹/₂ ounces	1 cup plus 3 tablespoons
Finely chopped toasted walnuts or hazelnuts (optional)	200 grams	7 ounces	2 cups

Additional oatmeal for the baking sheet

1. Combine the steel-cut oats, uncooked oatmeal, and water in a saucepan. Cover and bring to a boil. Uncover, stir, and reduce heat to low. Cook for 5 to 8 minutes until the cereal is softened. Continue cooking until all of the water has been absorbed. Set aside to cool completely before using.

2. Place the flour, salt, and yeast in a food processor fitted with the metal blade. Add the cooled oatmeal mixture. Using an instant-read thermometer, adjust the water temperature so that the combined temperatures of the flour and water give a base temperature of 130°F if using a Cuisinart or KitchenAid or 150°F if using a Braun. (See page 33 for other models.) With the machine running, pour all but 3 tablespoons of the water through the feed tube. Process for 15 seconds.

3. While the machine runs, check to see that the dough is coming together and forming a visible ball, adding the reserved water if it seems dry. If the dough seems too moist and is clinging to the shaft and sides of the bowl, sprinkle a few tablespoons of flour through the feed tube. Process 30 seconds longer, for a total of 45 seconds.

4. Stop the machine and take the temperature of the dough with an instant-read thermometer, which should read between 75°F and 80°F. If the temperature is lower than 75°F, process for an additional 5 seconds. If the temperature of the dough is still lower than 75°F, process for 5 seconds, up to twice more, until it reaches the desired temperature. If the temperature is higher than 80°F, remove the thermometer, scrape the dough from the food processor into an ungreased bowl, and refrigerate for 5 to 10 minutes. Check the temperature of the dough after 5 minutes; it should be 80°F or cooler by that time.

5. Remove the dough from the processor. If adding nuts, scrape the dough out onto a generously floured work surface and lightly sprinkle the surface of the dough with flour. Flatten the dough, sprinkle it with the walnuts or hazelnuts, and knead to distribute the nuts evenly throughout, adding flour as needed should the mixture be too sticky to work easily.

6. Transfer the dough to a large ungreased bowl, cover with plastic wrap, and allow to ferment for 2½ to 3 hours at room temperature, 70°F to 72°F. The dough will double in volume as it ferments.

7. Scrape the dough onto a floured work surface. With a dough scraper or kitchen knife, divide it into 2 equal pieces. Using additional flour as needed to work with this sticky dough, shape it into 2 football-shaped loaves (page 38).

8. Generously sprinkle a baking sheet with cornmeal or oatmeal flakes. Place the loaves on the sheet, spaced 4 inches apart. Dust them with flour, cover them with plastic wrap, and let them proof for 1 hour at room temperature.

9. One hour before baking, put the oven rack on the second shelf from the bottom of the oven and place the baking stone on the rack. Place a pan for water on the floor of the oven. Preheat the oven to 475°F.

10. Brush the loaves with water, then sprinkle them with a few tablespoons of uncooked oatmeal. Carefully transfer the loaves to a peel or the back of a baking sheet sprinkled with cornmeal. Dust the surface of the loaves with flour, then make one deep slash along the length of each loaf. Pour 1 cup of warm water into the pan in the oven to create steam. Use the peel or baking sheet to slide the bread onto the baking stone and immediately turn the heat down to 450°F.

11. Bake the loaves for 2 minutes. Open the oven and quickly pour another cup of water into the pan on the oven floor for more steam. Continue baking another 30 to 35 minutes, until the crust is golden brown. Insert an instant-read thermometer into a loaf, and if the internal temperature is 205°F to 210°F, the bread is done.

12. Remove from the oven and immediately place the loaves on a wire rack to cool. Let the loaves cool completely before serving and storing.

Store the bread in a paper bag or loosely covered with a kitchen towel at room temperature. It will remain fresh for up to three days. For longer storage, wrap the bread in plastic and freeze for up to three weeks.

Rye Porridge Bread

Two 10-inch
loaves

Fermentation:
2¹/₂ to 3 hours
at room
temperature

Proofing:
1 hour at room
temperature

Here is a loaf of bread with a thick, dark crust and a deep aroma; it invites nibbling. The flavor of this loaf improves if you can wait a few hours to taste it. The slight sweetness of the molasses and the rich rye taste develop as the bread matures.

Rye flakes are made when individual rye grains are flattened between rollers. The resilient flakes are hard and are still somewhat chewy even after cooking. If you cannot find rye flakes, substitute oatmeal or cream of wheat in this recipe. Molasses and butter give this bread a uniform crumb flecked with bits of rye cereal.

This long-keeping loaf is delicious sliced, buttered, and drizzled with honey.

FOR THE RYE CEREAL:

Water	335 grams	12 ounces	1¹/₂ cups
Rye flakes	100 grams	3¹/₂ ounces	1 cup
Unsalted butter	30 grams	1 ounce	2 tablespoons
Dark molasses	2 tablespoons	2 tablespoons	2 tablespoons

FOR THE DOUGH:

Whole wheat flour	250 grams	8 ounces	1²/₃ to 2 cups
Unbleached bread flour	250 grams	8 ounces	1²/₃ to 2 cups
Fine sea salt	15 grams	2³/₄ tablespoons	2³/₄ tablespoons
Instant yeast	2 teaspoons	2 teaspoons	2 teaspoons
Water	315 grams	10 ounces	1¹/₄ cups

Additional rye flakes for sprinkling on dough and baking sheet

1. To make the rye cereal, bring the water to boil in a 1-quart saucepan. Add the rye flakes, reduce heat to low, cover, and cook for 20 minutes until softened. Stir in the butter and molasses, then set aside to cool completely.

2. Place the flours, salt, and yeast in a food processor fitted with the metal blade. Add the cooled rye mixture. Using an instant-read thermometer, adjust the water temperature so that the combined temperatures of the flour and the water give a base temperature of 130°F if using a Cuisinart or KitchenAid or 150°F if using a Braun. (See page 33 for other models.) With the machine running, pour all but 3 tablespoons of the water through the feed tube. Process for 15 seconds.

3. While the machine runs, check to see that the dough is coming together and forming a visible ball, adding the reserved water if it seems dry. If the dough seems too moist and is clinging to the shaft and sides of the bowl, sprinkle a few tablespoons of flour through the feed tube. Process 30 seconds longer, for a total of 45 seconds.

4. Stop the machine and take the temperature of the dough with an instant-read thermometer, which should read between 75°F and 80°F. If the temperature is lower than 75°F, process the dough for an additional 5 seconds. If the temperature of the dough is still lower than 75°F, process for 5 seconds, up to twice more, until it reaches the desired temperature. If the temperature is higher than 80°F, remove the thermometer, scrape the dough from the food processor into an ungreased bowl, and refrigerate for 5 to 10 minutes. Check the temperature of the dough after 5 minutes; it should be 80°F or cooler by that time.

5. Scrape the dough from the processor bowl onto a lightly floured work surface. Dust the dough lightly with flour, gather it into a crude ball, and place it in a large ungreased bowl. Cover with plastic wrap. Ferment the dough for 2½ to 3 hours at room temperature, 70°F to 72°F. The dough will have just about doubled in volume.

6. Turn the dough onto a lightly floured work surface. With a dough scraper or kitchen knife, divide it into 2 equal pieces. Using additional flour as needed to work this sticky dough, shape it into 2 smooth round loaves (page 35). Cover them with plastic wrap and let rest for 15 to 20 minutes.

7. Generously sprinkle a baking sheet with rye flakes. Roll the loaves in the rye flakes, leaving a circle on the top of each loaf plain. Shake the sheet to redistribute the remaining rye flakes, then set the loaves back on the sheet, spaced about 4 inches apart so that they do not stick together as they rise. Dust the loaves with flour and cover with plastic wrap. Proof the loaves for about 1 hour at room temperature.

Store the bread in a paper bag or loosely covered with a towel at room temperature. It will remain fresh for up to three days this way.

8. One hour before baking, put the oven rack on the second shelf from the bottom of the oven and place the baking stone on the rack. Place a small pan of water on the bottom of the oven. Preheat the oven to 475°F.

9. Transfer the loaves to a peel or the back of a baking sheet sprinkled with cornmeal. Slash each loaf once horizontally and once vertically. Each slash should measure about 4 inches long. Steam the oven by pouring about ½ cup of water into the pan, then immediately slide the bread from the peel onto the stone and turn the heat down to 450°F.

10. Bake the loaves for 2 minutes, then quickly open the oven door and add another ½ cup of water to the pan. Continue baking another 25 to 30 minutes, until the crust is well browned. Insert an instant-read thermometer into the bread, and if the internal temperature is 205°F to 210°F, the bread is done.

11. Remove the bread from the oven and place the loaves on a wire rack to cool.

Crunchy Wheat Rolls

Nuggets of steel-cut oats give these savory rolls a crunchy exterior. Use cracked wheat, wheat bran, or regular oatmeal if you cannot locate steel-cut oats. (McCann's is a well-known brand imported from Ireland.)

    This recipe makes a solid dough that puffs noticeably after the rolls have been formed. Baked at a high temperature, these rolls cook rapidly and develop a crisp crust in a short time.

Twelve 3-inch rolls

Fermentation:
2½ to 3 hours at room temperature, 70°F to 72°F

Proofing:
45 minutes to 1 hour at room temperature

Unbleached all-purpose flour	500 grams	1 pound	3⅓ to 4 cups
Whole wheat flour	125 grams	4 ounces	1 cup
Graham flour	30 grams	1 ounce	3 tablespoons
Raw wheat germ	1 tablespoon	1 tablespoon	1 tablespoon
Steel-cut oats	85 grams	3 ounces	½ cup
Fine sea salt	10 grams	2 teaspoons	2 teaspoons
Instant yeast	1 teaspoon	1 teaspoon	1 teaspoon
Water	435 grams	14 ounces	1¾ cups

Cornmeal for the baking sheet

    1. Place the flours, wheat germ, oats, salt, and yeast in a food processor fitted with the metal blade. Using an instant-read thermometer, take the temperature of the flour, then adjust the water temperature so that the combined temperatures give a base temperature of 130°F if using a Cuisinart or KitchenAid or 150°F if using a Braun. (See page 33 for other models.) With the machine running, pour all but 2 tablespoons of the water through the feed tube. Process for 20 seconds, adding the remaining water if the dough appears dry and is not coming together into a ball. If the dough is wet and is sticking to the shaft and sides of the bowl, add a few spoonfuls of flour with the machine running. Process the dough for 25 seconds more.

    2. Stop the machine and take the temperature of the dough with an instant-read thermometer, which should read between 75°F and 80°F. If the temperature is lower than 75°F, process the dough for an additional 5 seconds, up to twice more, until it reaches the desired temperature. If the temperature is higher than 80°F, remove the thermometer, scrape the dough from the food processor into an ungreased bowl, and refrigerate for 5 to 10 minutes. Check the temperature after 5 minutes; it should be 80°F or cooler by that time.

3. Remove the dough from the processor, place it in a large ungreased bowl, and cover with plastic wrap. Allow it to ferment for 2½ to 3 hours at room temperature, 70°F to 72°F.

4. Scrape the dough onto a lightly floured work surface. Lightly press down to flatten it to a thickness of about 2 inches without pressing out too many of the air bubbles that formed during fermentation. With a dough scraper or kitchen knife, divide the dough into 12 pieces, each weighing about 3 ounces. Cover with plastic wrap and let rest for 15 to 20 minutes before forming into rolls.

5. Form into rolls (page 39). Dust them with flour. Place the rolls on a baking sheet dusted with cornmeal, spacing them a few inches apart so they don't grow together in the oven. Cover with plastic wrap and let them proof for 45 minutes to 1 hour. The dough will puff slightly.

6. One hour before baking, put the oven rack on the second shelf from the bottom of the oven and place the baking stone on the rack. Place a small pan for water on the bottom of the oven. Preheat the oven to 475°F.

7. Using a razor blade or sharp paring knife, make one horizontal and one vertical slash on the top of each roll. This cross will open up during baking.

8. Pour about 1 cup warm water into the pan in the oven. Immediately place the rolls in the oven and turn the heat down to 450°F. Bake for 5 minutes, then create steam in the oven by adding another cup of water to the pan on the oven floor. Bake for another 10 minutes. When the rolls are firm enough to handle, transfer them directly onto the baking stone in the oven. Bake them for another 10 to 15 minutes. (If you do not transfer the rolls to the baking stone, reduce the heat in the oven to 350°F and continue baking.) Insert an instant-read thermometer into the bread, and if the internal temperature is 205°F to 210°F, the rolls are done.

9. Remove the rolls from the oven and cool them on a wire rack.

Thai Jasmine Rice Rolls or Bread

An extraordinary bread full of the fragrance of jasmine rice and a hint of lemongrass, this dough bakes into a loaf with a thin crust that reminds me of rice crackers.

 For the opening of his French-inspired Thai restaurant, Vong, Chef Jean-Georges Vongerichten asked me to develop a bread that combined these two influences. The rice flour lightens the bread, resulting in a very pale, fluffy roll. Serve these rolls with spicy Indian or Southeast Asian food.

Fourteen 3-inch rolls, or two 8-inch round breads

Fermentation: 1½ to 2 hours at room temperature, 70°F to 72°F

Proofing: 1 hour at room temperature

FOR THE COOKED JASMINE RICE:

Jasmine rice	½ cup	½ cup	½ cup
Water	about 230 grams	about 8 ounces	1 cup

FOR THE LEMONGRASS WATER:

Water	450 grams	16 ounces	2 cups
Chopped dried or fresh lemongrass	2 tablespoons	2 tablespoons	2 tablespoons

FOR THE JASMINE RICE DOUGH:

Unbleached bread flour	400 grams	12 ounces	2⅓ to 3 cups
Rice flour	100 grams	4 ounces	½ cup
Fine sea salt	10 grams	2 teaspoons	2 teaspoons
Instant yeast	1 teaspoon	1 teaspoon	1 teaspoon
Lemongrass water	315 grams	10 ounces	1¼ cups
Cornmeal for the baking sheet			

1. The day before or earlier in the day, prepare the rice and the lemongrass water. Place the rice in a small saucepan, cover it with the water, cover, and bring to a boil. Remove the cover, stir the rice once, then reduce heat to low. Cover the rice again and cook it for 20 minutes. Remove from the heat, uncover, and fluff with a fork. Cool completely before using.

2. To prepare the lemongrass water, bring the water to a boil, add the lemongrass, and cover the pan. Turn off the heat and let the lemongrass steep for 1 hour. Strain, discard the lemongrass, and let the flavored water cool to room temperature, 70°F to 72°F, before proceeding.

3. Place the flours, salt, and yeast in a food processor fitted with the metal blade. Using an instant-read thermometer, adjust the lemongrass water temperature so that the combined temperatures of the flour and the water give a base temperature of 130°F if using a Cuisinart or KitchenAid or 150°F if using a Braun. (See page 33 for other models.)

4. With the machine running, pour all but 2 tablespoons of the water through the feed tube. Process for 30 seconds, adding the remaining water if the dough appears to be dry. If the dough appears too wet and is not forming a ball in the bowl of the processor, add a few tablespoons of bread flour through the feed tube with the machine running. Process the dough for 15 seconds longer, for a total of 45 seconds.

5. Stop the machine and take the temperature of the dough with an instant-read thermometer, which should read between 75°F and 80°F. If the temperature is lower than 75°F, process for an additional 5 seconds. If the temperature of the dough is still lower than 75°F, process for an additional 5 seconds, up to twice more, until it reaches the desired temperature. If the temperature is higher than 80°F, remove the thermometer, scrape the dough from the food processor into an ungreased bowl, and refrigerate for 5 to 10 minutes. Check the temperature after 5 minutes; it should be 80°F or cooler by that time.

6. Remove the dough from the processor and place it on a generously floured work surface. It will be creamy, white, and moist. Flatten the dough out into a 12 inch square. Spread all but ¼ cup of the cooled cooked jasmine rice over the surface, flour your hands, and roll the dough into a log shape. Fold it in half and knead for about 2 minutes, using a dough scraper to lift it from the table and fold it onto itself. Keep sprinkling your hands and the dough with flour as you manipulate the dough to incorporate the rice throughout.

7. Place the dough in a large ungreased bowl, cover with plastic wrap, and allow it to ferment for 1½ to 2 hours at room temperature, 70°F to

72°F. It will have increased in volume by about half and will appear well aerated.

8. Turn the dough onto a lightly floured work surface. Lightly sprinkle it with flour, then press it gently to remove some of the air bubbles that have formed. Using a dough scraper or knife, divide it into 14 pieces, each weighing about 2 ounces. Form the pieces into oblongs and place them on a cornmeal-covered baking sheet, spacing them about 2 inches apart so they don't grow together when baking. Cover the baking sheet loosely with plastic wrap and let the rolls proof for about 1 hour at room temperature.

9. One hour before baking, put the oven rack on the second shelf from the bottom of the oven and place the baking stone on the rack. Place a small pan for water on the bottom of the oven. Preheat the oven to 450°F.

10. Uncover the rolls. Press ½ teaspoon of the reserved rice into the center of each one.

11. Pour 1 cup of warm water into the pan in the oven. Immediately put in the rolls and turn the heat down to 425°F.

12. Bake for 10 minutes, then remove the baking sheet from the oven. Transfer the rolls to a peel or the back of a baking sheet, slide them directly onto the baking stone, and bake for another 12 to 15 minutes, until uniformly light brown.

13. Remove from the oven and transfer to a wire rack to cool.

Variation:

Another way to form this dough is to make larger rolls and bake them in round cake pans. The entire loaf is served and each guest breaks off a roll.

1. To make the loaves of rolls, generously sprinkle two 8-inch cake pans with cornmeal. Divide the dough into 14 pieces. Form the pieces into rolls by pinching and place 6 in a circle about 1 inch from the edge of each pan and 1 roll in the center. (As the bread proofs, the rolls will grow together to form a loaf.)

2. Cover with plastic wrap and let proof for about an hour at room temperature, 70°F to 72°F.

This bread freezes well. Store it tightly wrapped in a plastic bag in the freezer for up to three weeks. Thaw and reheat the bread by placing it in a preheated 350°F oven for 8 to 10 minutes. The crust will be crackled and the interior slightly warm and moist.

Store as instructed for the loaf, page 81.

3. An hour before baking, put the oven rack on the second shelf from the bottom of the oven and place the baking stone on the rack. Place a small pan for water on the bottom of the oven. Preheat to 450 °F.

4. Uncover the pans of rolls and press ½ teaspoon of the reserved rice into the center of each roll.

5. Pour 1 cup of warm water into the pan in the oven. Immediately place the pans in the oven. Turn the heat down to 425 °F.

6. Bake for 15 minutes, then remove the pans. Use a small knife to remove the rolls from the pans and return them to the oven to finish baking directly on the baking stone. Bake for another 5 to 8 minutes until they are uniformly light brown. Using an instant-read thermometer, they will be done when they reach an internal temperature of 205 °F to 210 °F.

7. Remove from the oven and transfer to a wire rack to cool completely before storing.

Savory Carrot and Leek Bread

When served with a simple green salad, this bread is almost a meal in itself. Or, slice this bread in half horizontally, layer with roasted chicken and garlic mayonnaise, and pack the sandwiches for a picnic.

   Slivered fresh fennel, zucchini, or summer squash also work in place of any of the vegetables in the mixture. Whatever combination you use, be certain to cook the vegetables long enough so all of their natural moisture evaporates. Excess moisture from the vegetables will saturate the bread dough, making it dense and soggy. Chill the filling thoroughly before layering it in the bread dough.

   Coarse black pepper on the outside of the bread adds crunch as well as flavor; the finer a peppercorn is ground, the hotter it will taste. Some peppermills will produce a coarse grind, but I prefer to crush whole peppercorns with a cast-iron skillet. Spread the peppercorns on a baking sheet and use the side of the heavy pan to crush each one roughly in half.

Two 10-inch flat loaves

Fermentation: 1 1/2 to 2 hours at room temperature, 70°F to 72°F

Proofing: 1 hour at room temperature

1 recipe The Best Bread Ever dough (page 50)	1 teaspoon chopped fresh marjoram, or 1/2 teaspoon dried marjoram
2 tablespoons olive oil	2 tablespoons chopped fresh parsley
4 peeled carrots, cut into 1/2-inch dices (about 1 cup)	Salt and pepper
4 cleaned leeks, cut into 1/2-inch pieces (about 4 cups)	1 tablespoon coarsely ground black pepper
3 cloves garlic, chopped	1 tablespoon cornmeal
	1 teaspoon red pepper flakes

1. While the dough is fermenting, heat the olive oil in a large skillet over medium heat. Add the carrots, leeks, garlic, and 2 tablespoons of water. Cover the pan and cook the vegetables for 10 minutes. Add the marjoram and parsley and season with salt and pepper. Raise the heat to medium-high. Continue to cook the vegetables about 15 minutes longer, uncovered, until the carrots soften and the vegetables begin to brown. Remove the pan from the heat, adjust the seasonings, and let the vegetables cool before proceeding.

2. One hour before baking, put the oven rack on the second shelf from the bottom of the oven and place the baking stone on the rack. Place a small

This bread will stay fresh at room temperature for a day covered with a towel. For longer storage, wrap the bread in plastic wrap and place in the refrigerator. Revive the crust in a 350°F oven for 8 to 10 minutes before serving.

pan for water on the floor of the oven. Preheat the oven to 475°F. Sprinkle a baking sheet with the tablespoon of coarse black pepper and the cornmeal. Set aside.

3. Scrape the dough onto a lightly floured work surface. With floured hands, gently pat it into a large rectangle about 2 inches thick. Use a dough scraper or kitchen knife to divide the dough into 2 equal pieces. Pat each piece into a crude oval measuring about 8 inches long and 6 inches wide.

4. Spread a quarter of the filling down the center of one piece of dough. Fold the dough over, seal the edges with your fingertips, then roll it back and forth across the work surface into a loose tube. Transfer the cylinder to one end of the baking sheet and press down on it to flatten it slightly. Spread another quarter of the filling over the surface of the loaf. Repeat with the second piece of dough and the filling. Space the loaves about 4 inches apart on the baking sheet so they don't grow together when baking. Sprinkle the loaves with the red pepper flakes. Cover with plastic wrap and let proof for about 1 hour at room temperature.

5. Just before baking, pour about 1 cup of water into the pan in the oven. Immediately place the baking sheet on the baking stone in the oven and turn the heat down to 400°F. Wait 5 minutes, then create steam by adding another cup of water to the pan in the oven.

6. Bake the breads for 20 to 25 more minutes until they are a uniform golden brown. Or, insert an instant-read thermometer into one of the loaves, and if the internal temperature is 205°F to 210°F, the bread is done.

7. Remove the baking sheet from the oven and transfer the loaves to a wire rack to cool.

Swiss Twist
Ham and Gruyère Loaves

This hearty loaf has a sweet fragrance, a fine crumb, and the delectable combination of ham and cheese.

    If it is available, use high-gluten flour to make this dough. When cheese is added to bread dough, it weighs it down. The extra protein in high-gluten flour gives the loaf great spring and the strength to make a buoyant bread with an even-textured crumb.

    The "twist" is the subtle curved shape achieved by bending the ends of the loaf in opposite directions. This bread makes great toast. I serve it with a salad of bitter greens and a mustard dressing.

One 12-inch loaf

Fermentation: 2½ to 3 hours at room temperature, 70°F to 72°F

Proofing: 45 minutes to 1 hour at room temperature

Unbleached bread flour	500 grams	1 pound	3⅓ to 4 cups
Fine sea salt	10 grams	2 teaspoons	2 teaspoons
Instant yeast	1 teaspoon	1 teaspoon	1 teaspoon
Water	315 grams	10 ounces	1¼ cups
Finely diced smoked ham	85 grams	3 ounces	¾ cup
Grated Gruyère or Swiss cheese	85 grams	3 ounces	1 cup

1. Place the flour, salt, and yeast in the bowl of the food processor fitted with the metal blade. Using an instant-read thermometer, adjust the water temperature so that the combined temperatures of the flour and the water give a base temperature of 130°F if using a Cuisinart or KitchenAid or 150°F if using a Braun. (See page 33 for other models.) With the machine running, pour all but 2 tablespoons of the water through the feed tube. Process for 20 seconds, adding the remaining water if the dough seems dry and does not come together into a ball during this time. Process 25 seconds longer for a total of 45 seconds.

2. Stop the machine and take the temperature of the dough with an instant-read thermometer, which should read between 75°F and 80°F. If the temperature is lower than 75°F, process the dough for an additional 5 sec-

onds. If the temperature of the dough is still lower than 75°F, process for an additional 5 seconds, up to twice more, until it reaches the desired temperature. If the temperature is higher than 80°F, remove the thermometer, scrape the dough from the food processor into an ungreased bowl, and refrigerate for 5 to 10 minutes. Check the temperature after 5 minutes; it should be 80°F or cooler by that time.

3. Scrape the dough onto a lightly floured work surface. Gather it into a loose ball, then cover it with plastic wrap. Let rest for 10 to 15 minutes.

4. Press the dough out into a 12-inch square. Sprinkle the surface with the diced ham and the cheese. Roll the dough into a log shape, fold it in half, and knead it for about 2 to 3 minutes to incorporate the ham and cheese. If the dough seems too tough to knead easily, cover it loosely with plastic wrap and let it rest for 5 to 10 minutes before continuing. After kneading in the ham and cheese, place the dough in a large ungreased bowl and cover with plastic wrap. Allow it to ferment for 2½ to 3 hours at room temperature, 70°F to 72°F. The dough will have increased in volume somewhat, but don't be concerned by how much.

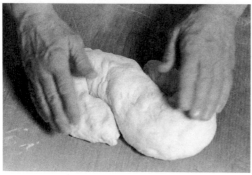

Shaping the Swiss Twist

5. Turn the dough onto a lightly floured work surface and shape it into a smooth ball. Cover with plastic wrap and let rest for 15 to 20 minutes.

6. Sift a fine coating of flour on the work surface. Gently pat the dough down to an even thickness of 1 inch. Fold it into a log shape, then roll into a thick baguette (page 36) about 16 inches long. To make the twist, shape the dough into an S: Fold one end about 4 inches up the side and fold the other end 4 inches down the opposite side. The ends of the dough should meet in the center along opposite sides of the loaf. Press the edges of the dough together so that the finished loaf resembles an S curve.

7. Using both hands, gently transfer the loaf to a baking sheet lightly dusted with cornmeal. Sprinkle the surface lightly with flour and cover the baking sheet loosely with plastic wrap or a kitchen

towel. Let proof for 45 minutes to an hour, until the dough increases by half its size. It should feel softer, but still spring back slightly when poked with your finger.

8. One hour before baking, put the oven rack on the second shelf from the bottom of the oven and place the baking stone on the rack. Place a small pan for water on the floor of the oven. Preheat the oven to 500°F.

9. Uncover the bread and again lightly sprinkle it with flour. Slash the top of the loaf several times diagonally with a razor blade.

10. Carefully pour about 1 cup of warm water into the pan on the oven floor. Immediately put the bread in the oven and turn the heat down to 450°F.

11. Bake the bread for 2 minutes. Open the oven door and quickly create steam by adding another cup of warm water to the pan. Continue baking for 25 to 30 minutes until the crust is a uniform rich brown. Insert an instant-read thermometer into the bread, and if the internal temperature is 205°F to 210°F, it is done.

12. Remove the loaf from the oven and place it on a wire rack to cool completely before storing.

Stored at room temperature covered with a towel, this bread will stay fresh for two days. For longer storage, wrap in plastic and freeze for up to three weeks.

New York Bagels

6 bagels

Fermentation:

12 to 16 hours in the refrigerator, 37°F to 45°F

Proofing:

20 to 25 minutes at room temperature, 70°F to 72°F

There is much debate about what constitutes a truly great bagel—chewy or crisp, dense or fluffy. I like a chewy bagel with a hardy, golden crust. My friend, Ray Frosti, an avid home baker with a bagel fixation, took it upon himself to conquer the bagel. He did the research, talked to the "old bagel guys" and learned their secrets, modifying their recipes for home use.

High-gluten or bread flour gives bagels their solid, chewy crumb. The food processor simplifies the mixing of the dough, ensuring that the gluten is well developed. When mixing the dough, you can tell it is dry without stopping the food processor; as the dough spins in the bowl, little pieces trail a larger ball of dough. This dough feels cool and dense when it is first removed from the processor. Don't be alarmed; as the dough ferments, it softens.

Form the bagels right after mixing the dough; the bagels develop their true flavor from a long fermentation in the refrigerator. "In a real bagel bakery, the dough is allowed to rise for 24 to 48 hours before final proofing," Ray says.

For morning-fresh bagels, mix the dough and form the bagels in the afternoon the day before you want them. Mix two batches of this dough to make an even dozen bagels. Just be certain to space them an inch apart on the baking sheet so that they don't grow together while fermenting and proofing. The bagels are boiled very briefly just before they are baked to give them their distinctive thick crust. The water gives the crust a sheen and allows the bagels to bake without burning. Bake them long enough to develop their dark, glistening surface.

If you enjoy seeded or savory bagels, sprinkle them with poppy, caraway, or sesame seeds, coarse salt, or minced dried onion just before baking.

Unbleached bread flour	500 grams	1 pound	3¹/₃ to 4 cups
Brown sugar	20 grams	4 teaspoons	4 teaspoons
Fine sea salt	10 grams	2 teaspoons	2 teaspoons
Instant yeast	1 teaspoon	1 teaspoon	1 teaspoon
Water	300 grams	9¹/₂ ounces	1 cup plus 3 tablespoons
Baking soda	1 teaspoon	1 teaspoon	1 teaspoon
Sugar	15 grams	1 tablespoon	1 tablespoon

Sesame, poppy, or caraway seeds, coarse salt, or dried onion (optional) for garnish

Cornmeal for the baking sheet

1. Generously sprinkle a baking sheet with cornmeal and set aside.

2. Place the flour, brown sugar, salt, and yeast in a food processor fitted with the metal blade. Using an instant-read thermometer, adjust the water temperature so that the combined temperatures of the flour and the water give a base temperature of 130°F if using a Cuisinart or KitchenAid or 150°F is using a Braun. (See page 33 for other models.) With the machine running, pour all but 2 tablespoons of the water through the feed tube. Process for 20 seconds, adding the remining water if the dough seems dry and does not come together into a ball during this time.

3. Stop the machine and let the dough rest in the processor bowl for 5 minutes. It will noticeably soften as it rests. Then process for 25 seconds longer, for a total mixing time of 45 seconds.

4. Stop the machine and take the temperature of the dough with an instant-read thermometer. It should be between 75°F and 80°F. If the temperature is lower than 75°F, process the dough for an additional 5 seconds, up to twice more, until it reaches the desired temperature. If the temperature is higher than 80°F, remove the thermometer, scrape the dough from the food processor into an ungreased bowl, and refrigerate for 5 to 10 minutes. Check the temperature after 5 minutes; it should be 80°F or cooler by that time.

5. Scrape the dough onto a lightly floured work surface. It will be relatively firm. With a dough scraper or kitchen knife, divide the dough into 6 equal pieces.

6. To form the bagels, take each piece of dough and roll it into a ball. Flatten the ball, then fold it in half, sealing the edges with your fingertips. Then fold again to form a tight cylinder. Roll the dough into a tube about 9 inches long. Wrap this piece around the palm of your hand, overlapping the dough about 2 inches. Pinch the ends together to form a ring. (The hole in a bagel formed this way will be the right proportion once the dough is proofed, boiled, then baked.) Repeat with the remaining balls and transfer the bagels to the baking sheet, spacing them 2 inches apart.

7. Rub a bit of flour on the top of each bagel, then cover the sheet loosely with plastic wrap. (The flour will keep the plastic wrap from sticking to the dough as it ferments.) Place the bagels in the refrigerator for 12 to 16 hours, preferably overnight.

8. The next day, one hour before baking, put the oven rack on the second shelf from the bottom of the oven and place the baking stone on the rack. Preheat the oven to 450°F.

9. Take the bagels from the refrigerator. Remove the plastic wrap and let them proof at room temperature, 70°F to 72°F, for 20 to 25 minutes. While the bagels are proofing, bring a 4-quart pot of water to boil. Add the baking soda and sugar. Sprinkle a baking sheet with cornmeal.

10. Test to see that the bagels are proofed: Insert an instant-read thermometer into the center of one to check the internal temperature of the dough; it should be between 55°F and 60°F.

11. Set a colander in the sink. Drop one bagel in the boiling water. If it floats this means the bagels are proofed and ready to be boiled and baked. Boil the bagel for 5 to 10 seconds. Use a slotted spoon to turn it over and boil it for another 5 to 10 seconds. Transfer the bagel from the boiling water to drain in the colander. Boil the remaining bagels, one at a time, in the rapidly boiling water for no more than 10 seconds on each side, then drain them in the colander. Do not be concerned if the bagels sit on top of each other while draining. They are resilient and will regain their shape when baked.

12. Transfer the drained bagels to the baking sheet, spaced 2 inches apart. While the bagels are still wet from boiling, sprinkle them with the optional toppings.

13. Place the baking sheet in the oven. Reduce the heat to 425°F and bake for about 10 minutes. Open the oven and rotate the tray of bagels so that they brown evenly. Continue baking for 10 to 15 minutes longer until the bagels are uniformly browned.

14. Remove the baking sheet from the oven and transfer the bagels to a wire rack to cool. Serve the bagels warm from the oven or let them cool completely before storing.

Store the bagels in a paper bag for up to 24 hours. For longer storage, put the bagels in a plastic bag and store in the freezer. They will keep, frozen, for up to a month. Thaw them at room temperature for 10 minutes before reheating.

Cinnamon Raisin Bagels

6 bagels

Unbleached bread flour	500 grams	1 pound	3¹/₃ to 4 cups
Brown sugar	20 grams	4 teaspoons	4 teaspoons
Cinnamon	2 teaspoons	2 teaspoons	2 teaspoons
Ground nutmeg	¹/₈ teaspoon	¹/₈ teaspoon	¹/₈ teaspoon
Fine sea salt	10 grams	2 teaspoons	2 teaspoons
Instant yeast	1 teaspoon	1 teaspoon	1 teaspoon
Water	300 grams	9¹/₂ ounces	1 cup plus 3 tablespoons
Raisins	¹/₂ cup	¹/₂ cup	¹/₂ cup

Cornmeal for the baking sheet

Fermentation:
12 to 16 hours in the refrigerator, 37°F to 45°F.

Proofing:
20 to 25 minutes at room temperature, 70°F to 72°F.

1. Follow steps 1 through 4 of the master recipe, adding the cinnamon and nutmeg to the ingredients in step 2.

2. Remove the dough from the processor. Turn the dough onto a lightly floured work surface. The dough will be dry and somewhat firm. Flatten the dough with the palm of your hand into a rectangle measuring about 10 × 12 inches. Sprinkle the dough with the raisins. Fold the dough in half, then loosely roll it up into a ball. Knead this dough for about 2 minutes to evenly distribute the raisins throughout the dough. If the dough seems too stiff, cover it with plastic wrap and let the dough rest 10 minutes before continuing with the kneading.

3. With a dough scraper or kitchen knife, divide the dough into 6 equal pieces each weighing about 5 ounces. Form the bagels, cover, ferment, then bake them as outlined in the master recipe steps 6 through 13.

Flatbreads: Pizza, Focaccia, Breadsticks, and Ciabatta

If you want to be the most popular person on your block, conquer the recipes in this chapter. Flatbreads have just about everything going for them: They taste like delicious bread, bake in an instant, and are as fun to make as they are to eat.

The godfather of Italian flatbreads is pizza. The pizzas in this chapter are inspired by those served in Naples, the official pizza capital of the world. The crust is thin and crunchy but there is enough dough to give it the taste of a good bread. Everyone loves pizza, and the recipes in this chapter include all varieties, from a traditional tomato and cheese pizza to a refined pizza with four cheeses.

Focaccia and schiacciata, Tuscan flatbreads baked on a roasting hearth, are kissing cousins. Focaccia is a dimpled pizza dough filled with olive oil. When baked, it fills the kitchen with the piney smell of rosemary and bubbling oil. Schiacciata is pizza dough about the size of a personal pizza baked into a puffy small pie. To make schiaciatta, divide the basic pizza dough into five pieces. Flatten each piece, then roll and top with thin slices of tomato or slivers of red onion and sweet bell peppers.

Make the dough for these flatbreads a day ahead of time and let them retard in the refrigerator. This will give the dough time to develop taste and to soften somewhat so it is easier to roll into a generous circle. Flatbreads cook quickly and prefer a hot oven with even bottom heat. That's why a baking stone is a must for making any of the flatbreads in this chapter.

Whole Wheat Pita Pockets (page 123) proof in a short time and puff into pleasing rolls in less than 10 minutes. And from southern France comes the fougasse and pissaladière, plaques of crisp dough that bring the smells and tastes of Provence to your kitchen.

Pizza

I love pizza, and when you love something, you hate to see it abused. Pizza remains the number-one selling item in the entire restaurant industry, yet it amazes me that so much inferior pizza is sold today—puffy, bland dough or brittle, cracker crust overflowing with toppings. Pizza is really a simple food: a great wheat dough baked into a chewy, crisp crust and enhanced with a thin layer of complementary toppings.

Treat pizza dough as you would any other. Mix it a day ahead and retard it to develop its flavor and relax the gluten in the dough for ease of handling. Use all-purpose flour, which has a lower gluten content, because it makes a more tender crumb.

Unlike bread dough, pizza dough can withstand the hottest oven temperature, but you must use a baking stone to maximize the heat. Pizza goes in the oven without a final proofing stage so it can use its full energy to burst in the intense heat. With its thin crust, it cooks in just minutes.

The basic recipe makes enough dough for three pizzas. If you are making just one, form the leftover dough into a loaf or focaccia and bake accordingly. You can even let the dough sit another 8 to 12 hours in the refrigerator, then shape it into Ciabatta (page 116).

Basic Pizza Dough

This dough makes a pizza crust with the taste of bread and the character of pizza—equal parts crunchy and chewy. I use it to make focaccia and breadsticks as well as schiacciata. It is best when it has a long, slow rise.

There is a widely held belief that the best pizza dough is made with high-gluten flour. I disagree, as do the great Italian pizza makers of Naples, the birthplace of pizza. They use a flour that has less gluten than our all-purpose flour. For the food processor, use all-purpose for similar results. This recipe hits a home run, so don't adulterate it with the most virgin of olive oils.

After the dough ferments, it will be softer and stickier than when it was first mixed. Sprinkle a generous amount of flour on your hands and work surface when rolling it out and shaping it.

Enough dough for three 10-inch pizzas or focaccia, or 5 individual pizzas

Fermentation: 2½ to 3 hours at room temperature, 70°F to 72°F

Retardation: 4 to 36 hours in the refrigerator, 37°F to 45°F

Unbleached all-purpose flour	500 grams	1 pound	3⅓ to 4 cups
Fine sea salt	10 grams	2 teaspoons	2 teaspoons
Instant yeast	½ teaspoon	½ teaspoon	½ teaspoon
Water	300 grams	9½ ounces	1 cup plus 3 tablespoons

Cornmeal for the peel or baking sheet

1. Place the flour, salt, and yeast in a food processor fitted with the metal blade. Using an instant-read thermometer, adjust the water temperature so that the combined temperatures of the flour and water give a base temperature of 130°F if using a Cuisinart or KitchenAid or 150°F if using a Braun. (See page 33 for other models.) With the machine running, pour all but 2 tablespoons of the water through the feed tube. Process for 30 seconds. Stop the machine and if the dough seems too dry, add the remaining water during the last 15 seconds of processing for a total of 45 seconds.

2. Stop the machine and take the temperature of the dough with an instant-read thermometer, which should read between 75°F and 80°F. If the temperature is lower than 75°F, process the dough for an additional 5 seconds, up to twice more, until it reaches the desired temperature. If the temperature is higher than 80°F, remove the thermometer, scrape the dough from the food processor into an ungreased bowl, and refrigerate for 5 to 10 minutes. Check the temperature after 5 minutes; it should be 80°F or cooler by that time.

3. Remove the dough from the processor, place it in a large ungreased bowl, and cover with plastic wrap. Allow the dough to ferment for 2½ to 3 hours at room temperature, 70°F to 72°F. It will not double at this point, but it will increase in volume somewhat.

4. Place the bowl of dough in the refrigerator and retard for at least 4 hours or up to 36 hours. Proceed with any of the recipes for pizza, focaccia, or schiacciata.

5. Leftover pizza dough may be formed and baked like The Best Bread Ever (page 50).

Pizza Toppings

Don't let your imagination stop at mushrooms and pepperoni when it comes to topping pizza. There is no limit to the variety of ingredients that can make a memorable topping. Just don't overload each pizza with too much of anything. You want the heat of the oven to penetrate the dough and cook the lovely crust. Two ounces each of three or four items is just about right. Each batch of pizza dough makes enough for three large pizzas or five individual pizzas. They bake quickly, so save some toppings for the next one.

Pizza cooks fast at a high temperature. Cut raw vegetables like peppers, onions, or mushrooms thin before you place them on a pizza, so they are thoroughly cooked in the time it takes to bake the pizza. Shred carrots and partially cook vegetables like broccoli. Pan-fry slices of eggplant or zucchini before you put them on.

Add raw shrimp 2 or 3 minutes after the pizza has been placed in the oven. (Shrimp will become rubbery if baked on the pie from the beginning.)

For a burst of flavor, sprinkle hot pepper oil, balsamic vinegar, or freshly grated Parmesan cheese on the pizza when it comes from the oven.

Some delicious combinations you may enjoy:

Sautéed onions, garlic, proscuitto, and shredded arugula
Minced garlic, littleneck clams, parsley, and red pepper flakes
Sautéed mushrooms, strips of uncooked chicken, scallions, and slivers
    of Parmesan cheese
Thinly sliced red onions, garlic, and bacon
Sautéed eggplant, sausage, and sun-dried tomatoes

Pizza Margherita

One 10-inch
pizza

Margherita is a fancy name for a simple pizza topped with a small amount of tomato sauce, slices of fresh mozzarella, and fresh basil leaves. Pizza Margherita is a universal favorite among children.

1/3 recipe Basic Pizza Dough (page 95), about 10 ounces

1/4 cup Bright Tomato Sauce (page 100)

4 to 5 slices fresh mozzarella cheese (about 3 ounces), broken into small pieces

Basil leaves

3 tablespoons freshly grated Parmesan cheese

Salt and freshly ground black pepper

1 tablespoon extra virgin olive oil

Cornmeal for the peel or baking sheet

1. One hour before baking, put the oven rack on the second shelf from the bottom of the oven and place the baking stone on the rack. Preheat the oven to 500°F.

2. While the oven is heating up, remove the dough from the refrigerator and turn it onto a lightly floured work surface. With the palms of your hands, flatten it to a thickness of about ½ inch. Generously sprinkle a baking sheet with flour, place the dough on the sheet, and cover it loosely with plastic wrap. Allow the dough to come to room temperature. This will take about 30 minutes, but do not let it sit longer than 1 hour before forming and baking.

3. If your kitchen is very cold, place the baking sheet of dough on top of the stove. The warmth of the oven will help it to warm up so that the dough is soft enough to stretch easily. Don't leave the dough there more than 10 minutes; it could overproof. Turn the dough over once or twice during this time so that the heat permeates it.

4. Place the dough on a generously floured work surface. Using your fingertips, press it all over so that it begins to stretch out. Gently pull to stretch it into a round disk. The dough will be noticeably soft when pulled. Lift it by the edges, place your fists underneath it, and move your fists outward to stretch the dough into a circle about 10 to 11 inches in diameter, or the size that fits your peel or the baking sheet you are using to slide it into the oven. If it resists shaping, cover it with plastic wrap and let it rest for another 10 minutes.

Use your fingertips to stretch out the dough

Stretch the dough into a round disk

To form
a pizza

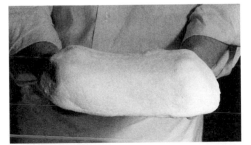

Place your fists underneath the dough

Using your fists, stretch the dough into a circle

Slide the dough carefully onto a peel

Gently shape dough into a circle

Spread the dough thinly with the tomato sauce,
leaving a 1/2-inch edge

5. Sprinkle a peel or the back of a baking sheet with cornmeal, then carefully transfer the stretched pizza dough onto it. Spread the dough thinly with the tomato sauce, leaving a 1/2-inch edge all around. Scatter the mozzarella over the tomato sauce. Sprinkle the pizza with the basil leaves and the

Parmesan and season it with salt and freshly ground pepper. Drizzle it all over with the olive oil.

6. Open the oven door and carefully slide the pizza directly onto the baking stone. (Hold the baking sheet or peel with two hands and reach deep into the oven, directly over the stone where you want the pizza to land. Use a firm back and forth movement to shake and slide the pizza from the peel or baking sheet onto the stone. As the pizza slides forward, gently pull the peel or baking sheet out from under it.)

7. Bake for 5 minutes. Check it and rotate so that it bakes evenly. Continue baking for another 5 to 7 minutes, until the edges of the crust are just beginning to get dark brown. To remove from the oven, slide the peel under the pizza and use it to lift the pie out. Or slide the baked pizza onto the back of a baking sheet. Transfer the pizza to a wire rack to rest for 2 minutes, so that some of the steam escapes and the crust doesn't get soggy.

8. Place the pizza on a cutting board and slice into 8 pieces.

Bright Tomato Sauce

Covered, this sauce will keep for a week in the refrigerator.

Even in the summer, I use canned tomatoes from California to make this sauce. I find the quality of Red Pack Italian-style Plum Tomatoes to be consistently sweet and a good value. This is a simple sauce and therein, like everything Italian, lies its genius.

1/4 cup extra virgin olive oil	1 teaspoon fine sea salt
3 cloves garlic, thinly sliced	2 pinches of sugar
One 28-ounce can Italian-style plum tomatoes	

1. In a small saucepan over medium heat, warm the olive oil. Add the garlic and soften it for 2 or 3 minutes without browning. Add the canned tomatoes and their liquid, the salt, and sugar. Simmer the sauce for 15 minutes, stirring occasionally with a wooden spoon to break up the tomatoes.

2. Pour the sauce through a food mill fitted with a medium or coarse plate, or press it through a sieve. The sauce is ready to use immediately, but

should be at room temperature before being spread on pizza dough. (If the sauce seems too watery, return it to the pan, set on heat, heat and simmer for another 5 to 10 minutes until it is reduced.)

Provençal Pizza

One 10-inch pizza

A good friend's son calls this the "pizza with sticks." In the intense heat of the oven, the thyme burns slightly leaving a scattering of flavorful twigs. I serve this pizza in the fall when tomatoes are at their peak, basil overtakes our garden, and it is cool enough to fire up the oven. If there is any left over, it is just as good served at room temperature.

⅓ recipe Basic Pizza Dough (page 95), about 10 ounces

¼ cup Bright Tomato Sauce (page 100), about 2 ounces

1 fresh medium tomato, sliced ¼ inch thick

½ cup crumbled feta cheese (about 2 ounces)

⅓ cup (about 12) pitted black olives

6 anchovy fillets

5 sprigs of fresh thyme, or ½ teaspoon dried thyme

3 or 4 large fresh basil leaves

1 tablespoon extra virgin olive oil

Freshly ground black pepper

Cornmeal for the peel or baking sheet

1. One hour before baking, put the oven rack on the second shelf from the bottom of the oven and place the baking stone on the rack. Preheat the oven to 500°F.

2. While the oven is heating up, remove the dough from the refrigerator, turn it onto a lightly floured work surface and flatten it to a thickness of about ½ inch with the palms of your hands. Generously sprinkle a baking sheet with flour, place the dough on the sheet, and cover it loosely with plastic wrap. Allow it to come to room temperature. This will take about 30 minutes, but do not let it sit longer than 1 hour before forming and baking.

3. If your kitchen is very cold, place the baking sheet of dough on top of the stove. The warmth of the oven will help the dough warm up so that the dough is soft enough to stretch easily. Don't leave it there more than 10 minutes; it could overproof. Turn the dough over once or twice during this time so that the heat permeates it.

4. Place the dough on a generously floured work surface. Using your fingertips, press it all over so that it begins to stretch out. Gently pull to stretch it into a round disk. The dough will be noticeably soft when pulled. Lift it by the edges, place your fists underneath it, and move your fists outward to stretch the dough into a circle about 11 to 12 inches in diameter.

5. Sprinkle a peel or the back of a baking sheet with cornmeal, then carefully transfer the stretched pizza dough onto it. Spread the dough thinly with the tomato sauce, leaving a ½-inch edge all around. Arrange the tomato slices about 2 inches apart on the top of the crust. (Don't crowd the pizza with tomatoes; they release moisture and can make the pizza soggy.) Scatter the feta, olives, and anchovies over the tomatoes. Strip the fresh thyme leaves from their stems and scatter on the pizza, or sprinkle with the dried thyme. Shred the basil leaves and distribute evenly on top. Drizzle olive oil over the pizza and season with a generous grinding of black pepper.

6. Open the oven door and carefully slide the pizza directly onto the baking stone. (Hold the peel or baking sheet with two hands and reach deep into the oven, directly over the stone where you want the pizza to land. Use a firm back and forth movement to shake and slide the pizza from the peel or baking sheet onto the stone. As the pizza slides forward, gently pull the peel or baking sheet out from under it.)

7. Bake for 5 minutes. Check it and rotate so that it bakes evenly. Continue baking for another 5 to 7 minutes, until the edges of the crust are just beginning to get dark brown. To remove from the oven, slide the peel under the pizza and use it to lift the pizza out. Or, using an oven mitt, slide it onto the back of a baking sheet. Transfer the pizza to a wire rack to sit for 2 minutes so that some of the steam escapes and the crust doesn't get soggy.

8. Place the pizza on a cutting board and slice it into 8 pieces.

Four-Cheese Pizza with Garlic

One 10-inch pizza

The scent of mellowed garlic and pungent cheeses combined with the spice of toasting wheat fills the kitchen when this pizza bakes. Because this is a rich pizza with a subtle taste, serve it with a simple salad of bitter greens like Belgian endive, arugula, and chicory dressed with a lemony vinaigrette, and don't forget the peppermill.

The optional addition of truffle oil makes this a regal pizza. Truffles, those priceless tubers with an indescribable mushroom and garlic taste found in the Piedmont region of Italy, are so precious and potent that just a few slivers will flavor a cup of mild olive oil. Use truffle oil to enliven risotto or any creamy dish with a delicate taste, like this pizza. Truffle oil is available at gourmet stores and through mail-order sources.

15 peeled garlic cloves	3 tablespoons (about 1½ ounces)
2 tablespoons olive oil	grated fontina cheese
⅓ recipe Basic Pizza Dough (page 95),	3 tablespoons freshly grated Parmesan
about 10 ounces	cheese
5 slices provolone cheese	Freshly ground black pepper and salt
1½ ounces mozzarella cheese, sliced	2 ounces white truffle oil (optional)
and crumbled	Cornmeal for the peel or baking sheet

1. Place the peeled garlic cloves in a small saucepan, cover them with water, and bring the water to boil. Cook for 2 minutes, drain the water, and cover the garlic again with fresh cold water. Bring the water to boil and cook the garlic for 5 minutes, until it begins to soften. Drain. Return the garlic to the pan, add the olive oil, and cook over medium heat, shaking the pan once or twice to turn the garlic, until it is lightly golden in color but not too brown, about 3 minutes. Set aside.

2. One hour before baking, put the oven rack on the second shelf from the bottom of the oven and place the baking stone on the rack. Preheat the oven to 500°F.

3. While the oven is heating up, remove the dough from the refrigerator and turn it onto a lightly floured work surface. With the palms of your hands, flatten it to a thickness of about ½ inch. Generously sprinkle a baking sheet with flour, place the dough on the sheet, cover it loosely with plastic wrap, and allow it to come to room temperature. This will take about 30 minutes, but do not let it sit longer than 1 hour before forming and baking.

4. If your kitchen is very cold, place the baking sheet of dough on top of the stove. The warmth of the oven will help the dough warm up so that the dough is soft enough to stretch easily. Don't leave it there more than 10 minutes; it could overproof. Turn the dough over once or twice during this time so that the heat permeates it.

5. Place the dough on a generously floured work surface. Using your fingertips, press it all over so that it begins to stretch out. Gently pull to stretch it into a round disk. The dough will be noticeably soft when pulled. Lift it by the edges, place your fists underneath it, and move your fists outward to stretch the dough into a circle about 10 to 11 inches in diameter, or the size that fits your peel or the baking sheet you are using to slide it into the oven. If it resists shaping, cover it with plastic wrap and let it rest for another 10 minutes.

6. Sprinkle a peel or the back of a baking sheet with cornmeal. Carefully transfer the stretched pizza dough onto it. Arrange the provolone slices on top, then sprinkle with the mozzarella and fontina. Scatter with the garlic cloves and then sprinkle with the grated Parmesan, freshly ground pepper, and salt.

7. Open the oven door and carefully slide the pizza directly onto the baking stone. (Hold the baking sheet or peel with two hands and reach deep into the oven, directly over the stone where you want the pizza to land. Use a firm back and forth movement to shake and slide the pizza from the peel or baking sheet onto the stone. As the pizza slides forward, gently pull the peel or baking sheet out from under it.)

8. Bake for 5 minutes. Check it and rotate so that it bakes evenly. Continue baking for another 5 to 7 minutes, until the edges of the pizza crust are just beginning to get dark brown. To remove from the oven, slide the peel under the pizza and use it to lift the pizza out. Or, using an oven mitt, slide it onto the back of the baking sheet. Transfer the pizza to a wire rack to sit for 2 minutes so that some of the steam escapes and the crust doesn't get soggy.

9. Place the pizza on a cutting board, drizzle it with the truffle oil, if using, and slice it into 8 pieces.

Broccoli Rabe and Sausage Pizza

A frequent dish on our dinner table combines orecchiette (pasta in the shape of "little ears"), broccoli rabe, and spicy fennel garlic sausage from the local Italian deli. Here, the pasta is replaced with pizza dough.

One 10-inch pizza

5 tablespoons olive oil

1/2 large red onion, thinly sliced

1 tablespoon (about 2 cloves) minced garlic

4 stems broccoli rabe, chopped into 1/2-inch pieces

Salt

1/4 teaspoon red pepper flakes, or more to taste

1/3 recipe Basic Pizza Dough (page 95), about 10 ounces

1 small link (about 3 ounces) uncooked hot Italian-style sausage

2 tablespoons freshly grated Parmesan cheese

Freshly ground black pepper

Cornmeal for the peel or baking sheet

1. Heat 2 tablespoons of the olive oil in a large skillet over medium-high heat. Add the red onion and sauté until soft, about 5 to 7 minutes. Add the garlic, broccoli rabe, and 2 tablespoons of water. Cover the pan and cook for 7 to 8 minutes. Remove the cover. Season the mixture with salt and red pepper flakes, then set aside to cool.

2. One hour before baking, put the oven rack on the second shelf from the bottom of the oven and place the baking stone on the rack. Preheat the oven to 500°F.

3. While the oven is heating up, remove the dough from the refrigerator and turn it onto a lightly floured work surface. With the palms of your hands, flatten it to a thickness of about 1/2 inch. Generously sprinkle a baking sheet with flour, place the dough on the baking sheet, cover it loosely with plastic wrap, and allow it to come to room temperature, 70°F to 72°F. This will take about 30 minutes, but do not let it sit longer than 1 hour before forming and baking.

4. If your kitchen is very cold, place the baking sheet of dough on top of the stove. The warmth of the oven will help the dough warm up so that the dough is soft enough to stretch easily. But don't leave it there more than 10 minutes; it could overproof. Turn the dough over once or twice during this time so that the heat permeates it.

5. Place the dough on a generously floured work surface. Using your fingertips, press it all over so that it begins to stretch out. Gently pull the dough to stretch it into a round disk. The dough will be noticeably soft when pulled. Lift it by the edges, place your fists underneath it, and move your fists outward to stretch the dough into a circle about 10 to 11 inches in diameter, or the size that fits your peel or the baking sheet you are using to slide it into the oven. If it resists shaping, cover it with plastic wrap and let it rest for another 10 minutes.

6. Sprinkle a peel or the back of a baking sheet with cornmeal. Carefully transfer the stretched pizza dough onto it. Brush the pizza dough with 2 tablespoons of the remaining olive oil. Spread the top with the onion and broccoli rabe mixture. Break up the uncooked sausage into walnut-size pieces and scatter them on top of the pizza. Sprinkle with the Parmesan and season with additional salt and freshly ground pepper. Drizzle the remaining 1 tablespoon of olive oil over the pizza crust and toppings.

7. Open the oven door and carefully slide the pizza directly onto the baking stone. (Holding the peel or baking sheet with two hands, place it deep in the oven, directly over the pizza stone where you want the pizza to land. Use a firm back and forth movement to shake and slide the pizza from the peel or baking sheet onto the stone. As the pizza slides forward, gently pull the peel or baking sheet out from under it.)

8. Bake for 5 minutes. Check it and rotate so that it bakes evenly. Continue baking for another 5 to 7 minutes, until the edges of the pizza crust are just beginning to get dark brown.

9. To remove the pizza from the oven, slide the peel under it and use it to lift the pizza out. Transfer it to a wire rack to sit for 2 minutes so that some of the steam escapes and the crust doesn't get soggy. Or, wearing an oven mitt, slide the baked pizza onto the back of a baking sheet and transfer it to a wire rack to sit.

10. Place the pizza on a cutting board and slice into 8 pieces.

Focaccia

One 10-inch flatbread

Proofing:
45 minutes at room temperature, 70°F to 72°F

There are as many versions of focaccia as there are regions in Italy. This focaccia is a basic bread to be served alone or with a colorful antipasto assortment. Like pizza, focaccia is made from a simple dough, flattened and baked in a hot brick oven. To make the focaccia puff, roll the dough as for pizza and then proof it for a short time. Before baking, dimple it with the tips of your fingers and sprinkle with a combination of olive oil, water, and coarse salt. When the focaccia hits the hot oven, the water evaporates creating steam which helps the crust puff and stay thin and crisp. Sprinkle the dough with coarse salt just before baking for a crunchy counterpoint to the tender crust.

Focaccia is the ideal bread to sprinkle with any type of herb or seasoning. Minced chives, chopped thyme, oregano, shredded prosciutto, green olives, or diced bacon cook evenly on the moist surface of focaccia.

¹/₃ recipe Basic Pizza Dough (page 95), about 10 ounces
¹/₄ cup extra virgin olive oil
4 cloves garlic, chopped

1 teaspoon coarse salt
1 tablespoon chopped fresh rosemary, or ¹/₂ teaspoon dried rosemary

1. One hour before baking, put the oven rack on the second shelf from the bottom of the oven and place the baking stone on the rack. Preheat the oven to 500°F.

2. While the oven is heating up, remove the dough from the refrigerator, turn it onto a lightly floured work surface and flatten it to a thickness of about ¹/₂ inch with the palms of your hands. Cover the dough with a clean towel and allow it to rest for about 15 minutes.

3. Brush a baking sheet or large round pizza pan with some of the olive oil. Using the pads of your fingers, flatten the dough so that it fits in the greased pan. Cover with a clean towel and let it proof, about 45 minutes to an hour.

Dimpling the focaccia

Brush the focaccia with the garlic-and-herb oil mixture

Dimple the oiled focaccia

4. In a small dish combine the garlic, ½ teaspoon of the salt, 1 tablespoon of water, and the rosemary with the remaining oil. Firmly press the tips of your fingers into the dough so that the surface of the focaccia is evenly dimpled. Brush the dough with the garlic and herb oil. Dimple again to spread out any oil that has pooled on the dough. Sprinkle with the remaining coarse salt.

5. Slide the focaccia onto the baking stone. Bake for 10 minutes, then turn the baking sheet front to back to allow for even baking. Continue baking for 7 or 8 more minutes, until the focaccia is crisp and golden. The focaccia will be finished when it reaches an internal temperature of 205°F to 210°F on an instant-read thermometer. Remove from the oven and place it on a wire rack.

6. Cool the focaccia on the wire rack for 5 minutes, then remove it from the pan onto the rack and allow it to cool completely. To crisp the focaccia before serving, place it directly on the preheated baking stone for 5 minutes.

Feta and Herb Focaccia

1 layered flatbread about 10 × 12 inches

Proofing:

45 minutes at room temperature, 70°F to 72°F

Fresh sage, garlic, and assertive feta cheese are layered between two rectangles of dough and then baked. This flatbread is delicious with cold roast pork or soup and a salad.

1 recipe Basic Pizza Dough (page 95), about 1½ pounds

¼ cup extra virgin olive oil

1 tablespoon chopped garlic

1 teaspoon fresh sage leaves, minced, or ½ teaspoon dried sage

3 ounces feta cheese, crumbled

Freshly ground black pepper

Red pepper flakes

1 tablespoon coarse salt

1. One hour before baking, put the oven rack on the second shelf from the bottom of the oven and place the pizza stone on the rack. Preheat the oven to 500°F.

2. While the oven is heating up, remove the dough from the refrigerator and place it on a lightly floured surface. With a dough scraper, divide it in 2 equal pieces. Place one piece on a baking sheet. Pour 1 tablespoon of the olive oil over the dough, spreading it carefully, and pat the dough into a thin rectangle measuring about 8 × 12 inches, and about ½ inch thick.

3. Sprinkle the flattened dough with the garlic, sage, and feta. Generously season with the freshly ground pepper and pepper flakes.

4. On a lightly floured work surface, drizzle the second piece of focaccia dough with 1 tablespoon of the olive oil. Spread the olive oil over the surface and flatten the dough into a rectangle the same size as the first piece. Place this on top of the herb and feta layer and stretch and shape to make an even fit.

5. Press the two layers firmly together so they adhere to one another. Using the pads of your fingers, dimple the focaccia, pressing to remove any air pockets that have formed between the two layers of dough. Cover with plastic wrap and allow the dough to proof for 45 minutes.

6. Combine the remaining 2 tablespoons of olive oil with 2 tablespoons water and the coarse salt. Brush the focaccia with the oil and salt mixture.

7. Slide the baking sheet of focaccia into the oven directly onto the baking stone.

8. Bake the focaccia for 10 minutes. Open the oven and pierce the focaccia with a fork in several places to keep it from rising like a balloon and developing large air bubbles. Continue baking the focaccia for 15 to 20 minutes, until it is well puffed and golden. The focaccia will be finished when it reaches an internal temperature of 205°F to 210°F on an instant-read thermometer. Remove the focaccia from the oven and cool on a wire rack for a few minutes before cutting into wedges and serving.

Pissaladière

A specialty of Provence is this highly seasoned pie with caramelized onions and garlic, decorated with a crisscross of anchovy fillets. Some make it with a butter and olive oil crust, but a pizza type dough is more traditional. Cook the onions very slowly so that all of their moisture evaporates but the onions do not brown. Cut the pissaladière into pieces to serve.

²/₃ recipe Basic Pizza Dough (page 95)	Freshly ground black pepper
2 tablespoons extra virgin olive oil	1 large red pepper
2 pounds onions, thinly sliced	About 40 anchovy fillets
1 teaspoon (about 1 clove) minced garlic	¹/₂ cup pitted, halved black olives
2 teaspoons fresh thyme leaves, or	5 fresh thyme sprigs (optional)
¹/₂ teaspoon dried thyme	Cornmeal for the baking sheet
Fine sea salt	

1. One hour before baking, remove the dough from the refrigerator. Put the oven rack on the second shelf from the bottom of the oven and place the pizza stone on the rack. Preheat the oven to 475°F.

2. Heat the olive oil in a large nonstick pan over medium heat. Add the onions, garlic, and thyme, cover the pan, and reduce the heat to low. Cook for 10 minutes. Remove the cover, stir the onions, and season with salt and pepper. Cover the pan and cook the onions another 20 minutes, until they are completely tender and softened. Remove the pan from the heat and cool completely before proceeding.

3. While the onions are cooking, prepare the roasted red pepper. Place it directly on a burner set to medium and cook until the skin chars. Using tongs or a long fork, turn the pepper and continue charring it on all sides. The skin will blacken all over and bubble. Place the roasted pepper in a paper bag, seal tightly, and let it cool for 10 minutes. Once it has cooled, open the bag and peel the pepper under cool running water. Remove the stem and seeds, then cut the pepper into strips ¹/₂ inch wide. Set aside.

4. Place the pizza dough on a generously floured work surface. With a lightly floured rolling pin, roll the dough into a rectangle measuring about

10×16 inches, roughly the size of a baking sheet. If it resists rolling, cover it with plastic wrap and let it rest for 5 to 10 minutes before continuing. Lift the dough by the edges and transfer it to a baking sheet sprinkled with cornmeal. Let the dough sit for 10 minutes, then stretch it to fit the baking sheet evenly, lifting it by the edges and pulling gently until it fits.

5. Evenly spread the cooked onions over the surface of the dough, leaving a ½-inch border along each edge. Starting in one corner, lay the anchovy fillets end to end, spaced about 2 inches apart, in a diagonal line across the center of the pan. Lay another line of anchovy fillets parallel to the first, spaced about 2 inches apart. Continue in this direction until the dough is covered with 4 or 5 parallel lines of anchovy fillets. Turn the pan around 180 degrees and repeat this pattern in the opposite direction.

6. Use the strips of red pepper to make crosses in several of the diamond spaces. Dot the center of each diamond with half a black olive. Scatter the fresh thyme sprigs over the pissaladière if you wish.

7. Place the pissaladière in the oven directly on the pizza stone. Reduce the heat to 450°F and bake it for about 20 to 25 minutes until the edges of the crust are evenly browned.

8. Remove the pissaladière from the oven and place it on a wire rack to cool slightly, then slide it from the baking sheet onto a cutting board. To serve, cut the pissaladière with a long sharp knife into 2×3-inch pieces.

Breadsticks

Here are two recipes for making breadsticks. The variations are endless. I use pizza dough as the base because it is slightly wetter and easier to handle than regular basic bread dough, but you could certainly use the techniques here with many of the savory doughs like Country Wheat Crown (page 183) or a sweeter dough like Classic Pullman Loaf (page 127).

A few pointers: Use dough that has already risen and fermented at least once. The dough will have developed its taste. When you knead in additional ingredients like garlic and cheese, be patient. The gluten may toughen, making the dough harder to handle as you work in these additions. If it seems impossible to knead, let the dough rest a minute or two before proceeding.

When you roll the tiny pieces of dough, they tend to resist rolling any longer than 7 or 8 inches. Don't worry, once the dough has rested, it is simple to stretch it to the desired length.

Sesame Breadsticks

4 dozen 12-inch breadsticks

Proofing:
20 minutes at room temperature, 70°F to 72°F

Seeded breadsticks are the most traditional, but try these with nigella or black sesame seeds, mustard seeds, fennel seeds, cracked pepper, and coarse salt, alone or in combination. Don't sprinkle the seeds on the dough before it is rolled. The seeds will act like ball bearings so the dough will no longer stick to the work surface and cannot be rolled at all.

> 1 recipe Basic Pizza Dough (page 95)
> 1 cup hulled sesame seeds

1. One hour before baking, put the oven rack on the second shelf from the bottom of the oven and place the baking stone on the rack. Preheat the oven to 500°F.

2. While the oven is heating up, remove the dough from the refrigerator. To divide the dough into 48 uniform pieces, with a knife or dough scraper cut the dough into 4 equal pieces. Divide each piece of dough into 12 pieces to get 48 pieces of dough each weighing approximately 1½ ounces.

3. Sprinkle a baking sheet with the sesame seeds. Have two clean baking sheets ready. Roll each piece of dough into a thin rope about 10 inches long. Don't worry about getting the length at this stage. The dough may resist rolling. If so, cover it with plastic wrap and allow it to rest for 5 to 10 minutes, then continue.

4. When they are all rolled to about the right length, coat each breadstick with the sesame seeds, turning them to coat all sides. Place the breadsticks lengthwise about 1 inch apart on the two clean baking sheets. Cover with plastic wrap and let proof for 20 minutes.

5. Remove the plastic wrap from one baking sheet. The dough will be quite soft. Pick up a strip at each end and gently stretch it so that the dough touches the edges of the tray to make a breadstick measuring about 12 inches. Repeat with all of the breadsticks on the baking sheet.

6. Place one sheet of breadsticks in the oven and immediately reduce the temperature to 450°F. Bake for 8 to 10 minutes. Open the oven and turn the baking sheet so the breadsticks brown evenly. (If the edges of the breadsticks are getting too dark, remove them from the oven. Switch their positions on the baking sheet, placing the breadsticks from the center of the sheet near the edge where they cook more quickly). Return the baking sheet to the oven and bake for another 8 to 10 minutes. The breadsticks will be golden brown and double in size.

7. Remove the baking sheet from the oven and place the breadsticks on a wire rack to cool. They will harden as they cool. Repeat with the remaining baking sheet of breadsticks.

Store the cooled breadsticks tightly sealed in cookie tins or plastic bags. They keep up to a month in the freezer. Thaw them at room temperature, then place them directly on a heated baking stone or on a baking sheet in a preheated 450°F oven. Bake for 5 minutes, then cool the breadsticks on a wire rack. They will regain their crisp texture.

Garlic Parmesan Breadsticks

....

4 dozen
12-inch
breadsticks

Proofing:

20 minutes at
room
temperature,
70°F to 72°F

The cheese and oil in these breadsticks change the texture of the pizza dough. It tends to spread apart as you roll them more than a few inches. Don't worry. Simply stick the ends of the dough back together and continue rolling. I like the gnarly look this gives to their shape once baked.

Some combinations I have tried as knead-ins include fennel seeds, aniseeds, grated lemon and/or orange zest, mixed chopped herbs like parsley, chives, and thyme, herbs de Provence blend, and hot red pepper flakes. This recipe calls for what may seem like a large quantity of garlic, but since it is cooked, the harsh taste is mellowed. These breadsticks look like a bundle of kindling or fagots. They brown irregularly.

1 recipe Basic Pizza Dough (page 95)	Salt and freshly ground black pepper
3 tablespoons olive oil	1/2 cup freshly grated Parmesan cheese
1/3 cup (about 1 large head or 15 cloves) minced garlic	Cornmeal for the baking sheets

1. One hour before baking, put the oven rack on the second shelf from the bottom of the oven and place the pizza stone on the rack. Preheat the oven to 500°F. Sprinkle three baking sheets lightly with cornmeal and set aside.

2. Heat the olive oil in a small saucepan over medium heat. Stir in the minced garlic and 1/4 cup of water. Season with a pinch of salt and freshly ground pepper. Cook the garlic over medium heat for 8 to 10 minutes, adding a little more water if the garlic appears to be browning and sticking. The goal is to soften the garlic without letting it brown and become bitter. Continue cooking until all of the liquid has evaporated and the garlic forms a soft paste. Scrape the paste into a small bowl and let it cool before kneading it into the pizza dough.

3. While the oven is heating up, remove the dough from the refrigerator. Place it on a lightly floured work table and flatten it to a thickness of about 1 inch. Spread the dough with half the Parmesan and half the garlic paste, fold it over onto itself, and begin kneading. Work the dough for a minute or two. As the oil in the garlic blends into the dough, it will soften and become easier to knead. You should not need to add additional flour to flatten the dough again. Spread it with the remaining Parmesan and garlic paste. Knead for another minute or two until the cheese and garlic are thoroughly incorporated.

4. To divide the dough into 48 uniform pieces, cut the dough in half with a knife or dough scraper. Cut each piece in half again, making 4 equal pieces. Cut each quarter into 12 pieces to get 48 pieces of dough, each weighing approximately 1½ ounces. Sprinkle the baking sheets lightly with cornmeal. Roll each piece of dough into a thin rope about 8 inches long. The dough may be difficult to roll, so don't worry about getting the length at this stage. If it breaks apart, simply stick the ends together. Place the strips of dough lengthwise on the baking sheets about 1 inch apart. Cover with a sheet of plastic wrap and let proof for 20 minutes.

5. Remove the plastic wrap from one baking sheet. The dough will be quite soft. Pick up a strip at each end and gently stretch it so that the dough touches the edges of the baking sheet to make a breadstick about 12 inches long. Repeat with all of the breadsticks on the baking sheet.

6. Place one sheet of breadsticks in the oven and immediately reduce the temperature to 450°F. Bake for 8 to 10 minutes. Open the oven and turn the baking sheet so that the breadsticks brown evenly. (If the edges of the breadsticks are getting too dark, remove them from the oven. Switch their position on the baking sheet, placing the breadsticks from the center of the sheet near the edge where they cook more quickly.) Return them to the oven and bake for another 8 to 10 minutes. The breadsticks will be golden brown and double in size.

7. Remove the baking sheet from the oven and place the breadsticks on a wire rack to cool. They will harden as they cool. Repeat with the remaining sheets of breadsticks.

Store the cooled breadsticks tightly sealed in cookie tins or plastic bags. They keep up to a month in the freezer. Thaw them at room temperature, then place them directly on a heated baking stone or on a baking sheet in a preheated 450°F oven. Bake for 5 minutes, then cool the breadsticks on a wire rack. They will regain their crisp texture.

Ciabatta

Four 8-inch
loaves

Fermentation:

3¹/₂ to 4 hours
at room
temperature,
70°F to 72°F

Proofing:

30 minutes,
then another
30 minutes

These loaves of Italian flatbread take their name from their shape, which resembles a dusty old slipper. Properly made, a ciabatta is thin and dimpled, with pronounced holes from its long fermentation.

This dough is very wet, liquid, and alive. Don't be tempted to add more flour to make it easier to handle. The secret to great ciabatta is not handling the dough too much. The unusual way the dough is stretched and shaped means that much of the airy structure is left intact.

Simple Wheat Starter (page 175)	about 180 grams	about 6 ounces	³/₄ cup
Unbleached all-purpose flour	500 grams	1 pound	3¹/₃ to 4 cups
Fine sea salt	10 grams	2 teaspoons	2 teaspoons
Instant yeast	¹/₂ teaspoon	¹/₂ teaspoon	¹/₂ teaspoon
Water	300 grams	9¹/₂ ounces	1 cup plus 3 tablespoons

1. Two to four hours before you plan to mix the dough, feed your starter as described on page 173. Allow the starter to sit at room temperature until it is frothy, bubbly, and visibly active.

2. Place the flour, salt, and yeast in a food processor fitted with the metal blade. Measure ³/₄ cup of the active starter and pour it into the processor. Using an instant-read thermometer, adjust the water temperature so that the combined temperatures of the flour and water give a base temperature of 130°F if using a Cuisinart or KitchenAid or 150°F if using a Braun. (See page 33 for other models.) With the machine running, pour all but 3 tablespoons of the water through the feed tube. Process for 30 seconds. The dough should be relatively wet and sticky. With the machine running, add the reserved water if the dough seems too dry. Process 15 seconds longer, for a total of 45 seconds.

3. Stop the machine and take the temperature of the dough with an instant-read thermometer, which should read between 75°F and 80°F. If the temperature is lower than 75°F, process the dough for an additional 5 seconds, up to twice more, until the dough reaches the desired temperature. If the temperature is higher than 80°F, remove the thermometer, scrape the dough from the food processor into an ungreased bowl, and refrigerate for 5 to 10 minutes. Check the temperature of the dough after 5 minutes; it should be 80°F or cooler by that time.

4. Moisten a rubber spatula with water and use it to scrape the dough from the processor into a large ungreased bowl, being sure to scrape off bits of dough that cling to the blade and the sides of the bowl. Cover with plastic wrap and allow the dough to ferment for 3½ to 4 hours at room temperature, about 70°F to 72°F. It will have doubled in volume and developed a light, airy structure.

5. Scrape the dough onto a heavily floured work surface, using moistened fingers and a wet spatula to remove all of the dough that clings to the bowl. Carefully scoop the dough into a rectangle; use the edges of your cupped hands to push the dough into a shape measuring about 6 × 12 inches and 3 inches high.

6. With a dough scraper or kitchen knife, divide the dough into 4 equal pieces, which will become the finished loaves. Dust each piece of dough with flour. Stretch each piece, pulling gently on each end to lengthen it to about 10 inches long and 2 inches high. Leave the loaves on the table or transfer them to heavily floured baking sheets. Cover with sheets of plastic and let them proof for 30 minutes.

7. One hour before baking, put the oven rack on the second shelf from the bottom of the oven and place the baking stone on the rack. Place a small pan for water on the bottom of the oven. Preheat the oven to 500°F.

8. Uncover the loaves and gently flatten them to a thickness of about 2 inches; use the palms of your hands to pat them gently into even shapes. Cover and let proof for 20 to 30 minutes.

9. Transfer two of the loaves to a peel or the back of a baking sheet that has been dusted with flour. Sprinkle the loaves lightly with flour, and dimple them with the tips of your fingers.

10. Pour about ½ cup warm water into the pan on the bottom of the oven. Immediately slide the loaves from the peel or baking sheet onto the stone. Transfer the remaining loaves onto a floured peel or back of a baking sheet. Flour and dimple them and immediately slide them from the peel or baking sheet onto the baking stone. Reduce the oven heat to 450°F. Bake the

Ciabatta will
stay fresh for
a few days
stored in a
paper bag
at room
temperature.
For longer
storage, wrap
the breads in
plastic and
freeze.

loaves for 2 minutes, then steam the oven again with another ½ cup of water. Continue baking for 25 to 30 minutes until the crusts are golden brown. The loaves will be finished when they reach an internal temperature of 205°F to 210°F on an instant-read thermometer.

11. Remove the bread from the oven and immediately place the loaves on a wire rack to cool.

Grape and Pear Pizza— Schiacciata all'uva e alle pere

One 10-inch
pizza

Proofing:

1 to 1½ hours
at room
temperature,
70°F to 72°F

Italy is famous for its sweet flatbreads and pizzas, elegant combinations of fresh figs, pine nuts, spices, and bread dough. This schiacciata is a striking combination of ripe pears and red grapes in a delicious anise syrup that is made when the juice from the fruits melts with the sugar on top. The fruit browns in the oven, releasing its caramel scent into the kitchen. Use a light olive oil so as not to overpower the delicate taste of the fruit. This is perfect for breakfast with a cup of tea or as an afternoon pick-me-up with a sweet apéritif.

⅓ recipe Basic Pizza Dough (page 95), about 10 ounces	¼ cup sugar
	½ teaspoon aniseeds
1 or 2 ripe pears	2 tablespoons extra virgin olive oil
12 seedless grapes	Cornmeal for the baking sheet

1. One hour before baking, put the oven rack on the second shelf from the bottom of the oven and place the baking stone on the rack. Preheat the oven to 500°F.

2. While the oven is heating up, remove the dough from the refrigerator and turn it onto a lightly floured work surface. With the palms of your hands, flatten the dough to a thickness of about ½ inch. Sprinkle a baking sheet lightly with flour, place the dough on the sheet, and cover it loosely with plastic wrap. Allow it come to room temperature. This will take about 30 minutes, but do not let it sit longer than 1 hour before forming and baking.

3. If your kitchen is very cold, place the baking sheet of dough on top of the stove. The warmth of the oven will help it to warm up so that the dough is soft enough to stretch easily. But don't leave the dough there more than 10 minutes; it could overproof. Turn the dough over once or twice during this time so that the heat permeates it.

4. Peel the pears and slice thinly into a small bowl. Cut the grapes in half and toss them with the pears, sugar, and aniseeds. Set aside.

5. Place the dough on a generously floured work surface. Using your fingertips, press it all over so that it begins to stretch out. Gently pull to stretch it into a round disk. The dough will be noticeably soft when pulled. Lift it by the edges, place your fists underneath it, and move your fists outward to stretch the dough into a circle about 11 to 12 inches in diameter.

6. Sprinkle a peel or the back of a baking sheet with cornmeal, then carefully transfer the stretched dough onto the peel or baking sheet. Arrange the pear slices in a circle around the rim of the dough, spacing the slices ½ inch apart. Scatter the grapes over the pear slices. Carefully brush the pears with the olive oil.

7. Open the oven door and carefully slide the schiacciata directly onto the baking stone. (Hold the peel or baking sheet with two hands and reach deep into the oven, directly over the stone where you want the schiacciata to land. Use a firm back and forth movement to shake and slide the dough from the peel or baking sheet onto the stone. As it slides forward, gently pull the peel or sheet out from under it.)

8. Bake the schiacciata for 5 minutes. Check it and rotate so that it bakes evenly. Continue baking for another 5 to 7 minutes until the edges of the crust are just beginning to get dark brown.

9. To remove the schiacciata from the oven, slide the peel under it and use it to lift it out of the oven. Or, wearing an oven mitt, slide it onto the back of a baking sheet. Transfer the schiacciata to a wire rack to sit for 2 minutes so that some of the steam escapes and the crust doesn't get soggy.

10. Move the schiacciata to a cutting board, cut it into 8 wedges, and serve each wedge with a glass of fruity red wine or vin santo.

Calzone

If the ciabatta is a dusty slipper, then the calzone is a rugged country shoe. Calzone, which means great big shoe in Italian, is pizza or ciabatta dough flattened, then folded over delicious fillings.

To make calzone, divide one batch of fermented Basic Pizza Dough (page 95) into 4 pieces. Shape them as for pizza. On one half of each piece of dough, spread about 2 cups of a favorite filling such as ground beef or sausage cooked with tomatoes and spices, fried slices of eggplant, tomatoes, and mozzarella cheese, or anything that would make a delicious pizza topping. Slide into a preheated oven and bake for 18 to 20 minutes.

Provençal Flatbread with Bacon
Fougasse aux Lardons

1 large
flatbread

Fermentation:

1½ to 2 hours
at room
temperature,
70°F to 72°F.

Proofing:

30 minutes

Fougasse, a rustic flatbread from Provence with decorative slashes, resembles a ladder or a gnarled tree with branches. Fougasse dough often includes chunks of bacon or fatback called lardons and snips of rosemary or other herbs found in southern France. I always use imported lean, slab bacon that I cut myself.

This recipe makes one large or two smaller fougasse. I have had terrific results making fougasse with Basic Pizza Dough (page 95) that has been fermented, then retarded for 12 to 24 hours. (If you use pizza dough, just knead in the bacon and rosemary and prepare the fougasse as outlined here.) The loaf can be dusted with flour or coarse salt right before baking. I like the fougasse for its high proportion of crust to crumb.

Lean slab bacon or thick-cut lean bacon	120 grams	4 ounces	½ cup
Fresh rosemary, chopped	10 grams	2 teaspoons	2 teaspoons
All-purpose flour	500 grams	1 pound	3⅓ to 4 cups
Fine sea salt	10 grams	2 teaspoons	2 teaspoons
Instant yeast	1 teaspoon	1 teaspoon	1 teaspoon
Water	315 grams	10 ounces	1¼ cups
Extra virgin olive oil	15 grams	1 tablespoon	1 tablespoon

1. Cut the bacon into ¼-inch-thick slices, then cut each slice, into ¼-inch-wide strips for the lardons. Remove the rosemary from its woody stem. Discard the stems and chop the needles coarsely. Combine the lardons and rosemary in a small bowl and set aside.

2. Place the flour, salt, and yeast in a food processor fitted with the metal blade. Using an instant-read thermometer, adjust the water temperature so that the combined temperature of the flour and water is a base temperature of 130°F if using a Cuisinart or KitchenAid or 150°F if using a Braun. (See page 33 for other models.) Add the olive oil to the water. With the machine running, pour all but 2 tablespoons of the water through the feed tube. Process for 30 seconds. If the dough seems too dry, add the remaining water during the last 15 seconds of processing for a total mixing time of 45 seconds. This dough will be soft, elastic, and moist.

3. Stop the machine, and take the temperature of the dough with an instant-read thermometer. It should be between 75°F and 80°F. If the temperature is lower than 75°F, process the dough for an additional 5 seconds, up to twice more, until the dough reaches the desired temperature. If the temperature is higher than 80°F, remove the thermometer, scrape the dough from the food processor into an ungreased bowl, and refrigerate for 5 to 10 minutes. Check the temperature of the dough after 5 minutes; the dough should be 80°F or cooler by that time.

4. Remove the dough from the processor and place it on a lightly floured work surface. Flatten the dough with the palms of your hands to a thickness of about 1 inch. Sprinkle the dough with the raw bacon and chopped rosemary. Fold the dough over several times to incorporate the bacon and herbs. Lightly knead the fougasse dough to distribute the bacon and herbs evenly throughout the dough. Form the dough into a smooth ball.

5. Place the dough into a large ungreased bowl. Cover the bowl with plastic wrap. Allow the dough to ferment for 1½ to 2 hours at room temperature, 70°F to 72°F. The dough will have increased in volume somewhat but don't be concerned by how much.

6. Scrape the dough onto a lightly floured work surface. With a rolling pin, flatten the dough into a rectangle measuring about 8 × 12 inches and about ½ inch thick. Transfer the flattened dough to a baking sheet dusted with flour. Cover with plastic wrap.

Using a dough scraper or knife . . .   make 4-inch slits in the dough   Use your fingers to widen the slits of the fougasse

Making a
fougasse

7. Let the fougasse proof another 30 minutes. The fougasse is ready to bake when the dough does not spring back when lightly touched with your finger. It will feel light and spongy.

8. One hour before baking, put the oven rack on the second shelf from the bottom of the oven and place the baking stone on the rack. Place a pan for water on the floor of the oven and preheat to 475°F.

9. Just before baking, score the fougasse; with a dough scraper or razor blade make 2 vertical slits, each about 4 inches long, down the center of the fougasse. To the right, make 3 or 4 diagonal slits in the dough. Each of these slits should be about 3 inches long and 2 inches from the edge of the dough. Repeat on the left side. Stretch the slits open by lifting the edges of the fougasse. Pull on the dough until the slits widen to about 1 inch. Lift the dough on each side to stretch all of the slits open. This will prevent the slits from closing when baked. The fougasse will have the pattern of the trunk and branches of a tree when baked. Lightly sift more flour on the surface of the fougasse.

10. Carefully pour about ½ cup of warm water into the pan on the bottom of the oven. Immediately slide the baking sheet of fougasse on to the baking stone and turn the heat down to 450°F. Bake the fougasse for 20 to 25 minutes. The fougasse is done when lightly browned and has a hollow sound when tapped lightly on the bottom. Or, the fougasse will be finished when it reaches an internal temperature of 205°F to 210°F, using an instant-read thermometer.

11. Remove the fougasse from the oven and slide it directly on a wire rack to cool before serving.

Whole Wheat Pita Pockets

No bread is easier to make and offers more pleasure than this pita bread. Children love to watch pita breads miraculously puff up in the oven. Because whole wheat flour absorbs more water than many wheat flours, this dough is relatively dry. If you use all-purpose flour, you may not need to add the reserved water.

    The key to successful pita is not to overbake it, especially if you plan to fill it for sandwiches. Any dark parts may become brittle when cool causing holes in the pita bread and making that piece unsuitable for stuffing.

Twelve 7-inch pocket breads

Fermentation: 3½ to 4 hours at room temperature 70°F to 72°F

Whole wheat flour	500 grams	1 pound	3⅓ to 4 cups
Fine sea salt	10 grams	2 teaspoons	2 teaspoons
Instant yeast	1 teaspoon	1 teaspoon	1 teaspoon
Water	315 grams	10 ounces	1¼ cups
Vegetable oil	15 grams	1 tablespoon	1 tablespoon

1. Place the flour, salt, and yeast in a food processor fitted with the metal blade. Using an instant-read thermometer, adjust the water temperature so that the combined temperatures of the flour and water is a base temperature of 130°F if using a Cuisinart or KitchenAid or 150°F if using a Braun. (See page 33 for other models.) Add the vegetable oil to the water. With the machine running, pour all but 2 tablespoons of the water through the feed tube. Process for 20 seconds. Stop the machine and using a wooden spoon break up any dough that has become stuck under the metal blade. Process 25 seconds longer, adding the remaining water during the last 10 seconds if the dough seems too dry, for a total mixing time of 45 seconds.

2. Stop the machine, and take the temperature of the dough with an instant-read thermometer, which should read between 75°F and 80°F. If the temperature is lower than 75°F, process the dough for an additional 5 seconds, up to twice more, until the dough reaches the desired temperature. If the temperature is higher than 80°F, remove the thermometer, scrape the dough from the food processor into an ungreased bowl, and refrigerate for 5

To keep the pita breads soft and pliable, store the cooled bread tightly sealed in a plastic bag until ready to use.

to 10 minutes. Check the temperature of the dough after 5 minutes; the dough should be 80°F or cooler by that time.

3. Scrape the dough into a large ungreased bowl and cover it with plastic wrap. Let the dough ferment for 3½ to 4 hours at room temperature, 70°F to 72°F.

4. One hour before baking, put the oven rack on the second shelf from the bottom of the oven and place the baking stone on the rack. Preheat the oven to 500°F.

5. Scrape the dough onto a lightly floured work surface and with a knife or dough scraper cut it into 12 equal pieces. Roll each piece of dough into a smooth ball, cover the balls with a towel or plastic wrap and leave them to rest on the floured work surface for 10 minutes.

6. Flatten each ball of dough with a rolling pin into a 7-inch circle. Cover with plastic wrap and let the dough rest 5 minutes.

7. Place 4 or 5 pieces of flattened dough on a peel or the back of a baking sheet that has been lightly dusted with flour. Use the peel or baking sheet to slide the pita breads directly onto the heated baking stone. Or bake the pita breads on an ungreased baking sheet placed directly in the oven. Bake the breads for 6 to 7 minutes until they are lightly browned and well puffed. Remove the breads to a wire rack to cool and bake the remaining pitas.

Enriched Breads

Is there a better way to start a hectic day than with a buttery breakfast bread and a rich cup of roasted coffee? One of life's small luxuries is the smell of these delightful doughs as they bake, a hint of spice and the mouthwatering aroma of yeast and butter filling the kitchen.

The recipes in this chapter use the food processor to mix doughs enriched with butter, milk, and eggs. These breads make special occasions out of everyday eating, and the food processor makes them easy to make any day of the week.

Even a humble sandwich loaf develops a beautiful honeycombed crumb and creamy color when the dough is mixed in the food processor. The Classic Pullman loaf (page 127), mixed in 45 seconds and fermented for just 3 hours, is a memorable bread that will earn you kudos from those lucky enough to sample it.

From challah to airy rum babas, breads made from dough rich with butter and eggs are surprisingly easy to make. A delightful babka, an Eastern European coffee cake, is mixed, proofed, and baked within two hours.

Sweet doughs with a high percentage of butter, sugar, or eggs are sticky and moist, and, unlike other bread doughs in this book, most cling to the sides of the food processor bowl when mixed and do not form into a smooth ball. Don't be concerned. These are forgiving doughs; since many are formed and baked in pans, if the dough seems more moist than usual, it will make little difference once the dough is baked.

To give many of the enriched doughs their fluffy cakelike crumb, the yeast is dissolved in a small amount of liquid before it is added to the dry ingredients. This, in turn, activates the yeast more quickly, giving a big rise to breads like challah or brioche. When sugar and sweeteners are added to bread dough, the yeast goes on a feeding frenzy and the breads ferment and rise rapidly.

To slowly develop the flavor in brioche and other sweet doughs in this chapter, the dough is often retarded in the refrigerator for several hours or longer. The chill of refrigeration slows the action of the yeast and allows the dough to develop a rich taste.

With the additional weight of the butter and eggs in these doughs, the brioche and stollen in particular, you may find it easier to mix the dough in two batches if your food processor tends to stall.

Keep an eye on these rich breads as they bake. With their high butter and egg content, you may need to lower your oven temperature by 50°F if the loaves are browning too quickly.

Classic Pullman Loaf

Late on Thanksgiving Day, after the relatives have fled, when I get a craving for a sandwich layered with turkey, mayonnaise, and cranberry sauce, this is the bread I use. It has a soft crumb with a hint of sweetness that is ideal for hearty American-style sandwiches.

This recipe makes one large loaf, pale gold in color. I also use this dough to make Pain de Mie (page 129), a bread baked in a loaf pan with its own lid. If you don't have one of these pans, grease a baking sheet and use it as a lid on your loaf pan. Fill the pan as described in the recipe, then cover it with the baking sheet before the dough proofs. As the bread proofs, it rises to fill all the air space in the pan. When the bread is baked with the lid in place, the result is a perfectly square loaf ideal for tea sandwiches or canapés. This recipe makes one long majestic loaf or two smaller 8 × 4-inch loaves.

One 12-inch loaf or two 8 × 4-inch loaves

Fermentation: 1¹/₂ to 2 hours at room temperature, 70°F to 72°F

Proofing: 1 to 1¹/₂ hours at room temperature

Unbleached bread flour	750 grams	1¹/₂ pounds	4³/₄ to 6 cups
Nonfat dry milk	10 grams	¹/₄ cup	¹/₄ cup
Fine sea salt	15 grams	2³/₄ tablespoons	2³/₄ tablespoons
Instant yeast	1¹/₂ teaspoons	1¹/₂ teaspoons	1¹/₂ teaspoons
Honey	2 tablespoons	2 tablespoons	2 tablespoons
Unsalted butter	60 grams	2 ounces	4 tablespoons (¹/₂ stick)
Water	375 grams	12 ounces	1¹/₂ cups

Vegetable oil or vegetable cooking spray for the bread pan

1. Place the flour, nonfat milk, salt, yeast, and honey in a food processor fitted with the metal blade. Melt the butter in a saucepan set over low heat. Set aside. Using an instant-read thermometer, adjust the temperature of the water so that the combined temperatures of the flour and the water give a base temperature of 130°F if using a Cuisinart or KitchenAid or 150°F if using a Braun. (See page 33 for other models.) Add the melted butter to the water. With the machine running, pour all but 2 tablespoons of the liquid through the feed tube. Process for 30 seconds. Then add the remaining water during the last 15 seconds of the mixing if the dough seems too dry and is not forming a smooth ball. Process the dough for a total of 45 seconds.

2. Stop the machine and take the temperature of the dough with an instant-read thermometer, which should read between 75°F and 80°F. If the temperature is lower than 75°F, process the dough for an additional 5 seconds, up to twice more, until the dough reaches the desired temperature. If the temperature is higher than 80°F, remove the thermometer, scrape the dough from the food processor into an ungreased bowl, and refrigerate for 5 to 10 minutes. Check the temperature of the dough after 5 minutes; it should be 80°F or cooler by that time.

3. Remove the dough from the processor and place it in a large ungreased bowl. Cover with plastic wrap and allow the dough to ferment for 1½ to 2 hours at room temperature, 70°F to 72°F.

4. Brush a 12-inch loaf pan with vegetable oil or coat it with vegetable cooking spray. Set aside.

5. Turn the dough onto a lightly floured work surface. Press it into a 14-inch square (slightly longer than the loaf pan in which it will be baked). Fold in the right- and left-hand edges about 2 inches each. Roll the dough into a log and place it in the prepared pan, seam side down, being careful that the dough doesn't touch the sides of the pan.

6. Loosely cover the loaf pan with plastic wrap. Let the dough proof for about 1 to 1½ hours at room temperature until it increases by half its size and crests slightly above the rim of the pan.

7. One hour before baking, put the oven rack on the second shelf from the bottom of the oven and place the baking stone on the rack. Place a small pan for the water on the bottom of the oven and preheat to 475°F.

8. Lightly dust the loaf with flour. Using a sharp knife or razor blade, slash the loaf right down the center about ½ inch deep.

9. Pour about 1 cup warm water into the pan in the oven. Immediately place the loaf pan in the oven on the baking stone and reduce the heat to 400°F.

10. Bake the bread for about 15 minutes. Once the crust on the loaf has set, you may remove the loaf from the oven and carefully slide it from the pan in which it has been baking. Use a peel or the back of a baking sheet to slide the loaf back into the oven directly onto the baking stone. Continue baking the bread for another 30 minutes, until the crust has browned. Insert an instant-read thermometer into the bread, and if the internal temperature is 205°F to 210°F, the bread is done.

11. Remove the bread from the oven and immediately place it on a wire rack to cool.

Variation:

For Pain de Mie, place the formed dough into an oiled 12-inch loaf pan. Generously grease a baking sheet and place it over the pan to form a lid. Proof the dough with its lid in place and bake, covered, following the steps outlined for Classic Pullman Loaf. After 15 minutes in the oven, remove the pan from the oven. Uncover it and take the loaf from its pan, then return the bread to the oven to finish baking. Cool and store as for the Pullman loaf.

This bread will keep for several days stored in a paper bag at room temperature.

Challah

Two 10-inch
loaves

Fermentation:

1¹/₂ to 2 hours
at room
temperature,
70°F to 72°F

First Proofing:

1 to 1¹/₂ hours
at room
temperature

Second
Proofing:

45 minutes
at room
temperature

This traditional Jewish egg bread is so easy to make using the food processor technique that you'll probably want to make it more often than just for the holidays. The aroma of honey and eggs perfumes the kitchen as the loaves bake. The dough mixes easily into a smooth mass well suited to forming into a majestic braid or a simple round turban shape typically served at the Jewish New Year.

This recipe comes from my friend Howard Kaplan, who says that many people like their challah on the sweet side, depending on where they come from in Europe. Don't hesitate to add another tablespoon of honey or sugar to suit your taste. This dough ferments and is then proofed twice. The extra proofing before forming gives the challah its light, spongy texture.

I like this bread coated with poppy seeds, sliced for sandwiches or toasted, and it makes excellent French toast.

Unbleached all-purpose flour	500 grams	1 pound	3¹/₃ to 4 cups
Fine sea salt	10 grams	2 teaspoons	2 teaspoons
Instant yeast	1 teaspoon	1 teaspoon	1 teaspoon
Vegetable oil	2 teaspoons	2 teaspoons	2 teaspoons
Honey	1 tablespoon	1 tablespoon	1 tablespoon
Large eggs	3	3	3
Water	250 grams	8 ounces	1 cup

Poppy seeds or sesame seeds for sprinkling on loaves before baking

1. Place the flour, salt, yeast, vegetable oil, and honey in a food processor fitted with the metal blade. Using an instant-read thermometer, adjust the temperature of the water so that the combined temperatures of the flour and the liquid give a base temperature of 130°F if using a Cuisinart or KitchenAid or 150°F if using a Braun. (See page 33 for other models.) Beat two of the eggs and add them to the liquid. With the machine running, pour all but 2 tablespoons of the liquid through the feed tube. Process for 30 seconds. If the dough seems too dry and is not forming a smooth ball, add the reserved liquid and process for 15 seconds more, for a total of 45 seconds.

2. Stop the machine, and take the temperature of the dough with an instant-read thermometer, which should read between 75°F and 80°F. If the temperature is lower than 75°F, process the dough for an additional 5 seconds, up to twice more, until the dough reaches the desired temperature. If the temperature is higher than 80°F, remove the thermometer, scrape the dough from the food processor into an ungreased bowl, and refrigerate for 5 to 10 minutes. Check the temperature of the dough after 5 minutes; it should be 80°F or cooler by that time.

3. Remove the dough from the processor and place it in a large un-greased bowl. Cover with plastic wrap and ferment for 1½ to 2 hours at room temperature, 70°F to 72°F. The dough will have noticeably increased in volume and will be light and soft.

4. Scrape the dough onto a lightly floured work surface. Gently flatten it with the palms of your hands, but do not punch out all of the air bubbles that have formed as the dough has fermented. Form the dough into a loose ball; lift up one edge and fold it into the center. Do this about 4 or 5 times until the dough is formed into a ball. Return it to the bowl, cover, and let proof at room temperature until it doubles in bulk, about 1 to 1½ hours.

5. One hour before baking, put the oven rack on the second shelf from the bottom of the oven and place the baking stone on the rack. Place a pan on the bottom of the oven and preheat to 425°F.

6. Scrape the dough onto a lightly floured work surface. Using a dough scraper or kitchen knife, divide it into 2 pieces. Form each piece into a log shape to be rolled like a baguette (page 36). Cover and let rest for 10 minutes.

7. To form the dough into round turban shapes, roll one piece into a strip about 14 inches long. Taper the dough so that it is noticeably thicker at one end; use both hands to roll the dough into a point on the other end. Starting with the thicker end, coil the dough so that it forms a tight spiral. Wrap it around, then tuck the thin end under the loaf to keep it from un-raveling. With the palms of your hands, press the top of the loaf lightly to

Store the cooled challah in a paper bag at room temperature for up to three days. For longer storage, wrap the freshly baked, cooled loaves in plastic and freeze for up to three weeks.

flatten it slightly, then transfer it to one corner of a parchment-lined baking sheet. Repeat with the second piece of dough. Place it diagonally across from the first loaf spaced about 2 inches so the loaves do not stick together as they bake. Cover with a towel and let proof for about 45 minutes at room temperature. The loaves will be visibly puffed and will increase in volume by at least half.

8. Just before baking, beat the remaining egg with 1 tablespoon of water. Brush each loaf with the egg wash, then sprinkle the loaves with poppy seeds or sesame seeds. Carefully pour about 1 cup of warm water into the pan in the oven. Immediately slide the baking sheet of dough onto the baking stone in the oven and turn the heat down to 400°F.

9. Bake for 2 minutes, then quickly open the oven door and add another 1 cup warm water to the pan in the oven. Continue baking the bread for another 30 minutes. Check to see if it is browning too quickly. Reduce the heat to 375°F if necessary, then continue baking for another 10 to 15 minutes. The bread is done when golden brown. Insert an instant-read thermometer into it, and if the internal temperature is 205°F to 210°F, the bread is done.

10. Remove the bread from the oven and place the loaves on a wire rack to cool completely before cutting and storing.

Basic Brioche Dough

Brioche is a refined bread more like a cake. In fact the "cake" Marie Antoinette promised the rebellious masses of the French Revolution was the sensuous brioche. The beauty of a brioche is the contrast between its fluffy golden interior and its buttery crisp crust. A good brioche will taste of butter but will not be greasy.

Using the food processor to mix this rich dough makes quick work of a sticky, time-consuming process. In order to achieve a light, fluffy crumb, the yeast in this recipe is dissolved in liquid, then blended into the flour. The butter should be soft, but still cool. If it is too warm, it will separate and leave greasy pools in the dough.

Should this moist and heavy dough cause your food processor to stall, divide the ingredients in half and mix it in two batches.

To keep the dough cool and easy to handle when forming into any of the shapes in these recipes, refrigerate any dough that is not being used immediately. If it warms and becomes too sticky to handle, put it in the refrigerator or freezer to firm up before proceeding.

Brioche dough freezes. Ferment the brioche dough as instructed, then wrap it well in plastic before freezing. Thaw the brioche in the refrigerator.

Makes about 3 pounds brioche dough, enough for Brioche à Tête, or one 9-inch pan loaf, 2 conical loaves, or 16 individual rolls

Fermentation:
2 hours at room temperature, 70°F to 72°F

Retardation:
6 to 24 hours in the refrigerator

Unsalted butter	275 grams	9 ounces	1 cup plus 2 tablespoons (2 1/8 sticks)
Instant yeast	1 teaspoon	1 teaspoon	1 teaspoon
Pastry flour, or			
unbleached all-purpose flour	500 grams	1 pound	3 1/3 to 4 cups
Sugar	30 grams	1 ounce	2 tablespoons
Fine sea salt	10 grams	2 teaspoons	2 teaspoons
Milk	125 grams	4 ounces	1/2 cup
Large eggs	5	5	5

1. Press the butter between two sheets of waxed paper or plastic wrap and smash it with a rolling pin to soften. Or, place it in the bowl of a mixer fitted with the paddle attachment and beat until it is soft and creamy but still cool. The butter should have the texture of a firm frosting. Set it aside at room temperature.

2. Dissolve the yeast in 2 tablespoons of cool water. Place the flour, sugar, and salt in the bowl of the food processor fitted with the metal blade. Scrape in the yeast. Pulse 3 or 4 times to incorporate the yeast mixture.

3. Using an instant-read thermometer, take the temperature of the flour mixture. In a small metal bowl beat the milk and eggs lightly until blended. Take the temperature of the eggs. Adjust the temperature of the eggs so that the combined temperature of the flour and eggs gives a base temperature of 130°F if using a Cuisinart or KitchenAid or 150°F if using a Braun. (See page 33 for other models.) (If it is necessary to warm the eggs, place the metal bowl in another bowl containing hot tap water and stir for 3 to 4 minutes or until the eggs reach the desired temperature. If the eggs are too warm, cool them by placing the metal bowl over ice water. Stir for 2 or 3 minutes or until the eggs reach the desired temperature.)

4. With the machine running, add the eggs to the mixture in the food processor. Process for 15 seconds. Stop the machine and scrape down the sides of the bowl.

5. With a rubber spatula, scrape the butter from the waxed paper, plastic wrap, or mixer bowl into the bowl of the food processor. Using a spatula, turn the dough over so that some of the butter is under the dough near the blade of the machine. Process for 30 seconds. (If the dough sticks to the bottom of the bowl and the processor has trouble starting, remove the dough from the processor. Return half of it to the processor bowl, spreading it out evenly. Repeat, processing the dough in two batches.)

6. Stop the machine and take the temperature of the dough with an instant-read thermometer, which should read between 75°F and 80°F. If the temperature is lower than 75°F, process the dough for an additional 5 seconds, up to twice more, until it reaches the desired temperature. If the temperature is higher than 80°F, remove the thermometer, scrape the dough from the food processor into an ungreased bowl, and refrigerate for 5 to 10 minutes. Check the temperature after 5 minutes; it should be 80°F or cooler by that time.

7. Remove the dough from the processor, place it in a large ungreased bowl, and cover with plastic wrap. Allow the dough to ferment for 2 hours at room temperature, 70°F to 72°F. It will increase in volume somewhat, but don't be concerned if it doesn't double.

8. Uncover the dough and gently press it down to remove some of the air bubbles. Cover it with plastic wrap and put it in the refrigerator for 6 to 24 hours, preferably overnight. From this point, the brioche dough may be formed into any of the following shapes, proofed, and baked. Or, wrapped tightly in plastic wrap, it may be frozen for up to a month, then thawed in the refrigerator before using.

Brioche à Tête

The classic shape for brioche dough is a round fluted loaf with a distinctive topknot or head. As the dough proofs and bakes, the small ball of dough on top turns a dark shiny brown, rising to crown this memorable treat.

One 9-inch loaf

Proofing:

1¹⁄₂ to 2 hours at room temperature, 70°F to 72°F

The trick to forming this loaf is to divide the dough in two pieces, one three times the size of the other, and keep the dough cool while forming. To make the topknot, the smaller piece of dough is rolled into a small cone and placed in an indentation pushed into the larger ball.

Never place brioche near the oven to speed the proofing time; the butter will melt and leak out. With its high butter and egg content, brioche browns easily. You may need to cover the loaf with a piece of aluminum foil if it is browning too quickly as it bakes.

The refined taste of brioche makes it the preferred accompaniment to pâté, foie gras, and smoked salmon. It is equally delicious served plain or toasted with preserves, and it makes excellent French toast.

1 tablespoon butter, melted   1 large egg
1 recipe Basic Brioche Dough
     (page 133)

1. Two to three hours before baking, lightly butter a 9-inch fluted brioche mold with the melted butter. Set aside.

Store the brioche at room temperature, wrapped in plastic, for a few days. For longer storage, freeze it tightly sealed in plastic wrap for up to three weeks.

2. Remove the brioche dough from the refrigerator and scrape it onto a lightly floured work surface. Cut the dough into 2 pieces, 1 piece three times the size of the other. Using lightly floured hands, roll the larger piece of dough into a round ball. (Work quickly as the butter-rich dough tends to warm and soften, becoming more difficult to handle.) Place this piece of dough in the prepared mold, lightly pressing it into the pan to flatten the surface slightly. Then, with two fingers, make an indentation 2 inches deep in the top center of the dough.

3. Roll the smaller piece of dough into a round ball and roll one end of the ball to form a slightly pointed cone. Fit the pointed end into the indentation in the larger ball of dough. Adjust so that the topknot sits perfectly centered in the larger ball of dough.

4. Cover the formed brioche with plastic wrap and allow it to proof at room temperature, 70°F to 72°F, until it rises by half its size. This may take 1½ to 2 hours, depending on how cold the dough became while fermenting in the refrigerator. When it is ready to bake, it will be almost double in size and puffy, but it will still spring back when pressed with a finger.

5. One hour before baking, adjust the oven rack so that it is on the second shelf from the bottom of the oven. Preheat the oven to 450°F.

6. Beat the egg with 1 teaspoon of water. Using a pastry brush, glaze the brioche, taking care not to let any egg wash settle in the seams or down the sides of the brioche mold, where it could cause sticking.

7. Place the brioche in the oven and bake for 20 minutes. Rotate the pan to allow it to bake evenly. (Lower the oven temperature to 425°F if it is browning too quickly.) Bake for another 25 minutes. Insert an instant-read thermometer; the brioche will be finished when it reaches an internal temperature of 205°F to 210°F.

8. Remove the brioche from the oven and allow it to cool for 10 minutes on a wire rack. Remove it from the mold and cool it completely before slicing.

Brioche Mousseline

When additional butter is added to brioche dough, as much as triple what is called for in a basic recipe, it is called brioche mousseline. The rich dough is so fragile that it could topple under its own weight as it proofs. To avoid this bakers customarily bake it in tall cans, the sides of which support the dough. While no extra butter is added to this dough, it bakes into a light loaf with a downy texture much like authentic brioche mousseline.

Brioche dough is both delicate and malleable. It can be molded into the most intricate shape, then baked. Its buttery crust retains the exact outline of the pan in which it was baked. Coffee cans make tall, elegant loaves. Use cans with smooth linings, because the brioche tends to get stuck in ridged cans.

Two 10-inch-tall loaves

Proofing:
1¹/₂ to 2 hours at room temperature, 70°F to 72°F

2 tablespoons butter, melted
1 recipe Basic Brioche Dough
    (page 133), proofed and refrigerated
    for at least 6 hours
1 large egg

1. A few hours before baking, lightly grease two clean 16-ounce coffee cans with the melted butter. Butter a sheet of parchment or waxed paper. Trace two circles to fit the coffee cans, cut them out, and place one in the bottom of each can. Set aside.

2. Remove the dough from the refrigerator and scrape it onto a lightly floured work surface. Cut it into 2 equal pieces, each one weighing almost a pound. Using lightly floured hands, roll one piece into a smooth ball. The dough will be firm, smooth, and cool. Work quickly, as the butter-rich dough tends to warm and soften, becoming more difficult to handle. Flatten the ball and roll it into a log shape roughly the size of the coffee can. Press the dough firmly into the can so that it touches the sides. The dough will fill the can about halfway. Repeat with the second piece of dough.

3. Cover the cans with plastic wrap and place them in a draft-free place to proof for 1¹/₂ to 2 hours (depending on how cold the dough became while fermenting in the refrigerator). The dough will rise almost to the tops of the cans and will be well puffed but still spring back when pressed with a finger.

4. One hour before baking, adjust the oven rack so that is it on the second shelf from the bottom of the oven. Preheat the oven to 425°F. Beat the egg with 1 teaspoon water. Using a pastry brush, glaze the brioche, taking care not to let any egg wash drip down inside the cans.

5. Place the cans of brioche in the oven, then turn it down to 400°F. Bake for 15 minutes, then rotate the cans to allow them to bake evenly. Lower the oven temperature to 375°F and bake them for another 10 to 15 minutes, or until a wooden skewer inserted in the center of the brioche comes out clean. The brioche will be finished when an instant-read thermometer shows an internal temperature of 205°F to 210°F.

6. Remove the brioche from the oven and allow them to cool for 10 minutes on a wire rack. Using a long thin knife to loosen the breads from the edges of the cans, remove them from the molds and let them cool completely before slicing.

Individual Chocolate-Orange Brioche Rolls

16 brioche rolls

Proofing:

1 to 1¹/₂ hours at room temperature, 70°F to 72°F

Spoil someone you love with these delightful chocolate-flecked rolls warm from the oven. These individual rolls are formed with the classic topknot of the large brioche à tête. Work quickly to form and fill these rolls with chocolate and orange zest, because the large percentage of butter in the dough melts quickly, making it difficult to handle.

For a special dessert, serve each warm brioche split in half and topped with a scoop of chocolate ice cream.

1 recipe Basic Brioche Dough (page 133), proofed and refrigerated for at least 6 hours	16 teaspoons bittersweet chocolate morsels 8 teaspoons grated orange zest 2 large eggs

1. Butter 16 small fluted brioche molds about 2 inches in diameter, or 16 cups in one or two muffin tins. Set aside.

2. Remove the brioche dough from the refrigerator. On a lightly floured work surface, divide the dough into 16 equal pieces with a knife or

dough scraper. Place the pieces on a floured baking sheet. Work with 1 piece of dough at a time, storing the remaining dough in the refrigerator to keep cool as you work.

3. Divide 1 piece of dough into 3 pieces roughly equal in size. With lightly floured hands, combine two of the pieces and roll them together to form a small ball. Flatten the dough and sprinkle it with about 1 teaspoon of the chocolate morsels and ½ teaspoon of the orange zest. Fold the dough over and lightly knead it to distribute the chocolate and zest. Roll it into a uniform ball, then pat the top lightly to flatten it. Place the ball into one of the prepared molds. Roll the smaller piece of dough into a small ball.

4. To make the brioche shape, press down on the center of the larger piece of dough with lightly floured fingertips to make an indentation. Place the smaller ball of dough directly into this indentation; it should fit down in snugly. When it rises and bakes, this head should rise evenly up and form a shiny golden brown dome on the brioche. Repeat with the remaining pieces of dough.

5. Beat the eggs with 1 teaspoon water. Using a pastry brush, glaze the brioche, taking care not to let any egg wash settle in the seams or down the sides of the molds. Loosely cover the dough with plastic wrap.

6. Let the brioche proof for 1 to 1½ hours at room temperature, 70°F to 72°F, until just barely double in bulk. Do not overproof; the brioche will continue to rise in the oven while baking. (In warmer weather over 75°F, brioche may proof in 45 minutes to an hour.)

7. One hour before baking, put the oven rack on the second shelf from the bottom of the oven and place the baking stone on the rack. Preheat the oven to 450°F.

8. Place the proofed brioche in the oven directly on the baking stone. Bake them for 20 to 25 minutes. The brioche are done when they are uniformly golden brown and a toothpick inserted into the center of one roll comes out clean. Or they will be finished when they reach an internal temperature of 205°F to 210°F on an instant-read thermometer.

9. Place the tray of brioche on a wire rack to cool for 10 minutes before unmolding.

Store the brioche at room temperature, covered in plastic wrap, for a few days. For longer storage, freeze them tightly sealed in a plastic bag for up to two weeks.

Cheddar Pepper Brioche with Sun-Dried Tomatoes

Three 10-inch
conical loaves

Fermentation:

2 to 2¹/₂ hours
at room
temperature,
70°F to 72°F

Retardation:

6 to 24 hours
in the
refrigerator,
37°F to 45°F

Proofing:

1¹/₂ to 2 hours
at room
temperature

Make this bread to accompany brunch or to pack in a picnic basket. It is delicious toasted and served with an apéritif.

Try to find coffee cans with smooth linings; in ridged cans, the brioche tends to get stuck.

Unsalted butter, melted	30 grams	1 ounce	2 tablespoons
Unsalted butter, softened	360 grams	12 ounces	1¹/₂ cups (3 sticks)
Milk	75 grams	2¹/₂ ounces	¹/₄ cup plus 1 tablespoon
Unbleached all-purpose flour	600 grams	20 ounces	4 to 5 cups
Instant yeast	1¹/₂ teaspoons	1¹/₂ teaspoons	1¹/₂ teaspoons
Fine sea salt	10 grams	2 teaspoons	2 teaspoons
Pepper	15 grams	1 tablespoon	1 tablespoon
Large eggs	6	6	6
Grated Cheddar cheese	230 grams	8 ounces	3 cups
Sun-dried tomatoes packed in oil, drained	35 grams	1¹/₂ ounces	¹/₄ cup

1. Lightly grease three clean 8- to 12-ounce coffee cans with the melted butter. Butter a sheet of parchment or waxed paper. Trace three circles to fit in the bottoms of the coffee cans. Cut them out and insert them. Set aside.

2. Press the softened butter between two sheets of waxed paper or plastic wrap and smash it with a rolling pin to soften. Or, place it in the bowl of a mixer fitted with the paddle attachment and beat until it is soft and creamy but still cool. (The butter should have the texture of a firm frosting.) Set it aside at room temperature.

3. Place the milk and 1 tablespoon of the flour in the bowl of a food processor fitted with the metal blade. Sprinkle the yeast over the liquid. Cover the machine and process for 5 seconds to blend. Add the remaining flour, the salt, and pepper. Pulse 3 or 4 times to incorporate the yeast mixture.

4. Using an instant-read thermometer, take the temperature of the flour mixture. In a small metal bowl beat the eggs lightly until blended. Take the temperature of the eggs. Adjust their temperature so that the combined temperature of the flour and the eggs will give a base temperature of 130°F if using a Cuisinart or KitchenAid or 150°F if using a Braun. (See page 33 for other models.) To warm the eggs, place the metal bowl in another bowl with hot tap water and stir for 3 to 4 minutes or until the eggs reach the desired temperature. If the eggs are too warm, cool them by placing the metal bowl over ice water. Stir for 2 to 3 minutes or until the eggs reach the desired temperature.

5. With the machine running, add the eggs and process for 15 seconds. Stop the machine and scrape down the sides of the bowl. With a rubber spatula, scrape the softened butter from the waxed paper, plastic wrap, or mixer bowl into the bowl of the food processor. Using a spatula, turn the dough over so that some of the butter is under the dough near the blade of the machine. Process for 30 seconds. (If the dough sticks to the bottom of the bowl and the processor has trouble starting, remove the dough from the processor. Return half to the processor bowl, spreading it out evenly. Process the dough in two batches.)

6. Stop the machine, and take the temperature of the dough with an instant-read thermometer, which should read between 75°F and 80°F. If the temperature is lower than 75°F, process for an additional 5 seconds, repeating up to twice more, until the dough reaches the desired temperature. If the temperature is higher than 80°F, remove the thermometer, scrape the dough from the food processor into an ungreased bowl, and refrigerate for 5 to 10 minutes. Check the temperature of the dough after 5 minutes; the dough should be 80°F or cooler by that time. Add the Cheddar and sun-dried tomatoes. Pulse 6 to 8 times to incorporate.

7. Scrape the finished dough onto a lightly floured work surface. Knead for about a minute or two to distribute the Cheddar and sun-dried tomatoes evenly. Use a dough scraper to gather the dough into a rough ball, then place it into a large ungreased bowl and cover with plastic wrap. Allow it to rise for 2 to 2½ hours at room temperature, 70°F to 72°F. It will have increased in volume somewhat, but don't be concerned by how much.

Store the brioche at room temperature, covered in plastic wrap, for a few days. For longer storage, freeze it tightly sealed in plastic wrap for up to two weeks.

8. Uncover the dough and lightly press it down to remove some of the air bubbles. Cover it with plastic wrap and retard it in the refrigerator for at least 6 to 24 hours, preferably overnight.

9. Remove the dough from the refrigerator and scrape it onto a lightly floured work surface. It will be firm and easy to handle. Divide it into 3 equal pieces, each weighing about 1 pound. Using lightly floured hands, roll one piece of dough into a smooth ball. Work quickly, as the butter-rich dough tends to warm and soften, becoming more difficult to handle. Flatten the ball and roll it into a log shape roughly the diameter of the coffee can. Press the dough firmly into the can so that it touches the sides. (The dough should fill the can halfway.) Repeat with the remaining pieces of dough.

10. Dust the top of each loaf with flour, cover the cans with plastic wrap, and place them in a draft-free place to rise at room temperature. This should take from 1½ to 2 hours, though it may take as long as 3 hours to reach baking stage, depending on the temperature in your kitchen. The dough will rise almost to the tops of the cans.

11. Thirty minutes before baking, place the oven rack in the center of the oven and preheat the oven to 400°F.

12. Place the cans in the oven, directly on the center rack. Bake for 15 minutes. Switch the position of the cans so that those in the back are moved to the front. Continue baking for another 15 to 20 minutes, or until a wooden skewer inserted in the center of the brioche comes out clean. Or, the brioche will be finished when it reaches an internal temperature of 205°F to 210°F on an instant-read thermometer.

13. Remove the cans from the oven and let them cool on a wire rack for 10 minutes. Using a long thin knife to loosen the breads from the edges of the cans, unmold them while still hot by tapping the bottom of each can on a table, then gently shaking until the bread slides out. Allow the loaves to cool completely before slicing.

Alsatian Kugelhopf

There is something noble about a kugelhopf, the yeasty, fruit and nut cake that epitomizes Alsace, the province that borders Germany on the northeastern part of France. Perhaps it is the shape from the fluted mold in which kugelhopf is baked. It always reminds me of a crown that would have adorned the head of a king or prince in the seventeenth century.

 Made from a rich brioche dough studded with currants and covered with sliced blanched almonds and confectioners' sugar, kugelhopf can be the centerpiece for a regal dinner party. What your guests won't know is just how easy it is to make, using the food processor recipe.

One 8-inch cake

Proofing:
3 to 3¹/₂ hours at room temperature, 70°F to 72°F

1 tablespoon unsalted butter

¹/₄ cup sliced blanched almonds

¹/₂ recipe Basic Brioche Dough
 (page 133)

¹/₂ cup dried currants

2 tablespoons confectioners' sugar

1. A few hours before baking, butter an 8-inch fluted kugelhopf mold or tube pan with about a 5-cup capacity. Sprinkle it with the sliced blanched almonds.

2. Remove the brioche dough from the refrigerator and scrape it onto a lightly floured work surface. Using a floured rolling pin, flatten the dough into a rectangle about 1 inch thick. Sprinkle it with half of the currants. Fold the dough over onto itself. Flatten it and sprinkle it with the remaining currants, then knead it 6 or 8 times until the currants are well distributed throughout the dough.

3. Flatten the dough again, then gather up the edges and pinch them together to form a firm ball. Roll it a few times in a circular motion across the work surface to make a uniform ball. Slightly flatten the dough with the palm of your hand. Gather all of the fingers of one hand into a point and press them into the center of the dough, working your fingers into the dough until a hole forms. Pick up the dough with both hands and stretch it until the hole opens up enough for it to fit over the cone in the center of the kugelhopf mold or tube pan. Place the dough in the mold or pan.

Store the kugelhopf tightly wrapped in plastic in the refrigerator. It will keep, frozen, for up to one month. Thaw the bread at room temperature for about 10 minutes before reheating it at 400°F for 8 to 10 minutes.

4. Cover the kugelhopf with plastic wrap and a towel and let it proof for 3 to 3½ hours in a draft-free place at room temperature, 70°F to 72°F. It will increase in volume by half, and just begin to crest the sides of the mold or pan.

5. One hour before baking, adjust the oven rack so that it is on the second shelf from the bottom of the oven. Place the baking stone on the rack. Preheat the oven to 400°F.

6. Place the kugelhopf in the oven and bake it for 40 to 45 minutes, then rotate it and bake it for another 10 to 15 minutes. Remove the kugelhopf from the oven, unmold it onto a peel or the back of a baking sheet, slide the kugelhopf directly onto the baking stone, and bake it for another 5 minutes until it is uniformly browned. Insert an instant-read thermometer to the cake; the kugelhopf will be ready when it reaches an internal temperature of 205°F to 210°F.

7. Remove the cake from the oven and slide it on a wire rack. Allow it to cool completely. Dust it with confectioners' sugar before serving.

Galette Pérougienne

One 12-inch flat cake

Fermentation:

1 hour at room temperature, 70°F to 72°F

Pérouges is a medieval walled city just outside of Lyon, France. Under the graceful branches of an aging linden tree, coffee, wine, sparkling cider, and this galette is served to tourists who come to explore its narrow streets and stone ramparts. Baked in a hot brick oven, this yeasted butter cake has a distinctive burnt sugar topping that makes an exciting textured contrast to the chewy center.

You'll never make shortcake again once you taste this galette cut into wedges and served with fresh fruit and whipped cream.

Unbleached all-purpose flour	350 grams	12 ounces	2^1/$_3$ to 3 cups
Sugar	30 grams	1 ounce	2 tablespoons
Grated lemon zest	1 teaspoon	1 teaspoon	1 teaspoon
Grated orange zest	1 teaspoon	1 teaspoon	1 teaspoon
Fine sea salt	5 grams	^{3}/$_4$ teaspoon	^{3}/$_4$ teaspoon
Instant yeast	1 teaspoon	1 teaspoon	1 teaspoon
Unsalted butter, softened	210 grams	7 ounces	^{3}/$_4$ cup plus 2 tablespoons
Large eggs	2	2	2
Water	85 grams	3 ounces	^{1}/$_4$ cup plus 2 tablespoons
FOR THE TOPPING:			
Unsalted butter, softened	45 grams	1^1/$_2$ ounces	3 tablespoons
Sugar	45 grams	1^1/$_2$ ounces	3 tablespoons

1. Place the flour, sugar, lemon and orange zest, salt, and yeast in a food processor fitted with the metal blade. Cut the softened butter for the dough into small pieces and add it to the processor bowl. Process this mixture for 5 seconds. Combine the eggs and the water in a metal bowl. Using an instant-read thermometer, adjust the temperatures so that the combined temperatures of the flour and the egg mixture give a base temperature of 130°F if using a Cuisinart or KitchenAid or 150°F if using a Braun. (See page 33 for other models.) To warm the eggs and water, place the metal bowl in another bowl containing hot tap water and stir for 3 to 4 minutes or until the mixture reaches the desired temperature. If too warm, cool by placing the metal bowl over ice water. Stir for 3 or 4 minutes until the desired temperature is reached.

2. With the machine running, pour all of the liquid through the feed tube. Process for 45 seconds.

3. Stop the machine and take the temperature of the dough with an instant-read thermometer, which should read between 75°F and 80°F. If the temperature is lower than 75°F, process the dough for an additional 5 seconds, up to twice more, until the dough reaches the desired temperature. If

Store the galette in the refrigerator, wrapped tightly in plastic wrap, for up to one week. Or cut it into wedges and store it tightly sealed in a cookie tin for up to two weeks.

the temperature is higher than 80°F, remove the thermometer, scrape the dough from the food processor into an ungreased bowl, and refrigerate for 5 to 10 minutes. Check the temperature after 5 minutes; the dough should be 80°F or cooler by that time.

4. Remove the dough from the processor and scrape it into a large ungreased bowl. It will be soft and elastic, with a distinctive buttery aroma. Cover the bowl with plastic wrap and allow it to ferment for about 1 hour at room temperature, 70°F to 72°F. The dough will have doubled in volume and be light and active.

5. One hour before baking, put the oven rack on the second shelf from the bottom of the oven and place a baking stone on the rack. Preheat the oven to 450°F.

6. Turn the dough onto a generously floured work surface and lightly sprinkle it with flour. Fold the edges over and gather the dough up to form a smooth ball. Sprinkle a peel or the back of a baking sheet with flour. Transfer the ball onto the peel or baking sheet and begin to press it out into a large circle. Use your fingertips to pat the dough into a circle about 12 inches in diameter and 1/4 inch to 1/2 inch thick. To make a decorative fluted edge on the galette, pinch the edge of the dough with one thumb and index finger. With the other index finger placed on top of the edge of the dough, push toward your thumb and forefinger. Repeat this motion all around the edge of the dough.

7. Spread the top of the galette with the softened butter for the topping, then sprinkle with sugar. Open the oven door and slide the galette directly onto the baking stone as you would for pizza. Reduce the oven temperature to 400°F. Bake the galette for 10 to 12 minutes. Turn on the broiler and broil the surface of the galette for about 2 minutes, watching carefully to be sure it doesn't brown too much.

8. Remove the galette from the oven. It will be evenly browned and will seem somewhat soft to the touch. Slide it onto a wire rack to cool for a few minutes. Slice the galette into 3-inch wedges and serve warm.

Grandma's Cherry Babka

When you want a homey dessert, a cross between a bread and a lightly sweet cake, try this simple fruit-laden babka. The supple dough, almost like a thick batter, is easily mixed in the food processor. A tall collar of parchment paper or aluminum foil fastened around a cake pan lets this light dough rise and form a crested top speckled with a crunchy topping.

If you can't find the tart dried cherries available in specialty food stores or gourmet food catalogs, substitute dried cranberries, currants, or raisins.

One 9-inch round cake

Fermentation:
1 to 1 1/2 hours at room temperature, 70°F to 72°F

Unsalted butter, room temperature	120 grams	4 ounces	1/2 cup (1 stick)
Unbleached all-purpose flour	600 grams	20 ounces	4 to 5 cups
Sugar	120 grams	4 ounces	1/2 cup
Fine sea salt	7.5 grams	1 teaspoon	1 teaspoon
Instant yeast	1 1/2 teaspoons	1 1/2 teaspoons	1 1/2 teaspoons
Milk	250 grams	8 ounces	1 cup
Large eggs	4 whole plus 1 yolk	4 whole plus 1 yolk	4 whole plus 1 yolk
Dried cherries	1/2 cup	1/2 cup	1/2 cup

FOR THE TOPPING:

Fine bread crumbs	60 grams	2 ounces	1/4 cup
Sugar	60 grams	2 ounces	1/4 cup
Ground cinnamon	1 teaspoon	1 teaspoon	1 teaspoon
Unsalted butter	60 grams	2 ounces	4 tablespoons (1/2 stick)
Large egg white, lightly beaten	1	1	1

Confectioners' sugar for garnish

1. Grease a 9-inch springform pan with a tablespoon of the butter. Cut a strip of parchment paper or aluminum foil measuring about 4 inches wide and long enough to fit as a collar around the pan. Set aside.

2. Place the flour, sugar, salt, and remaining butter in the bowl of a food processor fitted with the metal blade. Dissolve the yeast in ¼ cup of the milk. Add to the mixture in the processor and process for 10 seconds.

3. Combine the remaining milk, eggs, and egg yolk in a small metal bowl. Using an instant-read thermometer, adjust the temperature of the milk and egg mixture so that the combined temperature of the liquid and the flour blend gives a base temperature of 130°F if using a Cuisinart or KitchenAid or 150°F if using a Braun. (See page 33 for other models.) To warm the milk and eggs, place the bowl in another bowl with hot tap water. With a wire whisk, stir the mixture until it reaches the desired temperature. If the milk and eggs are too warm, cool them by placing the metal bowl over ice water. Stir for 2 or 3 minutes or until the liquid reaches the desired temperature. With the machine running, pour all the liquid through the feed tube. Process for 45 seconds.

4. Stop the machine and take the temperature of the dough with an instant-read thermometer, which should read between 75°F and 80°F. If the temperature is lower than 75°F, process the dough for an additional 5 seconds, up to twice more, until the dough reaches the desired temperature. If the temperature is higher than 80°F, remove the thermometer, scrape the dough from the food processor into an ungreased bowl, and refrigerate for 5 to 10 minutes. Check the temperature of the dough after 5 minutes; the dough should be 80°F or cooler by that time. Return the dough to the processor, add the dried cherries and pulse for 5 seconds to blend them into the dough.

5. Using a rubber spatula, scrape the dough directly into the prepared pan. Wrap the strip of parchment or foil collar around the top of the pan, letting it extend at least 3 inches above the rim. Tie the collar securely to the pan using a piece of butcher's twine. Cover the babka loosely with plastic wrap, then a cloth towel. Let rise for 1 to 1½ hours in a draft-free place at room temperature.

6. While the babka is rising, prepare the topping. Place the bread crumbs, sugar, cinnamon, and butter in the bowl of a food processor fitted with the metal blade. Process for 1 minute until all ingredients are completely blended. With a spatula, scrape the topping into a small bowl and set aside.

7. Thirty minutes before baking, put the oven rack on the middle shelf of the oven. Preheat to 350°F.

8. To bake the babka, remove the towel and plastic wrap. The babka should have risen and crested the top of the pan. If it has not, cover it with plastic wrap and let it proof for up to 1 hour longer. Brush the top of the babka with the egg white, then sprinkle with the topping mixture.

9. Using a spray bottle, mist the inside of the oven with water 2 or 3 times. Place the babka in the oven directly on the center rack. Bake for 5 minutes, then spray the oven with water again. Bake the babka for about 50 to 55 minutes longer until the cake is golden brown and a toothpick inserted in the center comes out clean. Or, it will be finished when it reaches an internal temperature of 205°F to 210°F on an instant-read thermometer.

10. Remove the babka from the oven and place it on a wire rack to cool and rest for 20 minutes. Use a paring knife to loosen it, then remove it from the pan. Cut into 2-inch wedges and serve immediately, dusted with confectioners' sugar.

Or, cool the cake completely and store at room temperature wrapped tightly with plastic wrap for a few days. For longer storage, freeze the babka, tightly sealed in a plastic bag, for up to three weeks.

Ginger Lemon Nut Rolls

12 large rolls

Fermentation:

2 to 2½ hours
at room
temperature,
70°F to 72°F

Retardation:

4 to 16 hours
in the
refrigerator,
37°F to 45°F

Proofing:

1 to 1½ hours
at room
temperature

The recipe for these sweet and spicy rolls was adapted from a professional book for the French baker entitled Pain, Evolution et Tradition. *The rolls are cleverly hand-formed to resemble lemons, and the candied ginger gives them an exotic flavor, making them perfect to serve with tea or at a brunch.*

Mix this dough using the mix and rest method described in "For Lighter, Fluffier Bread" on page 54. The resting produces a buoyant dough that swells as it ferments and bakes into rolls with a fluffy crumb.

As with many sweet breads, this enriched dough benefits from a long fermentation in the refrigerator. The cool temperature slows down the yeast action, allowing the dough to develop its aromatic flavor.

Instant yeast	1½ teaspoons	1½ teaspoons	1½ teaspoons
Milk	250 grams	8 ounces	1 cup
Unbleached all-purpose flour	500 grams	1 pound	3⅓ to 4 cups
Grated lemon zest	1 teaspoon	1 teaspoon	1 teaspoon
Sugar	30 grams	1 ounce	2 tablespoons
Fine sea salt	10 grams	2 teaspoons	2 teaspoons
Large eggs	2	2	2
Coarsely chopped almonds	60 grams	2 ounces	½ cup
Coarsely chopped candied ginger	70 grams	2¾ ounces	¼ cup
Dried currants	60 grams	2 ounces	½ cup

1. Dissolve the yeast in ¼ cup of the milk. Place the flour, lemon zest, sugar, salt, and yeast mixture in the bowl of a food processor fitted with the metal blade. Pulse 3 or 4 times to blend in the yeast mixture. Combine the remaining milk and 1 of the eggs in a small metal bowl. Using an instant-read thermometer, adjust the temperature of the milk and egg mixture so that the combined temperature of the liquid and the flour gives a base temperature of 130°F if using a Cuisinart or KitchenAid or 150°F if using a Braun. (See page

33 for other models.) To warm the eggs, place the metal bowl in another bowl with hot tap water and stir for 3 to 4 minutes, or until the eggs reach the desired temperature. If the eggs are too warm, cool the mixture by placing the metal bowl over ice water. Stir for 2 to 3 minutes or until the desired temperature is reached.

2. With the machine running, pour all but 2 tablespoons of the liquid through the feed tube. Process for 15 seconds, adding the remaining liquid as the dough mixes if it appears too dry and is not coming together into a smooth ball.

3. Turn off the processor and let the dough rest in the bowl of the machine for 5 minutes. The dough will be noticeably softer and slightly sticky to the touch. Process for 30 seconds longer, for a total of 45 seconds.

4. Stop the machine, and take the temperature of the dough with an instant-read thermometer, which should read between 75°F and 80°F. If the temperature is lower than 75°F, process the dough for an additonal 5 seconds, up to twice more, until the dough reaches the desired temperature. If the temperature is higher than 80°F, remove the thermometer, scrape the dough from the food processor into an ungreased bowl, and refrigerate for 5 to 10 minutes. Check the temperature of the dough after 5 minutes; the dough should be 80°F or cooler by that time.

5. Remove the dough from the processor and place it on a lightly floured work surface. Cover with plastic wrap and let rest for 15 to 20 minutes.

6. Press the dough out into a rough 12-inch square. Sprinkle the surface with the almonds, candied ginger, and currants. Roll the dough into a log shape, fold it in half, and knead it for about 2 minutes to incorporate the nuts and fruit throughout.

7. Place the dough in a large ungreased bowl and cover with plastic wrap. Ferment for 2 to 2½ hours at room temperature, 70°F to 72°F. It will have increased in volume somewhat, but don't be concerned by how much.

8. Turn the dough onto a lightly floured work surface, and gently form it into a smooth ball. Cut the ball into 12 pieces each weighing about 3 ounces. Pinch each piece into a roll shape (page 39) and roll each formed

piece a few times in a circular motion across the work surface. Slightly taper the ends of each roll to form a shape resembling a lemon. Place the rolls about 2 inches apart on a parchment paper–lined baking sheet. Cover with plastic wrap and place the baking sheet in the refrigerator for 4 to 16 hours.

9. About 2 hours before baking, remove the rolls from the refrigerator and place them in a warm place to come to room temperature. This should take about 1½ to 2 hours.

10. One hour before baking, put the oven rack on the second shelf from the bottom of the oven and place the baking stone on the rack. Preheat the oven to 450°F.

11. Beat the remaining egg with 1 tablespoon of water. Brush each roll with the egg wash, then place the rolls in the oven. Reduce the heat to 400°F.

12. Bake the rolls for 18 to 20 minutes, until they are lightly golden brown. Or, the rolls will be finished when they reach an internal temperature of 205°F to 210°F on an instant-read thermometer. Remove from the oven and transfer to a wire rack to cool.

Holiday Stollen

Two 12-inch loaves

Fermentation:

1½ to 2 hours at room temperature, 70°F to 72°F

Proofing:

1 to 1½ hours at room temperature

Stollen is a German sweet bread studded with candied fruits that have been steeped in brandy. The bread dough is rolled around a core of rich marzipan, then baked and dusted with a snowfall of powdered sugar.

I slice stollen and serve it toasted with coffee for a decadent breakfast. The marzipan, a smooth confection made from blanched almonds, sugar, and glucose, warms in the toaster to become an addictive spread over the fruit-studded toast. You will find marzipan or almond paste, made with slightly more almonds, in the baking section of large supermarkets or by mail order through the King Arthur Flour Company Baker's Catalogue.

Candied fruit	115 grams	4 ounces	1/2 cup
Raisins	115 grams	4 ounces	1/2 cup
Brandy	60 grams	2 ounces	1/4 cup
Milk	270 grams	9 ounces	1 cup plus 2 tablespoons
Unbleached all-purpose flour	600 grams	20 ounces	4 to 5 cups
Instant yeast	2 teaspoons	2 teaspoons	2 teaspoons
Sugar	60 grams	2 ounces	1/4 cup
Fine sea salt	10 grams	2 teaspoons	2 teaspoons
Nutmeg	a few gratings	a few gratings	a few gratings
Ground allspice	1/4 teaspoon	1/4 teaspoon	1/4 teaspoon
Large eggs	2	2	2
Unsalted butter, melted	180 grams	6 ounces	3/4 cup
Marzipan	250 grams	8 ounces	1 cup
Confectioners' sugar for garnish			

1. Place the candied fruit and raisins in a small bowl, cover them with the brandy, and set aside for 1 hour to 12 hours, preferably overnight. Line a baking sheet with parchment paper. Set aside.

2. Place 1/2 cup of the milk and 1 tablespoon of the flour in the bowl of a food processor fitted with the metal blade. Sprinkle the yeast over the liquid. Cover the machine and process for 5 seconds to blend.

3. Add the remaining flour, the sugar, salt, and spices to the food processor. Pulse 3 or 4 times to incorporate the yeast mixture. Beat the eggs in a small metal bowl until blended. Drain the candied fruit and raisins, saving the brandy and adding it to the eggs, and setting the fruit aside. Add the remaining milk and 1/2 cup of the melted butter to the beaten eggs.

4. Using an instant-read thermometer, adjust the temperature of the egg mixture so that the combined temperatures of the flour and the eggs give a base temperature of 130°F if using a Cuisinart or KitchenAid or 150°F if using a Braun. (See page 33 for other models.) To warm the egg mixture, place the bowl in another bowl with hot tap water and stir for 3 to 4 minutes or until the desired temperature is reached. If the egg mixture is too warm, cool it by placing the metal bowl over ice water and stirring for 2 or 3 minutes, or until the egg mixture reaches the correct temperature.

5. With the processor running, add the egg mixture. Process for 15 seconds. Stop the machine and scrape the sides of the bowl. If the dough sticks to the bottom of the bowl and the processor has trouble starting, remove the dough from the processor. Return half of it to the bowl, spreading it out evenly. Process in two batches, each for another 30 seconds. The dough will be soft, but will not cling to the sides of the processor bowl.

6. Stop the machine and take the temperature of the dough with an instant-read thermometer, which should read between 75°F and 80°F. If the temperature is lower than 75°F, process for an additional 5 seconds, up to twice more, until the dough reaches the desired temperature. If the temperature is higher than 80°F, remove the thermometer, scrape the dough from the food processor into an ungreased bowl, and refrigerate for 5 to 10 minutes. Check the temperature after 5 minutes; the dough should be 80°F or cooler by that time.

7. Scrape the dough from the processor onto a lightly floured work surface. Press the dough out into a 12-inch square 2 inches thick. Sprinkle the surface with half of the drained candied fruit and raisins and roll it into a log shape. Fold it in half and knead it for about 2 minutes to incorporate the dried fruit. If the dough feels too firm to knead, cover it with a towel and let it rest for 10 minutes. Flatten it and sprinkle it with the remaining half of the dried fruits. Roll the dough and knead it again for 2 minutes, or just enough to distribute the fruit throughout.

8. Form the dough into a ball, place it in an ungreased bowl, and cover with plastic wrap. Allow it to ferment for 1½ to 2 hours at room temperature, 70°F to 72°F. It will have doubled in volume.

9. Scrape the dough onto a lightly floured work surface and divide it into 2 equal pieces. To form the stollen, flatten each piece into an oval about 10 inches long, 8 inches wide, and 1 inch thick. Roll half of the marzipan into a smooth log about the length of the flattened dough and lay it down the center. Fold the dough over and press the edges with your fingertips to seal.

Repeat with the remaining dough and marzipan. Transfer the loaves to the prepared baking sheet, spaced 4 inches apart so that they don't stick together when baking. Brush the stollen with part of the remaining melted butter.

10. Cover with a sheet of plastic wrap and allow the loaves to proof at room temperature until the dough has increased by half its size. This may take 1 to 1½ hours, depending on the temperature in your kitchen. When the dough is ready to bake, it will be puffed but still spring back slowly when pressed with a finger.

11. One hour before baking, adjust the oven rack so that it is on the second shelf from the bottom of the oven. Preheat the oven to 400°F. Place the baking sheet of stollen directly on the baking stone. Reduce the heat to 375°F and bake the stollen for 35 minutes. Open the oven and rotate the baking sheet. Bake the stollen for another 25 to 30 minutes, or until the loaves are a deep golden brown. The stollen will be finished when it reaches an internal temperature of 205°F to 210°F on an instant-read thermometer.

12. Remove the stollen from the oven and immediately brush them with the remainder of the melted butter. Allow the loaves to cool completely on a wire rack, then dust them heavily with confectioners' sugar before serving.

Store the stollen in a paper bag overnight or at room temperature for a few days. For longer storage, freeze them, tightly sealed in a plastic bag, for up to three weeks.

Babas au Rhum

Twelve 2-inch
cakes or one
12-inch cake

Proofing:

1 hour at room
temperature,
70°F to 72°F

An old-fashioned dessert that was popular around the time the word gourmet entered our vocabulary, babas au rhum deserve to be rediscovered. Babas are made from a spongy yeast dough rich with butter and eggs poured directly into special molds where it ferments and proofs for about an hour. Once baked, babas look like inflated champagne corks and taste of butter and the potent rum syrup in which they are soaked. When served with fresh berries and a smidgen of whipped cream, babas fit the bill for an elegant sweet that is simple to prepare.

Babas may be made well ahead of time and kept refrigerated or frozen for many weeks. The syrup preserves the moisture in the dough. To serve, just bring the babas to room temperature and refresh them with a light sprinkling of rum. (If you prefer, you can substitute rum flavoring or lemon juice for the rum in this recipe.)

Traditional baba molds are about 2 inches wide and 3 inches deep, but any small muffin pan will work fine. When the baba dough is baked in a tube pan it is called a savarin, which is especially delicious when filled with sliced fresh cherries or berries.

Unsalted butter	140 grams	5 ounces	1/2 cup plus 2 tablespoons
Raisins	170 grams	6 ounces	1 cup
Dark rum	335 grams	12 ounces	1 1/2 cups
Unbleached all-purpose flour	255 grams	9 ounces	1 3/4 to 2 1/4 cups
Sugar	200 grams	7 ounces	3/4 cup plus 2 tablespoons
Fine sea salt	5 grams	3/4 teaspoon	3/4 teaspoon
Instant yeast	1/2 teaspoon	1/2 teaspoon	1/2 teaspoon
Milk	250 grams	8 ounces	1 cup
Large eggs	3	3	3
Water	170 grams	6 ounces	1 cup

1. Grease 12 individual rum baba molds or a 12-inch tube pan with 2 tablespoons of the butter. Combine the raisins with 1 cup of the rum and set aside.

2. Place the flour, 2 tablespoons of the sugar, and the salt in the bowl of a food processor fitted with the metal blade. Add the remaining butter cut into 1-inch chunks. Dissolve the yeast in ¼ cup of the milk and add it to the flour mixture. Process for 5 seconds to combine.

3. Beat together the remaining milk and the eggs in a small metal bowl. Adjust the temperature of the milk and the eggs so that the combined temperatures of the flour and liquid mixture give a base temperature of 130°F if using a Cuisinart or KitchenAid or 150°F if using a Braun. (See page 33 for other models.) To warm the milk and eggs, place the metal bowl in another bowl with hot tap water and stir for 3 to 4 minutes, or until the milk and eggs reach the desired temperature. If the milk and eggs are very cold, set the bowl over a pot of simmering water and use an instant-read thermometer to monitor the milk and eggs carefully as they heat to the desired temperature.

4. With the food processor running, add the milk and eggs all at once. Process for 30 seconds. Stop the machine and scrape the bottom and sides of the bowl to make certain all of the ingredients are incorporated and no flour clings to the bottom of the bowl. Process for another 15 seconds, for a total of 45 seconds. The dough will be smooth and elastic but quite soft and liquid.

5. Stop the machine and take the temperature of the dough with an instant-read thermometer, which should read between 75°F and 80°F. If the temperature is lower than 75°F, process the dough for an additional 5 seconds, up to twice more, until the dough reaches the desired temperature. If the temperature is higher than 80°F, remove the thermometer, scrape the dough from the food processor into an ungreased bowl, and refrigerate for 5 to 10 minutes. Check the temperature of the dough after 5 minutes; the dough should be 80°F or cooler by that time.

6. Scrape the dough into a large mixing bowl. Drain the raisins, reserving the rum for the syrup. Stir the raisins into the dough so that they are evenly distributed.

When completely immersed in rum syrup, the cakes will keep, covered, in the refrigerator for two to three weeks.

7. Fill each baba mold ⅔ full, using a measuring cup. Or pour the dough into the prepared tube pan. Cover with a towel and let proof at room temperature, 70°F to 72°F, until double in bulk, about 1 hour.

8. While the dough is proofing, prepare the rum syrup. Combine the remaining sugar and water in a 1-quart saucepan. Bring to a boil; lower the heat and simmer for 5 minutes. Remove the pan from the heat and stir in the rum in which the raisins soaked. Set aside.

9. Half an hour before baking, preheat the oven to 375°F. Place the individual baba molds on a baking sheet. Place the sheet of the individual babas or the tube pan on the center shelf in the oven and bake the baba molds 20 to 25 minutes or the large cake 30 to 35 minutes. Insert an instant-read thermometer; the babas will be finished when they reach an internal temperature of 205°F to 210°F and will have a golden brown exterior.

10. Cool the cakes on a wire rack for 5 minutes, then remove from the molds or pan. With a fork, prick each baba or the large baba in several places. Place the cooked cakes in a pan deep enough to hold the rum syrup and pour the syrup over the warm babas. Let them soak in the syrup for at least an hour. Turn the cakes over and let them soak for at least another hour before serving.

11. To serve, sprinkle each baba with a tablespoon of rum, or brush the remaining rum over the surface of the larger cake.

Danish Pastry Dough

What is sold in bakeries as Danish pastry today is nothing more than yeasted sweet bread. The crunchy layers of the finest Scandinavian pastries have been replaced by expedient doughs with more shortening that lack the crispness of authentic multilayered Danish pastries.

The most challenging part of making good Danish dough is the turning and folding in of butter. Think of it as making a book, sandwiching thin sheets of butter between many pages of dough created with each roll and fold.

This is the basic dough for making individual Danish pastries filled with creams or fruit purées. It also makes excellent braided breads and the pièce de resistance, Rose Crown Danish Pastry (page 164).

Makes about 4 pounds of dough, enough for 32 Danish pastries, 4 Poppy Seed Braids, or 1 Rose Crown Danish Pastry

Fermentation:

3 to 24 hours in the refrigerator, 35°F to 45°F

Unbleached all-purpose flour	750 grams	1½ pounds	4¾ to 6 cups
Sugar	45 grams	1½ ounces	3 tablespoons
Fine sea salt	7.5 grams	1 teaspoon	1 teaspoon
Ground cardamom	2 teaspoons	2 teaspoons	2 teaspoons
Unsalted butter, at room temperature	625 grams	1¼ pounds	2½ cups
Instant yeast	1 teaspoon	1 teaspoon	1 teaspoon
Water	250 grams	8 ounces	1 cup
Large eggs	3	3	3

1. Place the flour, sugar, salt, cardamom, and ¾ cup of the butter in the bowl of the food processor fitted with the metal blade. Dissolve the yeast in ¼ cup of the water. Add it to the flour. Process for 5 seconds.

2. Lightly beat the eggs and the remaining water in a metal bowl. Take the temperature of the flour with an instant-read thermometer. Adjust the temperature of the egg mixture so that the combined temperatures of the flour and the liquids gives a base temperature of 130°F if using a Cuisinart or KitchenAid or 150°F if using a Braun. (See page 33 for other models). With the machine running, add the egg mixture. Process for 45 seconds.

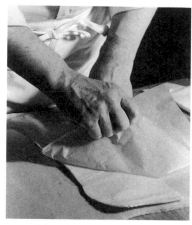

Place the butter in the center of the dough

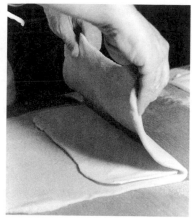

Fold the dough over the butter

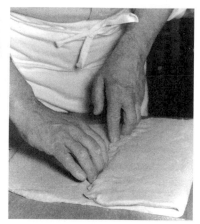

Seal the edges of the dough

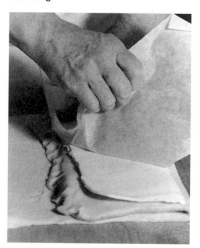

Place a second piece of butter onto the dough

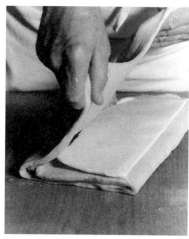

Fold the dough over the second piece of butter

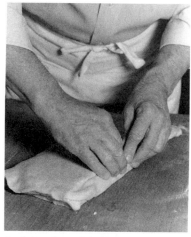

Seal the edges of the dough

3. Stop the machine and take the temperature of the dough with an instant-read thermometer, which should read between 75°F and 80°F. If the temperature is lower than 75°F, then process the dough for an additional 5 seconds, up to twice more, until the dough reaches the desired temperature. If the temperature is higher than 80°F, remove the thermometer, scrape the dough from the food processor into an ungreased bowl, and refrigerate for 5 to 10 minutes. Check the temperature of the dough after 5 minutes; the dough should be 80°F or cooler by that time.

4. Scrape the dough onto a lightly floured surface, and pat it into a rectangle about 2 inches thick. Use a rolling pin to flatten it slightly so that it measures about 6 × 8 inches. Wrap it in plastic wrap and place it in the refrigerator for 20 minutes.

5. While the dough is resting, place the remaining butter on a sheet of waxed paper or plastic wrap. Cover with a second sheet of waxed paper or plastic wrap and roll it into an 8 × 12 inch rectangle. Cut in half lengthwise, wrap each piece in plastic wrap, and chill the halves in the refrigerator for 10 minutes.

6. Remove the dough and butter from the refrigerator. On a lightly floured work surface roll the dough into a 12 × 16 inch rectangle about ¼ inch thick. Press a metal ruler or the back of a knife into the dough to divide it into 3 strips measuring about 5 × 12 inches each. Lightly dust with flour. Peel one piece of the butter from the plastic wrap. Position it in the center of the dough so that it almost reaches each side of the dough. Pick up the left side of the dough and fold it over the butter so that the butter is sandwiched between the two layers of dough. Seal the edges of the dough with the tips of your fingers to keep the butter completely encased. Place the second piece of butter on top of the stack, then fold the right side of dough over it. Again seal the butter inside with the tips of your fingers.

Press the rolling pin into the dough

7. With a floured rolling pin, press down on the dough about 1 inch from the edge. Continue pressing the rolling pin into the dough until it is covered with about 10 parallel lines. Turn the dough 90 degrees and repeat this until the dough looks slightly quilted. This keeps the butter evenly distributed in the dough layers. Wrap in plastic wrap and let chill for 30 minutes in the refrigerator.

8. Unwrap the dough and place it on a lightly floured work surface. With a floured rolling pin, roll the dough a few times in one direction to flatten slightly. Then roll it into a rectangle measuring about 12 × 16 inches. Fold the shorter sides in to meet in the center, then fold the whole package along the

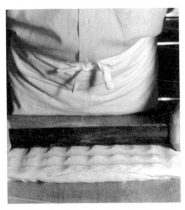

Turn the dough 90° and repeat until the dough looks slightly quilted

center seam to make 4 layers. Wrap in plastic wrap and chill for 30 minutes. This is the first turn. Repeat the above procedure twice more, chilling the dough for 30 minutes between each roll. After the dough has been rolled and folded a total of 3 times, chill it for 3 to 24 hours, preferably overnight, before forming into any of the Danish pastries.

9. The pastry dough may be tightly wrapped and frozen for up to three weeks before being thawed and used for pastries. Thaw the wrapped dough in the refrigerator for 4 to 5 hours or overnight before using.

Danish Twists

Thirty-two 4-inch pastries

Proofing:

30 to 45 minutes at room temperature, 70°F to 72°F

There are so many classic forms of Danish pastries: pinwheels, triangles filled with custard, fan shapes oozing with nut and fruit fillings, and others. I like these twists because the unusual fold makes a pastry with lots of crisp edges. The recipe is devised for two types of filling, but can easily be made with one.

Form the pastries in four waves. This staggers the baking so that there is enough room in the oven to bake this large batch of dough at one time. Or, divide the dough in half. Freeze half and make a half recipe.

Coarse sugar is sold by bakery supply companies. It consists of large crystal granules used to decorate festive breads and Danish pastries. To make your own coarse sugar, crush sugar cubes in a mortar and pestle to ⅛-inch pieces. Sift out the fine sugar and use the larger pieces in recipes that call for a coarse sugar garnish.

1 recipe Danish Pastry Dough (page 159)	2 egg whites
1 cup raspberry preserves	2 tablespoons water
1 cup apricot preserves	Coarse baker's sugar or crushed sugar cubes for garnish

1. Preheat the oven to 400°F. Line three baking sheets with parchment paper.

2. Unwrap the chilled dough and divide it into 4 pieces. Work with one piece at a time and keep the unused dough in the refrigerator as you are working. On a lightly floured work surface, roll one piece of the dough out into a rectangle measuring about 10 × 16 inches. Cut in half so that you have 2 rectangles measuring about 5 × 16 inches.

3. Spread the bottom half of one sheet of the pastry with some of the raspberry preserves, spreading the preserves in a thin layer; the jam oozes out of the dough when it is cut into individual pastries. Fold the dough over to cover the preserves, giving you a piece measuring about 5 × 8 inches. Using a sharp knife or pizza cutter and a metal ruler to help make a straight edge, cut the dough into 4 strips, each 5 × 2 inches. With a metal spatula or dough scraper, lift the pieces of pastry and separate them on the work surface. Cut a slit about 3 inches long in the center of each strip, starting and stopping about 1 inch from each end. Repeat this procedure with the remaining piece of dough, using the apricot preserves.

4. To make the twists, poke one end of each strip through the slit, then pull it up and out the other side. Flatten the pastry slightly and place it on one of the baking sheets. Repeat with the remaining pastries, spacing them 1 inch apart so that they don't stick together as they proof and bake.

5. Cover the formed pastries with a kitchen towel and allow the dough to proof at room temperature, 70°F to 72°F, for 30 to 45 minutes.

6. Beat the egg whites with the water. Uncover the pastries and gently brush each one with the egg glaze, then sprinkle with coarse sugar.

7. Bake them for 10 minutes. Rotate the baking sheet in the oven so the pastries bake evenly, then continue baking for another 5 to 10 minutes. They will be puffed and uniformly golden brown. Remove the pastries from the oven and transfer them immediately to a wire rack to cool. Serve immediately.

Store these pastries tightly wrapped in plastic. They may be frozen for up to three weeks, then thawed at room temperature. Reheat thawed pastries in a preheated 350°F oven for 5 to 7 minutes before serving.

Rose Crown Danish Pastry

One 10-inch
pastry

Proofing:

30 to 45
minutes at
room
temperature,
70°F to 72°F

This striking pastry is much easier to make than it sounds. It is the ideal centerpiece at a holiday brunch. Seven spirals of Danish Pastry Dough are positioned on top of a thin sheet of pastry covered with almond cream, apricots, and nuts. When baked, the pastry looks like a crown of roses. It is cut into thin wedges, the flaky butter pastry a contrast for the moist almond filling inside.

The almond filling used in this recipe may be used in place of jam for the Danish Twists (page 162).

1/4 cup plus 2 tablespoons unsalted
    butter
1/2 cup whole almonds
1/2 cup dried apricots

1/2 cup almond paste
1/4 cup sugar
1 recipe Danish Pastry Dough
    (page 159)

FOR THE GLAZE:

1 1/2 cups confectioners' sugar
1 tablespoon lemon juice

1/4 cup sliced blanched almonds

1. Lightly grease the bottom of a 10-inch pie pan or springform pan with a tablespoon of the butter. Cut a piece of parchment paper to fit the bottom of the pan, butter it, and place it in the pan. Set aside.

2. Place the almonds and dried apricots in the bowl of a food processor fitted with the metal blade. Pulse for 30 seconds to chop coarsely. Set aside in a small bowl.

3. Place the almond paste and sugar in the clean bowl of the food processor fitted with the metal blade. Process for 20 to 25 seconds until the mixture resembles coarse meal. Stop the machine, add the remaining butter, and process for 15 to 20 seconds longer until the mixture forms a smooth paste. Using a rubber spatula, scrape the mixture into a bowl and set aside.

4. Cut off about 1/3 of the pastry dough. Wrap the larger piece of dough and return it to the refrigerator. On a lightly floured work surface, roll the smaller piece of dough into a 10-inch circle about 1/4 inch thick. Use a paring knife to trim it into a circle to fit into the prepared pan. (Save any scraps of leftover dough for piecrust.) Sprinkle the dough with the chopped apricot and almond mixture. Use a rolling pin to press the mixture into the dough, then spread with a few tablespoons of the almond butter. Place the dough, spread side up, in the prepared pan.

5. On a lightly floured work surface, roll the remaining dough into a 14-inch square. Spread it with the remaining almond butter, fold it in half, then cut it into 7 strips, each about 2 inches wide.

6. To form a rosette, take one strip of the dough. Start from the folded end and roll it into a tight spiral. Tuck the end of the dough under to keep it from unrolling. Repeat with the other pieces of dough. Place one rosette in the center of the pastry-lined pan, with the 6 remaining spirals evenly spaced around the outside edge.

7. Cover the pan with plastic wrap and let proof at room temperature, 70°F to 72°F, for 30 to 45 minutes. The dough will puff and the spirals of pastry will fill the pan during this time.

8. About 30 minutes before baking, preheat the oven to 400°F. Place the pastry in the center rack of the oven and bake it for about 30 minutes. Check, and if it seems to be browning too quickly, reduce the oven temperature to 350°F. Continue baking for 25 to 30 more minutes. The pastry is done when it is uniformly browned and has reached an internal temperature of 205°F to 210°F on an instant-read thermometer.

9. Unmold the pastry. Combine the confectioners' sugar and lemon juice. While it is still warm, brush the pastry with the glaze, then sprinkle it with the sliced blanched almonds.

Store the Danish at room temperature covered in plastic wrap for two days. For longer storage, freeze it tightly sealed in a plastic bag for up to two weeks.

Poppy Seed Danish Braid

One 12-inch
pastry

Proofing:

30 minutes at
room
temperature,
70°F to 72°F

Old-time Danish pastries are still staples at classic New York bakeries like Kramer's in Yorktown or Rudi's in Ridgewood, Brooklyn. These recipes are two of my favorites, with either poppy seed filling or raspberry preserves with cream cheese and my "Baker's Secret Filling." (Not wanting to let anything go to waste, bakers have devised fillings using crumbled dry bread or leftover Danish pastries.) I like to spread the inside of this braid with red raspberry or apricot preserves and top it with my secret filling scented with cinnamon and lemon.

1/4 recipe Danish Pastry Dough
   (page 159)
2 teaspoons lemon juice
1 teaspoon Cognac or brandy

1/2 cup (about 6 ounces) prepared
   poppy seed filling
1 egg white
Confectioners' sugar for garnish

1. Line a baking sheet with parchment paper.

2. Stir the lemon juice and Cognac or brandy into the poppy seed filling. Set aside.

3. On a lightly floured work surface, roll the dough into a rectangle measuring about 14 × 10 inches. Use a metal-edged ruler to trim the edges of the dough to make it uniform. (Save the scraps to make piecrust.) Use a metal spatula or dough scraper to lift the pastry and place it on the prepared baking sheet. With the back of a knife, lightly score the dough (taking care not to cut through it): Make 2 indentations, each about 3 inches long, down the length of the pastry about 3 inches from each edge.

4. Spread the filling down the center section, taking care not to spread beyond the edges marked by the scored lines. To make the braided top, trim the short edges of each strip in a 1-inch diagonal. To form the braid, fold the top edge of the pastry over about 1/4 inch to keep the filling from leaking out during baking. Begin to braid the edge, folding the strip of dough on the left over the filling so that it touches the opposite side of the dough. Then fold the strip of dough on the right over the filling and continue, alternating strips, until you reach the bottom of the dough. To be certain the filling is safely contained, fold up the bottom edge 1/4 inch, then crisscross the remaining two strips. Tuck in the ends to make a seamless braid.

Scoring the pastry dough

Spread the poppy filling down the center of the dough

Trim the short edges of the dough into 1-inch strips

Fold the top edge of the pastry over about 1/4 inch

Braid the dough over the filling

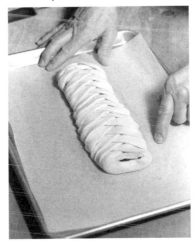

Finish the braid

5. Cover the braid with a kitchen towel and let it proof at room temperature, 70°F to 72°F, for 30 minutes. Twenty minutes before baking, preheat the oven to 400°F.

6. Beat the egg white with 1 tablespoon of water. Uncover the braid and gently brush it with the egg wash. Place the baking sheet in the oven and bake the pastry for 25 minutes. Open the oven and rotate the baking sheet so that the braid browns evenly. Bake for another 10 to 15 minutes, until the pastry is evenly browned and the poppy filling is bubbling.

Store the tightly wrapped braid in plastic wrap for two or three days in the refrigerator, or for up to three weeks in the freezer.

7. Remove the baking sheet from the oven and slide the parchment paper with the braid onto a wire rack. Cool completely before cutting. To serve, dust the pastry lightly with confectioners' sugar.

Variation: Raspberry Cheese Braid

FOR THE BAKER'S SECRET FILLING:

One 12-inch pastry

1 cup plain dry bread crumbs or crumbled stale Danish pastry

$^1/_4$ cup sugar

1 teaspoon grated lemon zest

$^1/_2$ teaspoon cinnamon

$^1/_4$ cup unsalted butter

1 large egg

$^1/_4$ recipe Danish Pastry Dough, (page 159)

$^1/_2$ cup raspberry preserves

$^1/_2$ cup cream cheese

1 egg white

Confectioners' sugar for garnish

1. Place the bread crumbs or crumbled pastry in the bowl of the food processor fitted with the metal blade. Process for about 30 seconds to grind into a fine crumb.

2. Add the sugar, lemon zest, and cinnamon. Process for a few seconds to combine. Add the butter, broken into several pieces, and the egg. Process for 10 seconds longer. Set aside in the refrigerator for later use.

3. Preheat the oven to 400°F. Line a baking sheet with parchment paper.

4. On a lightly floured work surface, roll the dough into a rectangle measuring about 10 × 14 inches. Use a metal-edged ruler to trim the edges of the dough to make it uniform. (Save the scraps to make piecrust.) Use a metal spatula or dough scraper to lift the pastry and place it on the prepared baking sheet. With the back of a knife, lightly score the dough (taking care not to cut through it): Make 2 indentations, each about 3 inches long, down the length of the pastry about 3 inches from each edge.

5. Remove the filling from the refrigerator. Spoon it down the center strip, taking care not to spread beyond the edges marked by the scored lines. Then spoon the raspberry preserves over the filling, again keeping within the edges marked in the dough. Crumble the cream cheese and distribute it evenly over the raspberry preserves.

6. To make the braided top, trim the short edges of each strip on a 1-inch diagonal. To form the braid, fold the top edge of the pastry over about 1/4 inch to keep the filling from leaking out during baking. Begin to braid the edge, folding the strip of dough on the left over the filling so that it touches the opposite side of the dough. Then fold the strip of dough on the right over the filling and continue, alternating strips, until you reach the bottom of dough. To be certain the filling is safely contained, fold up the bottom edge 1/4 inch, then crisscross the remaining two strips. Tuck in the ends to make a seamless braid.

7. Cover the braid with a kitchen towel and let it proof at room temperature, 70°F to 72°F, for 30 minutes. Beat the egg white with 1 tablespoon of water. Uncover the braid and gently brush it with the egg wash. Place the baking sheet in the oven and bake the pastry for 25 minutes. Open the oven and rotate the baking sheet so that the braid browns evenly. Bake for another 10 to 15 minutes, until the pastry is evenly browned and the filling is bubbling.

8. Remove the baking sheet from the oven and slide the parchment paper with the braid onto a wire rack. Cool completely before cutting. To serve, dust the pastry lightly with confectioners' sugar.

Store the braid tightly wrapped in plastic wrap for two or three days in the refrigerator, or for up to three weeks in the freezer.

Sourdough Breads
and Starters

Bread dough mixed in the food processor produces a loaf full of the earthy taste of grain, with a honeycombed crumb and crackly crust. This bread keeps its moist, chewy interior for a longer time than breads mixed by traditional methods, and is made with a fraction of the effort.

Using natural yeast starters alone or in combination with a small amount of commercial yeast opens up a whole array of breads with a complex taste and hearty texture. This chapter is full of breads with the tang of rye and a hint of sour, all of which depend on the use of a starter for their memorable taste. Should you want a bread that actually has a sour taste, the only way to develop that particular flavor is with a sour starter.

Use the Country Baguettes with Starter (page 180) as your introduction to working with starters.

Wild Yeast, the Natural Leavener

Before there was packaged yeast, the only way to make bread rise or to leaven bread was to use natural yeast. The air we breath is full of wild yeast organisms and bacteria, which turn an uncorked bottle of wine to vinegar or last week's leftovers to a sour stew. Something as simple as a blend of flour and water will encourage enough airborne yeast organisms to begin bubbling in a few hours.

A confusing array of expressions exists to describe natural yeast starters and how to use them. "Sourdough," "starter," "mother," and "chef" are some of the many terms coined for natural yeast starters at various stages. This variety underscores the challenges of working with slow-moving natural yeasts. While yeast organisms grow on everything from fruits and vegetables to wheat itself, capturing enough of these microbes and ensuring that there are enough yeast cells to leaven a batch of dough requires some practice and patience.

Commercial yeast is concentrated; there are many times more yeast cells in a packet of yeast than in a natural yeast starter. To develop enough natural yeast cells in a starter to leaven bread, flour and water are mixed in a loose dough and are left to attract wild yeast cells in the air. The mixture is then fed with more flour and water in continuing stages so that the yeast will multiply.

All breads made with a natural starter develop a different taste from breads made with commercial yeast. These natural yeast breads, so loved by artisan bakers, often have a degree of sourness to them because wild yeast (*saccharomyces exiquis*) is of a different genus than commercial yeast (*saccharomyces cerevisiae*). In simple terms, natural yeast and the surrounding bacteria thrive in an acidic environment, while commercial yeast feeds on the starches and sugars in the flour.

Commercial yeast feeds quickly and using excessive quantities contributes to the deterioration in quality and taste of bread baked in many bakeries. So it is no wonder that artisan bakers have gone back to the old ways to develop breads with character.

Learning to work with natural yeast starters alone and in combination with packaged yeast will open up a whole world of breads with character and old-world taste.

Preferments Over the years, professional bakers have devised many ways of balancing the benefits of natural yeast and long-fermented dough with the ease and reliability of commercial yeast. We add starters to bread dough along with the minimum amount of packaged yeast to infuse the dough with the flavor of bread that has benefited from a long fermentation. The starter in such doughs is called a "preferment."

The simplest preferment is a portion of dough reserved from the previous day's baking. For centuries, it was the only way to make bread dough rise. Bread dough that has fermented for up to 4 hours at room temperature or been retarded in a refrigerator for up to 24 hours is considered "old dough." I add a piece of "old dough" to Sour Raisin Rye (page 215) to lighten the texture of this dense bread. In the recipes in this chapter, an active starter with some commercial yeast gives the dough a head start on its way to developing the rich, wheaty taste of the best breads.

Raising a Natural Yeast Starter

There is really nothing to making a starter in your own kitchen. A small amount of flour and water are mixed and left to sit out for a few days at room temperature. As the yeast organisms feed on the sugars in the flour, they multiply and the starter begins to bubble. More flour and water are added to nourish the expanding mass of growing yeast cells. Within a few days, the starter becomes an active mass, which may bubble over the top of the container in which you've mixed it.

Keeping a starter alive is like having an undemanding house pet; it needs food and water at least once a week but benefits from more frequent feedings. Once you've raised a vigorous starter, it will last indefinitely in the refrigerator. Since the yeast continues to ferment, feeding on the nourishment in the flour, you must "feed" it regularly. Take it out at least once a week and feed it. Then leave it at room temperature for 2 to 4 hours until it becomes active before using or storing in the refrigerator for future use.

Activating and Maintaining Starter for Bread Dough

The recipes in this book call for active starters, ones that are bubbling, alive, and visibly expanded. To activate your starter, remove it from the refrigerator some hours before you plan to make dough. Feed it immediately, and, depending on the temperature, it will be full of yeast energy and ready to be used within hours. On a warm day, your starter may become active in a few hours; under cool conditions, the starter might take longer.

The first step in each recipe calls for feeding your starter; remove it from the refrigerator. Stir in about 1 cup flour and ½ cup water to keep it the consistency of a light pancake batter. If it seems too thick, moisten it with more water; if it's too thin, firm it up with more flour. Leave the starter out at room temperature, 70°F to 72°F, for 2 to 4 hours after feeding before using it or returning it to the refrigerator. Only once it is energized do you measure the exact amount called for in the recipe. Here are some tips for maintaining a starter.

1. Never feed your starter to more than double its bulk. If you have 2 cups of starter, feed it with the quantities of flour and water at 75°F given above. Feed your starters at least once a week and they will keep going for as long as a few years.

2. After one or two feedings, transfer your starter to a clean container. Sometimes old bits that cling to the sides of the bowl will contaminate a starter and kill it.

3. Rye starter ferments quickly and is easy to develop. Add a bit of rye grain to your active starter to change its character.

4. The wetter the starter the faster it ferments and becomes active. If you have an established starter that you want to revive quickly, add more water when you feed it. When you use that starter in a recipe, be prepared to add more flour to compensate for the extra moistness.

5. If you maintain a wet starter, it will develop a stronger sour taste. Taste it to see how sour it has become. If you want a starter with delicate, balanced flavor, discard about ⅓ of your starter with every feeding. Then feed it more frequently.

6. The longer you let your starter sit without feeding, the more sour it will become. Feed a starter regularly to keep it sweet.

7. When working with starters in bread dough, be prepared to make adjustments as you mix; you may need to add more flour or water depending on how wet you keep your starter.

Three reliable recipes for making starter are included here. If you have your own favorite, use it in any of the recipes in this book that call for starter. Always activate any starter before using it in these recipes.

Simple Wheat Starter

This recipe uses a pinch of commercial yeast to get going. It is a reliable and uncomplicated way to develop a starter in a short time, about three days at room temperature.

For best results, mix this starter in a clear glass or plastic container. A large measuring cup with graduated markings will make it easy for you to observe it as it doubles and triples in bulk. Mark the beginning level of your starter on the side of the container with a piece of masking tape. As the yeast becomes active, you will be able to see the starter become dotted with gas bubbles.

Once you have built a healthy starter, store it in the refrigerator until you are ready to use it.

About 5 cups

Fermentation:
3 to 4 days
at room
temperature,
70°F to 72°F

Unbleached all-purpose flour	about 335 grams	about 12 ounces	2 cups
Whole wheat flour	about 125 grams	about 2 ounces	1/2 cup
Water	about 500 grams	16 ounces	2 cups
Instant yeast	1/4 teaspoon	1/4 teaspoon	1/4 teaspoon

1. In a small bowl, combine 1/2 cup of the all-purpose flour, the whole wheat flour, 1 cup of the water with the yeast. Stir to blend well. The mixture will be sticky, with the texture of thick wallpaper paste. Scrape the starter into a large plastic container with about a 2-quart capacity. Cover it with plastic wrap. Mark the level of the starter and the time it was mixed with a piece of tape on the side of the container and let it sit at room temperature, 70°F to 72°F, for 18 to 24 hours.

2. Uncover the starter. It will have almost doubled in bulk. Add 3/4 cup of the all-purpose flour and 1/2 cup of the water. Stir to combine. Cover it with plastic wrap. Mark the level of the starter and the time it was mixed with a piece of tape on the side of the container and let it sit at room temperature, 70°F to 72°F, for 18 to 24 hours.

3. Uncover the starter. It will have doubled in bulk and be full of air bubbles. Add the remaining flour and water to the balance and mix well. It will have the consistency of thick pancake batter. If it seems too thick, add more water; if it seems too runny, add more flour. Cover with plastic wrap. Mark the level of the starter and the time it was mixed with a piece of tape on the side of the container and let it sit at room temperature, 70°F to 72°F, for 6 to 8 hours.

4. This basic starter is ready to use.

5. For the next three days, keep the starter covered at room temperature. Continue to feed it with about 1 cup all-purpose flour and ½ cup water every day for three more days to continue to build its strength.

6. At this point, if you are not going to use the starter right away, refrigerate it and feed it every four to five days: each time, stir in about 1 cup all-purpose flour and ½ cup water. As the starter grows in volume, after 3 or 4 feedings, discard half or give it to a friend.

Natural Sour Wheat Starter

About 4 cups

Fermentation:

3 to 4 day at room temperature, 70°F to 72°F

Our small Connecticut town of three thousand is home to a number of bakers. My friend Howard Kaplan, an accomplished home baker with a wood-burning oven in his basement, brought this recipe back from the Moulin de la Vierge Bakery in Paris, where Basil Kamir makes his natural starter using fresh orange juice. The juice from fresh grapes is another good medium for this starter. The mixture ferments readily, becoming creamy and vigorous in only a few days.

Juice from 2 oranges	about 185 grams	about 3 ounces	about ⅓ cup
Whole wheat flour	about 60 grams	about 2 ounces	½ cup
Unbleached all-purpose flour	about 425 grams	about 15 ounces	3 cups
Cool water, about 75°F	about 500 grams	16 ounces	2 cups

1. In a small bowl, combine the orange juice and whole wheat flour. Stir to blend well. The mixture will be a soft, sticky dough. Scrape the starter into a large plastic container with about a 2-quart capacity. Let it stand, covered, for 12 to 24 hours. Bubbles will begin to form visibly on the surface of the dough.

2. Uncover the starter and add 1 cup of the all-purpose flour and 1 cup of water. Stir to combine. Cover, then let stand at room temperature, 70°F to 72°F, for about 12 hours or until bubbles form on the surface.

3. Uncover and discard half the mixture or give to a friend. Add ½ cup of the all-purpose flour and ¼ cup of the water. Cover, then let stand at room temperature, 70°F to 72°F, for about 12 hours or until bubbles form on the surface of the starter. Transfer the starter to a large bowl if it seems to be rising over the top edge of the container.

4. Feed the starter two more times, adding ½ cup all-purpose flour and ¼ cup of water with each feeding and allowing the starter to ferment for 12 hours at room temperature between feedings.

5. Discard ⅓ of the mixture and feed one more time with ½ cup all-purpose flour and ¼ cup of water. After 12 to 24 hours, the starter is ready to use.

6. Store this starter in the refrigerator. Feed it every four to five days with ½ cup flour and ¼ cup water. If you like, at every fifth feeding, discard ½ cup of the starter and feed with it whole wheat instead of all-purpose flour.

7. From this point on, store this sour starter covered in the refrigerator. To maintain it, feed at least once a week; remove it from the refrigerator and add ½ cup of water and 1 cup of all-purpose flour. Cover the starter loosely and let it sit out at room temperature for 2 to 4 hours before using.

European Rye Starter

About 4 cups

Fermentation:

4 days at room temperature, 70°F to 72°F

Rye flour ferments quickly, making it a simple medium for a sour starter. This starter has the dense texture of wet cement. If you have an active wheat starter on hand, substitute ¼ cup of it for the instant yeast in this recipe.

To make a quick rye starter, feed 2 cups of any active wheat starter with 1 cup rye flour and ½ cup cool water. Within 4 to 6 hours, you will have a mild rye sour starter suitable for any of the recipes in this book.

American deli rye breads are often based on rye starters flavored with caraway seeds or minced onion. To 1 cup of this starter, add 1 teaspoon of minced caraway seeds and 1 teaspoon of minced onion for a variation on this classic European starter.

FOR THE INITIAL RYE STARTER:

Stone-ground rye flour	250 grams	8 ounces	1²/₃ to 2 cups
Water	500 grams	16 ounces	2 cups
Dry buttermilk, (see Note) two .8 ounce packages	1.6 ounces	1.6 ounces	1.6 ounces
Instant yeast	⅛ teaspoon	⅛ teaspoon	⅛ teaspoon

FOR THE RYE SOUR FEEDING:

Stone-ground rye flour	about 425 grams	about 15 ounces	3 cups
Water	about 280 grams	10 ounces	2½ cups

1. In a deep plastic or glass bowl with enough capacity to accommodate the starter if it triples in bulk, combine all the ingredients for the initial rye starter. Stir the mixture with a wooden spoon until it comes together into a wet gruel. It will be dense and have a texture like wet cement. Cover it loosely with plastic wrap and let it sit at room temperature, 70 to 72°F, for 24 hours.

2. The next day, uncover the starter. It will appear bubbly on the surface and will have risen slightly. Begin to feed it by adding 1 cup of rye flour and ½ cup of water. Cover loosely and let it sit out another 24 hours. The next day, uncover and stir in 1 cup of rye flour and 1 cup of water. (If the quantity you are producing is too much to handle, discard half of it or give it to a friend.) Again, cover and let it sit out for another 24 hours.

3. The third day, feed the sour with 1 cup of rye flour and 1 cup of water. After 24 hours, this sour will be ready to use in any of the recipes calling for rye sour.

4. From this point on, store covered in the refrigerator. To maintain, feed the starter at least once a week: Remove it from the refrigerator and add ½ cup of water and 1 cup of rye flour. Cover loosely and let it sit out at room temperature for 2 to 4 hours before using.

Note: Most grocery stores stock cultured dry buttermilk in the baking aisle. It comes packed in foil pouches, three or four to a box, or in bulk. It has a long shelf life and is a handy way to enrich any bread dough.

Country Baguettes with Starter

Three 14-inch
loaves

Fermentation:

2¹/₂ to 3 hours
at room
temperature,
70°F to 72°F

Retardation:

2 to 12 hours
in the
refrigerator,
37°F to 45°F

Proofing:

45 minutes to 1
hour at room
temperature

The Best Bread Ever dough (page 50) makes bread with a honeycombed sweet crumb and crisp crust. The addition of a starter to the dough creates a bread with some subtle differences, the flavor of an active starter perfuming the loaf. With a longer fermentation, the crumb becomes slightly dense and develops a hint of tang that suggests sourdough bread.

Whether you want a long loaf with lots of crust, a plump loaf for slicing, or dinner rolls, this recipe makes a versatile dough to use when you want to experiment with making bread with an active starter. Like its cousin, The Best Bread Ever, it may be formed in any of the shapes described on pages 35–42; it may be mixed with herbs, fruits, or nuts as described on pages 54–55, and it is a dough that benefits from long fermentation and retardation.

Because I am using a starter in this and other recipes in this chapter, I use less commercial yeast, just enough to promote the fermentation of the dough. Since starters work more slowly than packaged yeast, let the dough ferment for a longer time at room temperature.

Forming the dough and then retarding the shaped loaves slows down the proofing stage, allowing me a great deal of flexibility when I want to bake bread. This is an important part of my summer baking strategy, one you should adapt if you bake in a hot and humid climate. I can mix this dough, ferment it, and form the loaves. Then, I have a large window of time during which I can bake the bread. If it is very hot and humid in my kitchen, I can control how quickly the dough proofs by retarding the formed loaves.

This versatile dough also makes excellent sandwich rolls and round loaves.

Simple Wheat Starter (page 175) or Natural Sour Wheat Starter (page 176)	about 150 grams	about 5 ounces	¹/₂ cup
Unbleached bread flour	500 grams	1 pound	3¹/₃ to 4 cups
Raw wheat germ	15 grams	³/₄ ounce	¹/₄ cup
Fine sea salt	15 grams	2³/₄ teaspoons	2³/₄ teaspoons
Instant yeast	¹/₂ teaspoon	¹/₂ teaspoon	¹/₂ teaspoon
Water	275 grams	9 ounces	1 cup plus 2 tablespoons

Cornmeal for the baking sheet

1. Two to four hours before you plan to mix the dough, feed your starter as described on page 173. Allow the starter to sit at room temperature until it is frothy, bubbly, and visibly active.

2. Place the flour, wheat germ, salt, and yeast in a food processor fitted with the metal blade. Measure out ½ cup of active starter and pour it into the processor. (Cover the remaining active starter with plastic wrap and return it to the refrigerator for future use.) Using an instant-read thermometer, take the temperature of the flour. Adjust the water temperature so that the combined temperatures of the flour and water give a base temperature of 130°F if using a Cuisinart or KitchenAid or 150°F if using a Braun. (See page 33 for other models.) With the machine running, pour all but 2 tablespoons of the water through the feed tube. Process for 20 seconds, adding the remaining water if the dough seems dry and does not come together into a ball during this time. Process 25 seconds longer, for a total of 45 seconds.

3. Stop the machine and take the temperature of the dough with an instant-read thermometer, which should read between 75°F and 80°F. If the temperature is lower than 75°F, process for an additional 5 seconds. If the temperature is still lower than 75°F, process for 5 seconds, up to twice more, until it reaches the desired temperature. If the temperature is higher than 80°F, remove the thermometer, scrape the dough from the food processor into an ungreased bowl, and refrigerate for 5 to 10 minutes. Check the temperature after 5 minutes; it should be 80°F or cooler by that time.

4. Remove the dough from the processor and place it in an ungreased bowl large enough to allow it to double in volume. Cover with plastic wrap. Ferment the dough at room temperature, 70°F to 72°F, for 2½ to 3 hours. It will have increased in volume somewhat but don't be concerned by how much.

5. Turn the dough onto a lightly floured work surface. With a dough scraper or kitchen knife, divide it into 3 equal pieces. Form each piece into a smooth ball. Cover with a sheet of plastic, and let rest for 15 to 20 minutes.

6. In preparation for the final proofing, spread a sheet of canvas or a heavy linen cloth on a baking sheet. The cloth should measure twice the width of the sheet. Sprinkle it lightly with flour.

7. Roll each piece of dough into the baguette shape (page 36). Using both hands, gently transfer each loaf, seam side up, to the lightly floured cloth. Fold the fabric up to form 3 channels between which the loaves will rise. Place the baguettes close together so that they don't spread out. Dust the loaves lightly with flour and cover them loosely with a plastic bag or a sheet of plastic. Set the baking sheet of formed dough in the refrigerator, and retard the baguettes for 8 to 12 hours. The dough will increase by half its size.

8. One hour before baking, put the oven rack on the second shelf from the bottom of the oven and place the baking stone on the rack. Place a small pan for water on the floor of the oven. Preheat the oven to 475°F. About 30 minutes to an hour before baking, remove the bread from the refrigerator to warm to a temperature of 60°F to 62°F to be ready for baking.

9. Gently transfer the loaves, seam sides down, to a peel or baking sheet that has been lightly dusted with cornmeal. Dust each loaf with more flour and slash the tops several times diagonally with a razor blade.

10. Pour 1 cup of warm water into the pan in the oven, then slide in the baguettes and turn the heat down to 450°F. Bake the loaves for 2 minutes, then quickly open the oven door and create steam by adding another cup of water to the pan on the oven floor. Continue baking for 18 to 20 minutes longer, until the crust is well browned. Insert an instant-read thermometer into a loaf, and if the internal temperature is 205°F to 210°F, the bread is done.

11. Remove from the oven and immediately place the loaves on a wire rack to cool completely before storing.

Country Wheat Crown

Simple Wheat Starter (page 175) or Natural Sour Wheat Starter (page 176)	about 150 grams	about 5 ounces	1/2 cup	One 12-inch round loaf
Whole wheat flour	500 grams	1 pound	3 1/3 to 4 cups	Fermentation:
Graham flour	30 grams	1 ounce	3 tablespoons	2 1/2 to 3 hours at room temperature, 70°F to 72°F
Powdered milk	10 grams	2 teaspoons	2 teaspoons	
Fine sea salt	15 grams	2 3/4 teaspoons	2 3/4 teaspoons	Proofing:
Instant yeast	1/2 teaspoon	1/2 teaspoon	1/2 teaspoon	40 to 45 minutes
Water	300 grams	9 1/2 ounces	1 cup plus 3 tablespoons	at room temperature

Cornmeal for the baking sheet

1. Two to four hours before you plan to mix the dough, feed your starter as described on page 173. Allow the starter to sit at room temperature until it is frothy, bubbly, and visibly active.

2. Place the flours, powdered milk, salt, and yeast in a food processor fitted with the metal blade. Measure 1/2 cup of the active starter and pour it into the processor. Using an instant-read thermometer, adjust the water temperature so that the combined temperatures of the flour and the water give a base temperature of 130°F if using a Cuisinart or KitchenAid or 150°F if using a Braun. (See page 33 for other models.) With the machine running, pour all but 2 tablespoons of the water through the feed tube. Process for 20 seconds, adding the remaining water if the dough seems dry and does not come together into a ball during this time. Process 25 seconds longer, for a total of 45 seconds.

3. Stop the machine and take the temperature of the dough with an instant-read thermometer, which should read between 75°F and 80°F. If the temperature is lower than 75°F, process for an additional 5 seconds. If the temperature is still lower than 75°F, process for 5 seconds up to twice more, until it reaches the desired temperature. If the temperature is higher than 80°F, remove the thermometer, scrape the dough from the food processor

Store at room
temperature
covered with a
towel or in a
paper bag. The
bread will stay
fresh for up to
three days
at room
temperature.

into an ungreased bowl, and refrigerate for 5 to 10 minutes. Check the temperature after 5 minutes; it should be 80°F or cooler by that time.

4. Remove the dough from the processor and place it in an ungreased bowl large enough to allow it to double in volume. Cover with plastic wrap. Allow the dough to ferment for 2½ to 3 hours at room temperature, 70°F to 72°F. It will have increased in volume somewhat but don't be concerned by how much.

5. Turn the dough onto a lightly floured work surface. Gently form it into a loose ball, trying not to deflate all of the air bubbles that have formed as it has fermented. Cover with a sheet of plastic, and let rest for 15 to 20 minutes.

6. Form the dough into a crown (page 41). Gently transfer the loaf onto a peel or the back of a baking sheet that has been dusted with cornmeal. Dust the loaf with more flour, cover it with plastic wrap, and let it proof for 40 to 45 minutes, until dough increases by half its size. It should feel softer but still spring back slightly when poked with your finger.

7. One hour before baking, put the oven rack on the second shelf from the bottom of the oven and place the baking stone on the rack. Place a small pan for water on the floor of the oven. Preheat to 450°F.

8. Sprinkle the loaf lightly with flour. Holding a sharp knife or razor blade almost parallel to the top of the loaf, score it in several places.

9. Pour a cup of water into the pan in the oven. Using the peel or baking sheet, immediately slide the loaf of bread onto the stone in the oven. Reduce the heat to 425°F. Bake the loaf for a total of 40 to 45 minutes. Check after the first 30 minutes to see if the loaf is browning too quickly. If the crust appears to be too dark, turn the oven down to 400°F and continue to bake for another 10 to 15 minutes, until the crust is a deep brown. Insert an instant-read thermometer into the loaf; if the internal temperature is 205°F to 210°F, the bread is done.

10. Remove the bread from the oven and place on a wire rack to cool completely before storing.

Walnut Bread

A rich loaf studded with nuts and the full flavor of whole wheat, walnut bread is one of our family favorites. This bread bakes into a chubby loaf, the color of the crumb delicately stained a pale purple by the walnuts. You can substitute hazelnuts, if you choose. Either version is delicious when toasted for breakfast and spread with butter and preserves. These nut loaves are an essential part of a fine cheese course.

The food processor mixing produces a well-aerated dough with a spongy texture. If you have an oval cloth-lined basket, this dough retains the lovely impressions left on its surface by the basket.

One 12 × 4-inch oval loaf

Fermentation: 2½ to 3 hours at room temperature, 70°F to 72°F

Proofing: 45 minutes to 1 hour at room temperature

Simple Wheat Starter (page 175) or European Rye Starter (page 178)	about 150 grams	about 5 ounces	½ cup
Unbleached bread flour	300 grams	9½ ounces	2 to 2½ cups
Whole wheat flour	100 grams	3¼ ounces	¾ cup
Rye flour	100 grams	3¼ ounces	¾ cup
Fine sea salt	15 grams	2¾ teaspoons	2¾ teaspoons
Instant yeast	½ teaspoon	½ teaspoon	½ teaspoon
Water	300 grams	9½ ounces	1 cup plus 3 tablespoons
Walnuts, roasted and blanched	200 grams	7 ounces	1¾ cups
Cornmeal for the peel or baking sheet			

1. Two to four hours before you plan to mix the dough, feed your starter as described on page 173. Allow the starter to sit at room temperature until it is frothy, bubbly, and visibly active.

2. Place the flours, salt, and yeast in a food processor fitted with the metal blade. Measure out ½ cup of active starter and pour it into the processor. (Cover the remaining active starter with plastic wrap and place it in the refrigerator for future use.)

3. Using an instant-read thermometer, adjust the water temperature so that the combined temperatures of the flour and the water give a base temperature of 130°F if using a Cuisinart or KitchenAid or 150°F if using a Braun. (See page 33 for other models.) With the machine running, pour all but 2 tablespoons of the water through the feed tube. Process for 20 seconds, adding the remaining water if the dough seems dry and does not come together into a ball during this time.

4. Stop the machine and let the dough rest in the food processor bowl for 5 minutes. It will soften noticeably as it rests. Then process for 25 seconds longer, for a total of 45 seconds.

5. Stop the machine and take the temperature of the dough with an instant-read thermometer, which should read between 75°F and 80°F. If the temperature is lower than 75°F, process for an additional 5 seconds, up to twice more, until it reaches the desired temperature. If the temperature is higher than 80°F, remove the thermometer, scrape the dough from the food processor into an ungreased bowl, and refrigerate for 5 to 10 minutes. Check the temperature after 5 minutes; it should be 80°F or cooler by that time.

6. Scrape the dough from the processor onto a lightly floured work surface and gather it into a rough ball. Loosely cover with plastic wrap and let rest for 15 to 20 minutes.

7. Press the dough into a 12-inch square and about 1 inch thick. Sprinkle the surface with the walnuts, fold the dough over, and knead it for about 2 minutes to distribute the nuts throughout. Place in a large ungreased bowl and cover with plastic wrap. Allow the dough to ferment for 2½ to 3 hours at room temperature, 70°F to 72°F. It will have increased in volume somewhat but don't be concerned by how much.

8. Turn the dough onto a lightly floured work surface. Gently form it into a loose ball, trying not to deflate all of the air bubbles that have formed as it has fermented. Roll it into one football-shaped loaf (page 38). Place it on a flour-coated baking sheet or in a floured cloth-lined basket. Dust with flour and cover it loosely with plastic wrap.

9. Proof the loaf for 45 minutes to an hour at room temperature, until it increases by half its size. The dough should feel softer but still spring back slowly when poked with your finger.

10. One hour before baking, put the oven rack on the second shelf from the bottom of the oven and place the baking stone on the rack. Place a small pan for water on the floor of the oven and preheat to 475°F.

11. Lightly dust a peel or the back of a baking sheet with cornmeal. Carefully transfer the loaf to the peel or baking sheet, sprinkle it lightly with flour, and slash the top diagonally with a razor blade. (About 8 slashes spaced 1 inch apart should fit this size loaf.)

12. Pour about 1 cup of warm water into the pan in the oven. Using the peel or baking sheet, immediately slide the loaf onto the baking stone. Turn the heat down to 425°F. Bake for 35 to 40 minutes until the crust is deep brown. Insert an instant-read thermometer into the bread; if the internal temperature is 205°F to 210°F, the bread is done.

13. Remove the bread from the oven and place on a wire rack to cool completely before storing.

This bread will keep for three days at room temperature when covered with a kitchen towel.

Olive Rosemary Bread

One 12 × 4-inch oval loaf

Fermentation:

2½ to 3 hours at room temperature, 70°F to 72°F

Proofing:

30 to 45 minutes at room temperature

You can knead olives and herbs into any wheat bread in this book, but I like the contrast in tastes between the sweet whole wheat and rye flours and the briny olives. I stick the woody stem ends of short sprigs of rosemary into the dough just before it goes into the oven. The herb burns slightly in the oven as the loaves bake, giving the surface of the loaf the look of a porcupine.

Once the dough has been fermented, it becomes alive and bouncy. If it resists forming into a plump, round loaf, let it rest for a few minutes to relax the gluten in the bread flour.

If you use salty Greek olives, like kalamata, rinse them to remove some of their brine. Oil-cured olives give the bread a more mellow flavor.

Simple Wheat Starter (page 175) or Natural Sour Wheat Starter (page 176)	about 150 grams	about 5 ounces	½ cup
Unbleached bread flour	300 grams	9 ounces	1¾ to 2¼ cups
Whole wheat flour	170 grams	6 ounces	1¼ cups
Rye flour	30 grams	1 ounce	¼ cup
Fine sea salt	15 grams	2¾ teaspoons	2¾ teaspoons
Instant yeast	½ teaspoon	½ teaspoon	½ teaspoon
Water	300 grams	9½ ounces	1 cup plus 3 tablespoons
Extra virgin olive oil (optional)	1 teaspoon	1 teaspoon	1 teaspoon
Pitted black olives	140 grams	5 ounces	½ cup
Chopped rosemary	1 tablespoon	1 tablespoon	1 tablespoon
A few whole sprigs of rosemary for garnish			
Cornmeal for the peel or baking sheet			

1. Two to four hours before you plan to mix the dough, feed your starter as described on page 173. Allow the starter to sit at room temperature until it is frothy, bubbly, and visibly active.

2. Place the flours, salt, and yeast in a food processor fitted with the metal blade. Measure out ½ cup of active starter and pour it into the processor. (Cover the remaining active starter with plastic wrap and place it in the refrigerator for future use.) Using an instant-read thermometer, adjust the temperature of the water so that the combined temperatures of the flour and water give a base temperature of 130°F if using a Cuisinart or KitchenAid or 150°F if using a Braun. (See page 33 for other models.) If using, add the olive oil to the water.

3. With the machine running, pour all but 2 tablespoons of the water through the feed tube. Process for 20 seconds, adding the additional water if the dough seems too dry and crumbly and is not forming a smooth ball in the bowl of the machine. If the dough seems too wet and is sticking to the shaft and sides of the bowl, add a few additional spoonfuls of flour through the feed tube. Process for 25 more seconds, for a total of 45 seconds.

4. Stop the machine and take the temperature of the dough with an instant-read thermometer, which should read between 75°F and 80°F. If the temperature is lower than 75°F, process for an additional 5 seconds. If the temperature of the dough is still lower than 75°F, process the dough for an additional 5 seconds, up to twice more, until it reaches the desired temperature. If the temperature is higher than 80°F, remove the thermometer, scrape the dough from the food processor into an ungreased bowl, and refrigerate 5 to 10 minutes. Check the temperature after 5 minutes; it should be 80°F or cooler by that time.

5. Scrape the dough from the processor onto a lightly floured work surface. Gather it into a rough ball and place it in a large ungreased bowl. The dough will be slightly wet and springy. Cover the bowl with plastic wrap. Allow it to ferment for 2½ to 3 hours at room temperature, 70°F to 72°F. The dough will have increased in volume somewhat but don't be concerned by how much.

6. Turn the dough onto a lightly floured work surface. Flatten it with the palms of your hands into a 12-inch square. Sprinkle with the pitted olives and chopped rosemary, fold the dough over onto itself, and knead for about 3 to 4 minutes to thoroughly incorporate the olives and rosemary. If it resists kneading, cover with a towel and let rest for 10 minutes.

7. Form the dough into a round loaf (page 35), cover with a towel, and let rest while you prepare a basket or banneton.

8. Sprinkle a cloth-lined basket or banneton with flour. Place the ball of dough in the basket with the bottom of the loaf on top. Dust with flour and loosely cover the bread with a sheet of plastic wrap. Allow to proof 30 to 45 minutes, at room temperature, until the dough has visibly risen and springs back when pressed gently with your finger.

9. One hour before baking, put the oven rack on the second shelf from the bottom of the oven and place the baking stone on the rack. Place a small pan for water on the floor of the oven and preheat to 475°F.

10. Invert the dough onto a peel or the back of a baking sheet dusted with cornmeal and dust the top of the loaf with more flour. Score the dough in a star pattern: Starting from the center of the loaf, make a short slash about 3 inches long with a razor blade. Rotate the bread and continue slashing the loaf until a star pattern is formed on the top. Stick a few 1-inch sprigs of rosemary into the surface of the dough.

11. Pour a cup of warm water into the pan in the oven, then slide the loaf onto the baking stone. Turn the heat down to 450°F. Bake 5 minutes, then create steam by adding another cup of water to the pan on the floor of the oven. Bake the loaf for 30 minutes, then reduce the temperature to 425°F. Bake for about 15 more minutes until the crust is well browned. Insert an instant-read thermometer into the bread, and if the internal temperature is 205°F to 210°F degrees, the bread is done.

12. Remove the bread from the oven and immediately place it on a wire rack to cool.

The King of Bread—Peasant Wheat Loaf

There is probably no other bread that has as much mystique as this rustic country loaf. Formed by hand, no two loaves are ever exactly the same, but all are dark, almost burned in spots, with the signature of the baker etched in the slashes marked on the loaf's surface before baking. The crust appears impenetrable because of its thickness, but when it is cut, bits of the crust go flying in every direction, revealing its springy, moist interior. When it comes out of the oven, this steaming peasant loaf whistles as it hits the cool air outside the oven. French bakers call this "singing," and if you are ever lucky enough to be around when a load of these loaves is cooling on a baker's rack, you'll never forget the delicate sound or spicy scent.

This giant loaf cannot be rushed. You must wait for it to be ready to bake. To develop the complex flavor, slow down the fermentation action by placing the formed loaf in the refrigerator overnight before baking. (This process requires enough space in the refrigerator to hold the covered loaf.) If you are baking in the fall or winter in a cool climate, the garage, or attic stairs, or some other cool spot between 37°F and 45°F will work.

When this loaf sits in the banneton, moisture in the dough can make it stick to the basket. Heavily flour the cloth in the basket or banneton before you place the loaf in the basket. If it does stick, use your fingers to pry the dough from the basket. If there is a slight dent in the loaf, don't be concerned. Unless the surface is torn, most dents will disappear once the bread is baked. Besides, irregularities give this bread its hand-formed character.

Bake until the outside is a deep, dark brown. This will flavor the loaf and make for a thick, chewy crust.

This bread is for keeping. It can be shaped into baguettes, pan loaves, or dinner rolls. This is the dough that I use to make the Presentation Loaf (page 68).

One 12-inch loaf

Fermentation: 2¹/₂ to 3 hours at room temperature, 70°F to 72°F

Retardation: 12 to 16 hours in the refrigerator, 37°F to 40°F

Proofing: 1 to 2 hours at room temperature

Simple Wheat Starter (page 175) or European Rye Starter (page 178)	about 150 grams	about 5 ounces	1/2 cup
Whole wheat flour	75 grams	3 ounces	½ cup
Unbleached bread flour	400 grams	12 ounces	2⅓ to 3 cups
Stone-ground rye flour	75 grams	3 ounces	½ cup
Instant yeast	½ teaspoon	½ teaspoon	½ teaspoon
Fine sea salt	15 grams	2¾ teaspoon	2¾ teaspoon
Water	335 grams	11 ounces	1¼ cups plus 2 tablespoons

Cornmeal for the baking sheet

1. Two to four hours before you plan to mix the dough, feed your starter as described on page 173. Allow it to sit at room temperature until it is frothy, bubbly, and visibly active.

2. Place the flours, yeast, and salt in a food processor fitted with the metal blade. Measure ½ cup of the active starter and pour it into the processor. Using an instant-read thermometer, adjust the water temperature so that the combined temperatures of the flour and water give a base temperature of 130°F if using a Cuisinart or KitchenAid or 150°F if using a Braun. (See page 33 for other models.)

3. With the machine running, pour all but 2 tablespoons of the water through the feed tube. Process for 20 seconds, adding the remaining water if the dough seems dry and does not come together into a ball during this time. Process 25 seconds longer, for a total of 45 seconds.

4. Stop the machine and take the temperature of the dough with an instant-read thermometer, which should read between 75°F and 80°F. If the temperature is lower than 75°F, process the dough for an additional 5 seconds. If the temperature is still lower than 75°F, process for 5 seconds, up to twice more, until the dough reaches the desired temperature. If the temperature is higher than 80°F, remove the thermometer, scrape the dough from the food processor into an ungreased bowl, and refrigerate for 5 to 10 minutes. Check the temperature after 5 minutes; it should be 80°F or cooler by that time.

5. Remove the dough from the processor, place it in a large ungreased bowl, and cover with plastic wrap. Allow to ferment for 2½ to 3 hours at room temperature.

6. Turn the dough onto a lightly floured work surface and shape it into a large round loaf (page 35). Generously dust a banneton or cloth-lined basket with flour and place the loaf, seam side up, in the basket. Dust with flour and cover loosely with a sheet of plastic wrap. Place in the refrigerator for 12 to 16 hours.

7. Remove the dough from the refrigerator; it will be visibly puffed. Let the covered dough warm to a temperature of 60°F to 62°F. It will be soft but still spring back slowly when pressed with your finger. This may take from 1 to 2 hours, depending on how warm your kitchen is.

8. One hour before baking, put the oven rack on the second shelf from the bottom of the oven and place the baking stone on the rack. Place a small pan for water on the floor of the oven and preheat to 475°F.

9. Uncover the loaf and invert it onto a peel or the back of a baking sheet that has been sprinkled with cornmeal. If it seems to stick to the basket, use your fingers to pry the dough gently from the basket. Don't worry if you slightly dent the loaf. Unless the surface is torn, most dents will disappear once the bread is baked.

10. Make 4 slashes around the edges of the loaf, 2 horizontal and 2 vertical, to form a large square in the center of the top. Dust lightly with flour.

11. Pour about 1 cup warm water into the pan in the oven, then slide the loaf directly onto the baking stone. Reduce the heat to 450°F. Bake for 2 minutes, then quickly open the oven door and create steam by adding another cup of water to the pan on the floor of the oven. Close the oven door and continue baking for 15 more minutes. Then rotate the bread so that it bakes evenly. Should it appear to be browning too quickly, reduce the heat to 400°F and continue baking for another 25 to 30 minutes. Bake until the crust is a deep, dark brown. Or, insert an instant-read thermometer into the bread, and if the internal temperature is 205°F to 210°F, the bread is done.

12. Remove the bread from the oven and place it on a wire rack to cool completely before cutting.

Store this loaf covered with a cloth towel or in a paper bag at room temperature. It will stay fresh for four or five days at room temperature.

Pain au Levain Bread
Made From a Natural Starter

Schedule:

Activating the
Starter:

4 to 6 hours
at room
temperature,
70°F to 72°F

Fermentation
of Levain:

8 to 12 hours
at room
temperature

Fermentation
of Dough:

4 to 6 hours
at room
temperature

Proofing:

1¹/₂ to 3 hours
at room
temperature

This recipe is for the truly adventurous, for those who appreciate the joy of accidental discovery. The term pain au levain *refers to a particular method of fermenting dough to make bread rise, a method created before the advent of manufactured yeast. Best known in this country as sourdough, levain bread dough is fermented with yeast that is naturally present in flour and the air around us.*

As with making wine, making bread using the levain method requires patience and some experience to get it just right. When you succeed, there is a sense of accomplishment in having mastered this elemental bread-making method. (But since the bread you will produce using The Best Bread Ever method is considerably easier and produces controllable and consistent results, I believe the scale is tilted in favor of using minimum amounts of yeast and mixing dough in the food processor.)

The levain for this bread is quite dry, like a firm bread dough. It is essential that you begin with an active starter, one that is visibly bubbling like a fermenting swamp. Like the pain au levain in France, this dough will produce a bread with a true wheat flavor and little sour taste. If you would like to produce a bread with a real tang, experiment with this recipe by making the initial levain more moist; add as much as ¹/₂ cup more water in the initial mix. Tighten the dough in the last mixing stage with additional flour and proceed with the recipe.

When handling dough made only with natural yeast, it is important to treat the fragile dough very gently to preserve as many air bubbles as possible.

This is bread dough that doesn't keep to a firm schedule. If your kitchen is especially cold, it may take as long as 8 hours for your starter to become active. Depending on the vitality of your starter, the dough may ferment in 4 or 5 hours or it may take much longer to develop the strength to rise perceptibly.

Bakers have been making bread in this manner for centuries; don't be discouraged if it takes two or three tries to master it. The solid loaves this recipe produces have a tighter crumb than a classic baguette and the texture and taste of the best peasant loaf.

Natural Sour Wheat Starter (page 176)	about 60 grams	about 2 ounces	1/4 cup
Unbleached bread flour	255 grams	9 ounces	about 2 cups
Water	115 grams	4 ounces	1/2 cup

1. Two to four hours before you plan to make your levain, remove your starter from the refrigerator and feed it as described on page 173. Allow it to sit at room temperature until it is frothy, bubbly, and visibly active.

2. To mix the levain, measure 1/4 cup of the active starter and combine it with the flour in the bowl of a food processor fitted with the metal blade. With an instant-read thermometer, take the temperature of the flour. Adjust the temperature of the water so that the combined temperatures of the flour and water give a base temperature of 130°F if using a Cuisinart or KitchenAid or 150°F if using a Braun. (See page 33 for other models.) With the machine running, add all of the water and process for 45 seconds. The levain should be like a firm bread dough. Scrape it into a clear plastic container and cover it with plastic wrap.

3. Let the levain stand for 8 to 12 hours at room temperature before proceeding. It will be noticeably lighter by then, with bubbles throughout the dough indicating that the yeast organisms are active and alive.

FOR THE DOUGH

Levain	all of the Levain		
Unbleached bread flour	550 grams	18 ounces	about 4 cups
Fine sea salt	15 grams	2 3/4 teaspoons	2 3/4 teaspoons
Water	385 grams	12 1/2 ounces	1 1/2 cups plus 1 tablespoon
Cornmeal for the baking sheet			

1. Place all of the levain, flour, and salt in the bowl of a food processor fitted with the metal blade. Take the temperature of the flour. Adjust the temperature of the water so that the combined temperatures of the flour and water give a base temperature of 130°F if using a Cuisinart or KitchenAid or 150°F if using a Braun. (See page 33 for other models.) With the machine running, add all but 3 tablespoons of the water. Process for 20 seconds, adding the reserved water if the dough seems dry and crumbling. If the dough is not forming a ball and is clinging to the shaft and sides of the bowl, add a few spoonfuls of flour through the feed tube. Process 25 seconds longer, for a total of 45 seconds.

2. Stop the machine and take the temperature of the dough with an instant-read thermometer, which should read between 75°F and 80°F. If the temperature is lower than 75°F, process for an additional 5 seconds. If the temperature is still lower than 75°F, process for 5 seconds up to twice more, until it reaches the desired temperature. If the temperature is higher than 80°F, remove the thermometer, scrape the dough from the food processor into an ungreased bowl, and refrigerate for 5 to 10 minutes. Check the temperature after 5 minutes; it should be 80°F or cooler by that time.

3. Scrape the dough onto a lightly floured surface and form it into a loose ball. Place the ball in a clear glass or plastic container, cover with plastic wrap, and let it ferment for 4 to 6 hours at room temperature, 70°F to 72°F. During that time, it will double in bulk and bubbles will be visible throughout.

4. Gently scrape the dough onto a lightly floured surface, taking care not to deflate any air bubbles that have formed during fermentation. Use a dough scraper or kitchen knife to divide the dough into 2 pieces. Once the dough has fermented, form it into a round shape by folding up the sides of the loose dough on your work surface and proof the loaves in cloth-lined baskets or a banneton. The baskets will keep the shape of the loaf as it proofs. Transfer the loaves to a flour- or cornmeal-coated baking sheet, cover, and let proof for about 1 to 3 hours, until the dough has visibly risen by about ⅓.

5. One hour before baking, put the oven rack on the second shelf from the bottom of the oven and place the baking stone on the rack. Place a small pan for water on the bottom of the oven and preheat to 475°F.

6. Gently transfer each loaf to the back of the prepared baking sheet or peel. Dust the surface of each loaf with flour, then score in a cross pattern, making one 4-inch horizontal and one 4-inch vertical slash.

7. Pour about 1 cup of hot water into the pan in the oven, then slide the bread directly onto the baking stone. Turn the heat down to 425°F. Bake for 2 minutes, then create steam by adding another cup of water to the pan in the oven. Bake another 2 minutes, then steam the oven a third time. Continue baking the bread for another 10 minutes. Rotate bread in the oven, then turn the heat down to 400°F. Continue baking for 20 to 25 more minutes, until it is deep brown. Insert an instant-read thermometer into the bread, and if the internal temperature is 205°F to 210°F, it is done.

8. Remove the bread from the oven and immediately place the loaves on a wire rack to cool.

Store this bread covered with a cloth towel or in a paper bag at room temperature. It will stay fresh for two to three days at room temperature.

Altamura Loaf

The region of Altamura in Puglia, in the boot of Italy, is renowned for its exceptional breads made from the golden durum wheat grown on the neighboring plains. This appealing loaf is typical of the style of country bread found in that area. The high percentage of starter gives the loaf a thin crust with a slight tangy taste.

To develop the flavor in this bread, ferment the dough, then retard it before forming the loaf. When it has been retarded, you won't need to slash before baking, because it will naturally split down the center. As it bakes, the crust will develop small blisters, meaning that this dough has fermented for as long as possible.

This loaf speaks many languages; it goes with all types of food, and is delicious fresh or toasted.

This recipe is adapted from a recipe in Carol Field's informative book, The Italian Baker.

One 10-inch loaf

Fermentation: 2¹/₂ to 3 hours at room temperature, 70°F to 72°F

Retardation: 2 to 12 hours in the refrigerator, 37°F to 45°F (optional)

Proofing: 45 minutes to 1 hour at room temperature

Simple Wheat Starter (page 175) or Natural Sour Wheat Starter (page 176)	about 250 grams	about 8 ounces	1 cup
Durum wheat flour	500 grams	1 pound	3⅓ to 4 cups
Fine sea salt	20 grams	1 tablespoon	1 tablespoon
Instant yeast	¾ teaspoon	¾ teaspoon	¾ teaspoon
Water	265 grams	8½ ounces	1 cup plus 1 tablespoon
Cornmeal for the baking sheet			

1. Two to four hours before you plan to mix the dough, feed your starter as described on page 173. Allow the starter to sit at room temperature until it is frothy, bubbly, and visibly active.

2. Place the flour, salt, and yeast in a food processor fitted with the metal blade. Measure 1 cup of the active starter and pour it into the processor. Using an instant-read thermometer, adjust the water temperature so that the combined temperatures of the flour and water give a base temperature of 130°F if using a Cuisinart or KitchenAid or 150°F if using a Braun. (See page 33 for other models.)

3. With the machine running, pour all but 2 tablespoons of the water through the feed tube. Process for 20 seconds, adding the remaining water if the dough seems dry and does not come together into a ball during this time.

4. Stop the machine and let the dough rest in the food processor bowl for 5 minutes. It will soften noticeably as it rests. Process for 25 seconds longer, for a total of 45 seconds. It will feel firm but moist and will stick slightly to your fingertips.

5. Stop the machine, and take the temperature of the dough with an instant-read thermometer, which should read between 75°F and 80°F. If it is lower than 75°F, process for an additional 5 seconds. If it is still lower than 75°F, process for an additional 5 seconds, up to twice more, until the dough reaches the desired temperature. If the temperature is higher than 80°F, remove the thermometer, scrape the dough from the food processor into an ungreased bowl, and refrigerate for 5 to 10 minutes. Check the temperature after 5 minutes; it should be 80°F or cooler by that time.

6. Remove the dough from the processor, place it in a large ungreased bowl, and cover with plastic wrap. Allow to ferment for 2½ to 3 hours at room temperature, 70°F to 72°F. It will have increased in volume somewhat but don't be concerned by how much. (At this point the dough may be retarded for up to 12 hours; place it, covered, in the refrigerator.)

7. Turn the dough onto a lightly floured work surface and with lightly floured fingertips, pat it to flatten slightly. Shape into a small round loaf (page 35).

8. Transfer the loaf to a baking sheet lightly sprinkled with cornmeal, dust the top with flour, and cover loosely with plastic wrap. Let it proof for 45 minutes to 1 hour at room temperature before baking. (If the dough is cool from having been retarded in the refrigerator, this final proofing may take from 1 to 2 hours. It is ready to be baked when it reaches an internal temperature of 60°F to 62°F. Use an instant-read thermometer check.)

9. One hour before baking, put the oven rack on the second shelf from the bottom of the oven and place the baking stone on the rack. Place a small pan for water on the floor of the oven and preheat to 475°F.

10. Uncover the bread and generously dust it with flour. If the surface has not naturally split, make one slash about ¼ inch deep across the top.

11. Pour about 1 cup of warm water into the pan on the floor of the oven. Immediately place the baking sheet in the oven. Reduce the heat to 450°F. Bake for 2 minutes, then create steam by adding another cup of water to the pan in the bottom of the oven. Continue baking for 15 more minutes. Rotate the bread so that it bakes evenly, then bake for another 8 to 10 minutes, until the crust develops a deep, golden brown color. Insert an instant-read thermometer into the loaf, and if the internal temperature is 205°F to 210°F, the bread is done.

12. Remove the bread from the oven and place it on a wire rack to cool completely before cutting.

Store this bread covered with a towel or in a paper bag at room temperature. It will keep for three or four days at room temperature. For longer storage, wrap the bread in plastic and freeze for up to three weeks.

Stout Bread

One 9-inch
round loaf

Fermentation:

2¹/₂ to 3 hours
at room
temperature,
70°F to 72°F

Retardation:

2 to 6 hours
in the
refrigerator,
37°F to 45°F
(optional)

Proofing:

30 to 45
minutes
at room
temperature

The name of this bread doesn't refer to its size or shape, but rather to the heavy, strongly flavored ale that flavors this dark loaf. With microbreweries springing up all over, try a stout from a local producer, or use Guinness, available in many supermarkets.

With a large percentage of wheat flour, this bread has a springy interior crumb. The flavor of the dough improves with long fermentation, and cracked rye grain on the surface gives it an earthy look. Substitute oatmeal, wheat bran, or a dusting of whole wheat flour if cracked rye is not available.

European Rye Starter (page 178)	about 150 grams	about 5 ounces	¹/₂ cup
Unbleached bread flour	425 grams	14 ounces	2³/₄ to 3¹/₂ cups
Stone-ground rye flour	75 grams	2¹/₂ ounces	about ¹/₂ cup
Fine sea salt	15 grams	2³/₄ teaspoons	2³/₄ teaspoons
Instant yeast	¹/₂ teaspoon	¹/₂ teaspoon	¹/₂ teaspoon
Guinness stout or dark beer, at room temperature	250 grams	8 ounces	1 cup
Cracked rye grain	150 grams	4 ounces	¹/₂ cup
Cornmeal for the baking sheet			

1. Two to four hours before you plan to mix the dough, feed your European Rye Starter as described on page 173. Allow it to sit at room temperature until it is frothy, bubbly, and visibly active.

2. Place the flours, salt, and yeast in a food processor fitted with the metal blade. Measure ¹/₂ cup of the active starter and pour it into the processor. (Cover the remaining starter with plastic wrap and place it in the refrigerator for future use.)

3. Using an instant-read thermometer, adjust the temperature of the beer so that the combined temperatures of the flour and the beer give a base temperature of 130°F if using a Cuisinart or KitchenAid or 150°F if using a Braun. (See page 33 for other models.) To warm the beer, place it in a metal bowl set over hot water, stir for a few seconds, and measure the temperature with an instant-read thermometer. Or cool the beer by placing it in a metal bowl set over chilled or ice water. Stir for a few seconds, then measure the temperature with an instant-read thermometer. Repeat until desired temperature is reached.

4. With the machine running, pour all but 2 tablespoons of the beer through the feed tube. Process for 20 seconds, adding the remaining beer if the dough seems too dry and does not come together into a ball during this time. Process 25 seconds longer, for a total of 45 seconds.

5. Stop the machine and take the temperature of the dough with an instant-read thermometer. It should be between 75°F and 80°F. If the temperature is lower than 75°F, process for an additional 5 seconds, up to twice more, until it reaches the desired temperature. If the temperature is higher than 80°F, remove the thermometer, scrape the dough from the food processor into an ungreased bowl, and refrigerate for 5 to 10 minutes. Check the temperature after 5 minutes; it should be 80°F or cooler by that time.

6. Scrape the dough from the processor onto a lightly floured work surface. Gather the dough into a loose ball. It will feel soft and springy. Place it in a large ungreased bowl and cover it with plastic wrap. Allow to ferment for about 2½ to 3 hours at room temperature. The dough will have increased in volume somewhat but don't be concerned by how much.

7. Turn the dough onto a lightly floured work surface. Handling gently, form it into a loose round shape (page 35). Cover and let rest.

8. Sprinkle a cloth-lined basket with flour and sprinkle half of the cracked rye grain into the bottom of the basket. Place the ball of dough in the basket, seam side up. Cover with a kitchen towel and let proof for 30 to 45 minutes. (The dough may be retarded in the refrigerator at this point for up to 6 hours. Remove the formed loaf from the refrigerator and let it warm to a temperature of 60°F to 62°F, which may take 1 to 2 hours, before baking.)

9. One hour before baking, put the oven rack on the second shelf from the bottom of the oven and place the baking stone on the rack. Place a small pan of water on the floor of the oven. Preheat the oven to 475°F.

It will stay
fresh for three
days at room
temperature
when covered
with a kitchen
towel.

10. Invert the loaf onto a peel or the back of a baking sheet sprinkled with cornmeal. Brush the sides with water and sprinkle the remaining cracked rye over the wet dough. Score the dough with a deep cross, making the slashes about 5 inches long in each direction.

11. Pour about 1 cup of warm water into the pan in the oven. Immediately slide the loaf onto the baking stone and turn the heat down to 425°F. Bake 45 to 50 minutes, until the crust is a rich, dark brown. Using an instant-read thermometer, the loaf will be finished when it reaches an internal temperature of 205°F to 210°F.

12. Remove the bread from the oven and immediately place it on a wire rack to cool.

Normandy Cider Bread

Sparkling fermented cider, a specialty of Normandy, France, is made in this country as well, but if you can't find it, use apple cider. The apples' musky sweetness lingers in these loaves.

Form this dough into two round loaves or one large oblong loaf and serve with strong cheeses such as a ripe blue cheese or a creamy Camembert.

If your processor tends to stall, divide the dough in half and mix it in two batches.

Two 10-inch loaves

Fermentation: 2½ to 3 hours at room temperature, 70°F to 72°F

Proofing: 1½ to 2 hours at room temperature

European Rye Starter (page 178) or Simple Wheat Starter (page 175)	about 150 grams	about 5 ounces	½ cup
Unbleached bread flour	500 grams	16 ounces	3⅓ to 4 cups
Whole wheat flour	125 grams	4 ounces	about 1 cup
Rye flour	125 grams	4 ounces	about 1 cup
Fine sea salt	20 grams	1 tablespoon	1 tablespoon
Instant yeast	1 teaspoon	1 teaspoon	1 teaspoon
Still or sparkling cider, at room temperature	225 grams	7½ ounces	¾ cup plus 3 tablespoons
Water	225 grams	7½ ounces	¾ cup plus 3 tablespoons
Cracked wheat for garnish (optional)			
Cornmeal for the baking sheet			

1. Two to four hours before you plan to mix the dough, feed your starter as described on page 173. Allow it to sit at room temperature until it is frothy, bubbly, and visibly active.

2. Place the flours, salt, and yeast in a food processor fitted with the metal blade. Measure ½ cup of the active starter and pour it into the processor. (Cover the remaining starter with plastic wrap and place it in the refrigerator for future use.)

3. Combine the cider and the water. Using an instant-read thermometer, adjust the temperature of the liquids so that the combined temperatures of the flour and liquid mixture give a base temperature of 130°F if using a Cuisinart or KitchenAid or 150°F if using a Braun. (See page 33 for other models.) To warm the liquids, place them in a metal bowl set over hot water, stir for a few seconds, and measure the temperature with an instant-read thermometer. Or, cool the liquids by placing them in a metal bowl set over chilled or ice water. Stir for a few seconds, then measure the temperature with an instant-read thermometer. Repeat until the desired temperature is reached.

4. With the machine running, pour all but 3 tablespoons of the liquid through the feed tube. Process for 20 seconds, adding the remaining liquid if the dough seems dry and does not come together into a ball during this time. Process 25 seconds longer, for a total of 45 seconds.

5. Stop the machine and take the temperature of the dough with an instant-read thermometer, which should read between 75°F and 80°F. If the temperature is lower than 75°F, process for an additional 5 seconds, up to twice more, until it reaches the desired temperature. If the temperature is higher than 80°F, remove the thermometer, scrape the dough from the food processor into an ungreased bowl, and refrigerate for 5 to 10 minutes. Check the temperature after 5 minutes; it should be 80°F or cooler by that time.

6. Scrape the dough from the processor onto a lightly floured work surface. Gather the dough into a loose ball. It will be firm and slightly sticky. Place it in a large ungreased bowl, cover with plastic wrap, and allow to ferment for about 2½ to 3 hours at room temperature, 70°F to 72°F. It will have increased in volume somewhat but don't be concerned by how much.

7. Turn the dough onto a lightly floured work surface and gently divide it into 2 equal pieces. Form each piece into a round shape (page 35).

8. Sprinkle a baking sheet with cornmeal and transfer the loaves to the sheet, spaced 4 inches apart. Dust them with flour and cover the baking sheet loosely with plastic wrap. Proof the loaves at room temperature for 1½ to 2 hours.

9. One hour before baking, put the oven rack on the second shelf from the bottom of the oven and place the baking stone on the rack. Place a small pan of water on the floor of the oven and preheat to 475°F.

10. Uncover the bread. Spray the surface of each loaf with water, then sprinkle with some of the cracked wheat, if using, then more flour. Score each loaf with 5 diagonal slashes, each about 5 inches long, across the tops. Rotate the baking sheet and make 5 more diagonal slashes across the top of each loaf to create a checkerboard effect.

11. Pour a cup of warm water in the pan in the oven. Immediately place the baking sheet on the baking stone and turn the heat down to 425°F. Bake 5 minutes, then create steam by adding another cup of water to the pan on the floor of the oven.

12. Bake the loaves for 20 minutes, then remove them from the oven, transfer them directly onto the baking stone, and continue baking 25 to 30 minutes longer, until the crust is a rich, dark brown. Insert an instant-read thermometer: The loaves will be finished when they reach an internal temperature of 205°F to 210°F.

13. Remove the loaves from the oven and immediately place them on a wire rack to cool.

Stored at room temperature covered with a kitchen towel, this bread will stay fresh for two to three days. For longer storage, wrap in plastic wrap and freeze for up to three weeks.

Multigrain Sandwich Loaf

One 8-inch pan
loaf

Fermentation:

1¹/₂ to 2 hours
at room
temperature,
70°F to 72°F

Proofing:

1 to 1¹/₂ hours
at room
temperature

This is a loaf full of the nutty taste of whole grains. The dough is firm enough to be hand-formed into a chubby round, but I prefer to bake it in a loaf pan for sandwich bread. When toasted, it is delicious with a wedge of sharp Cheddar cheese and spicy fruit chutney.

Really an 11-grain loaf, this bread gets its taste from a 7-grain cereal blend sold in most grocery and health food stores. A combination of oat, wheat, rye, barley and other grains, these cereals are sold to be served hot at breakfast.

This dough benefits from long fermentation; you could let it sit at room temperature for as long as 3 hours. But it will provide delicious results in half that time. You can retard this loaf after it is formed for 2 to 6 hours in the refrigerator, a great help if you need some extra time to schedule your baking. Just remember that dough that has been retarded in the refrigerator may take from 1 to 3 hours to proof and come to room temperature before it can be baked.

Simple Wheat Starter (page 175)	about 180 grams	about 6 ounces	³/₄ cup
Unbleached bread flour	275 grams	10 ounces	2 to 2¹/₂ cups
Whole wheat flour	75 grams	2 ounces	about ¹/₂ cup
Rye flour	75 grams	2 ounces	about ¹/₂ cup
Graham flour	75 grams	2 ounces	about ¹/₂ cup
7-grain cereal	60 grams	2 ounces	about ¹/₂ cup
Fine sea salt	10 grams	2 teaspoons	2 teaspoons
Instant yeast	³/₄ teaspoon	³/₄ teaspoon	³/₄ teaspoon
Water	315 grams	10 ounces	1¹/₄ cups

1. Two to four hours before you plan to mix the dough, feed your starter as described on page 173. Allow it to sit at room temperature until it is frothy, bubbly, and visibly active.

2. Place the flours, 7-grain cereal, salt, and yeast in a food processor fitted with the metal blade. Measure ³/₄ cup of the active starter and pour it into the processor. (Cover the remaining starter with plastic wrap and place it in the refrigerator for future use.)

3. Using an instant-read thermometer, adjust the water temperature so that the combined temperatures of the flour and the water give a base temperature of 130°F if using a Cuisinart or KitchenAid or 150°F if using a Braun. (See page 33 for other models.) With the machine running, pour all but 3 tablespoons of the water through the feed tube. Process for 15 seconds.

4. With the machine running, check to see that the dough is coming together and forming a visible ball in the processor, adding the reserved water if it seems dry and crumbly. If the dough seems too moist and is clinging to the shaft and sides of the bowl, sprinkle a few tablespoons of flour through the feed tube. Process 30 seconds longer, for a total of 45 seconds. This dough will be soft, moist, and somewhat sticky.

5. Stop the machine and take the temperature of the dough with an instant-read thermometer, which should read between 75°F and 80°F. If the temperature is lower than 75°F, process for an additional 5 seconds. If it is still lower than 75°F, process for 5 seconds up to twice more, until the dough reaches the desired temperature. If the temperature is higher than 80°F, remove the thermometer, scrape the dough from the food processor into an ungreased bowl, and refrigerate for 5 to 10 minutes. Check after 5 minutes; it should be 80°F or cooler by that time.

6. Scrape the dough from the processor onto a lightly floured work surface. Lightly flour the dough, gather it into a rough ball, and place it in a large ungreased bowl. Cover with plastic wrap. Allow to ferment for 1½ to 2 hours at room temperature, 70°F to 72°F. The dough will double in volume.

7. Brush a loaf pan measuring about 8 × 4 inches with vegetable oil. Turn the dough onto a generously floured work surface. With the tips of your fingers, lightly pat it into a rectangle about 2 inches longer than the loaf pan and about 2 inches thick. Roll it into a log. Tuck in the ends and place the dough in the bread pan, seam side down. Lightly dust with flour and cover the pan loosely with plastic wrap or a kitchen towel. Let proof for 1 to 1½ hours at room temperature.

Store this
bread under a
towel or in a
paper bag
at room
temperature. It
will stay fresh
at room
temperature
for three days.

8. One hour before baking, put the oven rack on the second shelf from the bottom of the oven and place the baking stone on the rack. Preheat the oven to 475°F.

9. Dust the proofed loaf with flour and make a ¼-inch slash down the center with a sharp knife or razor blade. Slide the loaf pan into the oven and turn the heat down to 425°F.

10. Bake the bread for about 20 minutes, then open the oven and rotate the pan so that it bakes evenly. Continue baking 15 to 20 minutes longer, until the crust is deeply browned. Remove the loaf from the oven, take it out of the pan, and return the bread to bake directly on the stone for another 5 minutes. Insert an instant-read thermometer into it, and if the internal temperature is 205°F to 210°F, the bread is done.

11. Remove the loaf from the oven and immediately place it on a wire rack to cool completely before storing.

Idaho Potato Rolls

These moist dinner rolls with a crackling crust are delectable. Because of its low moisture content, the Idaho potato makes a rich, creamy mash.

    The potato starch in this recipe helps reduce the moisture in the rolls. As with any recipe that calls for a porridge, a starter, or liquid, be prepared to add a bit more flour if the dough seems too wet to come together in the bowl of the food processor. (For convenience, I use instant mashed potatoes in this recipe.) Serve these rolls with soups and stews or filled with a curried chicken salad.

Fifteen 3-inch rolls

Fermentation: 2 hours at room temperature, 70°F to 72°F

Proofing: 45 minutes to 1 hour at room temperature

Simple Wheat Starter (page 175) or Natural Sour Wheat Starter (page 176)	about 150 grams	about 5 ounces	1/2 cup
Unbleached bread flour	500 grams	1 pound	3 1/3 to 4 cups
Potato starch	80 grams	3 ounces	1/2 cup
Fine sea salt	15 grams	2 3/4 teaspoons	2 3/4 teaspoons
Instant yeast	1 teaspoon	1 teaspoon	1 teaspoon
Mashed Idaho potatoes, cooled	360 grams	12 ounces	1 1/4 cups
Water	250 grams	8 ounces	1 cup

1. Two to four hours before you plan to mix the dough, feed your starter as described on page 173. Allow it to sit at room temperature until it is frothy, bubbly, and visibly active.

2. Place the flour, potato starch, salt, yeast, and mashed potatoes in a food processor fitted with the metal blade. Measure 1/2 cup of the starter and pour it into the processor. (Cover the remaining starter with plastic wrap and place it in the refrigerator for future use.)

3. Using an instant-read thermometer, adjust the temperature of the water so that the combined temperatures of the flour and water give a base temperature of 130°F if using a Cuisinart or KitchenAid or 150°F if using a Braun. (See page 33 for other models.) With the machine running, pour all but 3 tablespoons of the water through the feed tube. Process for 30 seconds.

With the machine running, check the dough and add the reserved water if it seems too dry and is not coming together in a visible ball. (Or, stop the machine and add more flour if the dough is too soft to form a ball during the mixing process.) Process 15 seconds longer, for a total of 45 seconds. This dough will be relatively moist, soft, and sticky.

4. Stop the machine and take the temperature of the dough with an instant-read thermometer, which should read between 75°F and 80°F. If the temperature is lower than 75°F, process for an additional 5 seconds, up to twice more, until it reaches the desired temperature. If the temperature is higher than 80°F, remove the thermometer, scrape the dough from the food processor into an ungreased bowl, and refrigerate for 5 to 10 minutes. Check the temperature after 5 minutes; it should be 80°F or cooler by that time.

5. Scrape the dough from the processor into a large ungreased bowl. (Wet your hands and a rubber spatula and remove the processor blade from the dough, scraping off bits that cling to the blade and sides of the bowl.) Cover the bowl with plastic wrap and allow to ferment for 2 hours at room temperature, 70°F to 72°F.

6. Scrape the dough onto a well-floured work surface. With floured fingers, gather it into a rough ball and, using a dough scraper or kitchen knife, divide it into 15 pieces. Form each piece of dough into a roll shape (page 39), then roll each one into an oval shape that resembles an Idaho potato. Place the rolls on a parchment-lined baking sheet, sprinkle with more flour, and cover them loosely with plastic wrap. Let proof for 45 minutes to 1 hour at room temperature.

7. One hour before baking, put the oven rack on the second shelf from the bottom of the oven and place the baking stone on the rack. Place a small pan of water on the bottom of the oven and preheat to 450°F.

8. Uncover the rolls and score each one with a short deep cut, about 2 inches long, along the length. This will help them to burst open in the oven while baking.

9. Pour about 1 cup of warm water into the pan in the oven. Immediately place the baking sheet of rolls on the baking stone and turn the heat down to 425°F. Bake 5 minutes, then create steam in the oven by adding another cup of water to the pan on the oven floor.

10. Bake the rolls for 15 minutes, then remove the baking sheet from the oven. Carefully transfer the partially baked rolls to a peel or the back of a baking sheet and slide them back into the oven directly onto the baking stone. Bake for another 10 to 15 minutes, until they are a uniform golden brown. Insert an instant-read thermometer into one of the rolls, and if the internal temperature is 205°F to 210°F, they are done.

11. Remove the rolls from the oven and immediately place them on a wire rack to cool.

Store the rolls in a paper bag or covered with a towel. The rolls will stay fresh, covered at room temperature, for two days.

European Rye Breads

The tradition of rye breads in Europe is long and revered. The pronounced flavor of this grain finds a home in a classic bread from every country in Europe.

Classic rye breads include at least 30 percent wheat flour to reinforce the gluten structure in the dough. Rye ferments quickly and overproofs if left to rise too long.

Brittany Rye Bread

One 12-inch loaf

Fermentation:
1½ hours at room temperature, 70°F to 72°F

Proofing:
1 to 1½ hours at room temperature

What better bread to eat with shellfish than a rye from Brittany, the oyster capital of France? Made with a rye and wheat flour blend called méteil *in France, this dense dough produces a compact loaf with a substantial crust.*

Like an oyster nestled on the ocean floor, this dough seems motionless. Only when it is formed and proofed does the solid loaf expand. As with any bread made with a high percentage of rye flour, this loaf ferments rapidly, but the rye flour has little gluten. The food processor mixing ensures that the gluten in the recipe is fully developed, giving the loaf a fine, even crumb and a creamy rye flavor.

If you have a narrow oval basket or banneton, proof this dough in it. Or, form the loaf, proof, and bake it on a cornmeal-dusted baking sheet.

Serve this bread, thinly sliced and buttered, with shellfish or smoked fish.

European Rye Starter (page 178)	about 150 grams	about 5 ounces	½ cup
Stone-ground rye flour	300 grams	10 ounces	2 to 2½ cups
Unbleached bread flour	200 grams	6 ounces	about 1½ cups
Fine sea salt	15 grams	2¾ teaspoons	2¾ teaspoons
Instant yeast	½ teaspoon	½ teaspoon	½ teaspoon
Water	250 grams	8 ounces	1 cup
Cornmeal for baking sheet			

1. Two to four hours before you plan to mix the dough, feed your starter as described on page 173. Allow it to sit at room temperature until it is frothy, bubbly, and visibly active.

2. Place the flours, salt, and yeast in a food processor fitted with the metal blade. Measure ½ cup of the active starter and pour it into the processor. (Cover the remaining starter with plastic wrap and place it in the refrigerator for future use.)

3. Using an instant-read thermometer, adjust the water temperature so that the combined temperatures of the flour and water give a base temperature of 130°F if using a Cuisinart or KitchenAid or 150°F if using a Braun. (See page 33 for other models.) With the machine running, pour all but 2 tablespoons of the water through the feed tube. Process for 20 seconds.

4. With the machine running, check to see that the dough is coming together and forming a visible ball in the food processor, adding the reserved water if the dough seems dry. If the dough seems too moist and is clinging to the shaft and sides of the bowl, sprinkle a few spoonfuls of flour through the feed tube. Process 25 seconds longer, for a total of 45 seconds.

5. Stop the machine and take the temperature of the dough with an instant-read thermometer, which should read between 75°F and 80°F. If the temperature is lower than 75°F, process for an additional 5 seconds. If it is still lower than 75°F, process for 5 seconds up to twice more, until it reaches the desired temperature. If the temperature is higher than 80°F, remove the thermometer, scrape the dough from the food processor into an ungreased bowl, and refrigerate for 5 to 10 minutes. Check the temperature after 5 minutes; it should be 80°F or cooler by that time.

6. Remove the dough from the processor. It will be slightly sticky and dense with a claylike texture. If it feels hard, lumpy, and uneven, divide it in half and process each piece separately for another 5 seconds. Place the dough in an ungreased bowl large enough to allow it to double in volume. Cover the bowl with plastic wrap or a plastic bag and allow the dough to rise and ferment for 1 to 1½ hours at room temperature, 70°F to 72°F. The dough will have increased in volume somewhat but don't be concerned by how much.

7. Scrape the dough out onto a lightly floured work surface and form it into a plump loaf about 4 inches in diameter and 10 inches long. Using both hands, gently transfer the loaf, seam side up, to a baking sheet lightly sprinkled with cornmeal. Dust the top of the loaf with flour and cover it loosely with plastic wrap or a kitchen towel. Let it proof for 1 to 1½ hours until it increases by half its size.

8. One hour before baking, put the oven rack on the second shelf from the bottom of the oven and place the baking stone on the rack. Place a small pan for water on the floor of the oven and preheat to 475°F.

9. Gently transfer the loaf onto a peel or the back of a baking sheet dusted with cornmeal. Sprinkle with flour, then slash the top diagonally. About 8 slashes spaced 1 inch apart should fit this size loaf.

10. Pour 1 cup warm water into the pan in the oven. Using the peel or baking sheet, immediately slide the loaf of bread into the hot oven. Turn the heat down to 425°F. Bake for 35 to 40 minutes, until the crust is a rich, golden brown. Insert an instant-read thermometer into the loaf, and if the internal temperature is 205°F to 210°F, the bread is done.

11. Remove the bread from the oven and immediately place on a wire rack to cool.

Sour Raisin Rye

A loaf studded with moist raisins and spiced with rye and cardamom, this is a bread to enjoy toasted for breakfast, or layered with smoked ham and honey mustard.

Old dough gives this plump loaf a fine open crumb. Save a lump of dough (about 4 to 6 ounces) covered in the refrigerator the next time you mix *The Best Bread Ever* (page 50), or any bread dough, to give this loaf its unique taste. (Old dough is any dough that is at least 4 hours old. Freeze a piece for this purpose or keep it covered in plastic in the refrigerator for up to 24 hours before using. When stored in the refrigerator, a lump of dough can be used for up to 48 hours in any recipe that calls for old dough or in any bread dough where you want to add a hint of the rich taste of prefermented bread.) If you don't have old dough, the recipe will still make a delicious loaf.

For a sophisticated variation, substitute tart dried cherries or pieces of diced figs for the raisins.

One 14-inch oval loaf

Fermentation:
2¹/₂ to 3 hours at room temperature, 70°F to 72°F

Proofing:
1¹/₂ to 2 hours at room temperature

FOR THE CORNSTARCH GLAZE:

Cornstarch	1 tablespoon	1 tablespoon	1 tablespoon
Cold water	250 grams	8 ounces	1 cup

FOR THE RAISIN DOUGH:

European Rye Starter (page 178)	about 150 grams	about 5 ounces	¹/₂ cup
Dark raisins	335 grams	12 ounces	2 cups
Unbleached bread flour	600 grams	20 ounces	4 to 5 cups
Rye flour	75 grams	2 ounces	¹/₂ cup
Graham flour	75 grams	2 ounces	¹/₂ cup
Ground cardamom	¹/₂ teaspoon	¹/₂ teaspoon	¹/₂ teaspoon
Fine sea salt	15 grams	2³/₄ teaspoon	2³/₄ teaspoon
Instant yeast	1 teaspoon	1 teaspoon	1 teaspoon
Old dough (see above)	about 150 grams	about 5 ounces	about ²/₃ cup
Water	400 grams	13 ounces	1¹/₂ cups plus 2 tablespoons

Cornmeal for the baking sheet

1. Two to four hours before you plan to mix the dough, feed your starter as described on page 173. Allow the starter to sit at room temperature until it is frothy, bubbly, and visibly active.

2. Dissolve the cornstarch in 2 tablespoons of the cold water. Bring the remaining water to a boil in a small saucepan. Stir in the cornstarch mixture. Whisk the glaze to cook the cornstarch for about 2 minutes. Set aside.

3. Bring 4 cups of water to boil in a medium saucepan. Add the raisins. Cook until the water comes back to a boil, about 3 minutes. Drain the raisins in a colander and spread them on a paper towel to dry before using.

4. Place the flours, cardamom, salt, and yeast in a food processor fitted with the metal blade. Measure ½ cup of the active starter and pour it into the processor. (Cover the remaining active starter with plastic wrap and place it in the refrigerator for future use.) Break the old dough into 6 pieces and spread it out in the processor bowl.

5. Using an instant-read thermometer, adjust the water temperature so that the combined temperatures of the flour and water give a base temperature of 130°F if using a Cuisinart or KitchenAid or 150°F if using a Braun. (See page 33 for other models.) With the machine running, pour all but 2 tablespoons of the water through the feed tube. Process for 20 seconds. With the machine running, add the remaining water if the dough seems too dry and crumbly, processing 25 seconds longer, for a total of 45 seconds.

6. Stop the machine and take the temperature of the dough with an instant-read thermometer, which should read between 75°F and 80°F. If the temperature is lower than 75°F, process for an additional 5 seconds, up to twice more, until it reaches the desired temperature. If the temperature is higher than 80°F, remove the thermometer, scrape the dough from the food processor into an ungreased bowl, and refrigerate for 5 to 10 minutes. Check the temperature after 5 minutes; it should be 80°F or cooler by that time.

7. Remove the dough from the processor and place it on a lightly floured work surface. To relax the gluten and make it easier to knead in the raisins, cover the dough with a sheet of plastic wrap and let it rest for 20 minutes. Uncover the dough, press it out into a rectangle, and sprinkle it with the drained raisins. Fold the dough over onto itself and knead it for 2

to 3 minutes until the raisins are incorporated. Use a dough scraper to lift the dough from the work surface should it seem sticky and difficult to handle.

8. Form the dough into a rough ball, place it in a bowl about twice its size, and cover with plastic wrap. Allow the dough to ferment for 2½ to 3 hours at room temperature, 70°F to 72°F. It will have increased in volume somewhat but don't be concerned by how much.

9. Turn the dough onto a lightly floured work surface and press it gently to deflate some of the air bubbles that may have formed. Form it into a football shape (page 38) about 14 inches long. Dust the loaf with flour, transfer it to a cornmeal-coated baking sheet, and cover loosely with plastic wrap. Let proof for 1 to 1½ hours until the dough increases by half its size. It should feel softer but still spring back slightly when poked with your finger.

10. One hour before baking, put the oven rack on the second shelf from the bottom of the oven and place the baking stone on the rack. Place a small pan of water on the floor of the oven and preheat to 450°F.

11. Carefully transfer the loaf to a peel or the back of a baking sheet lightly dusted with cornmeal. Brush the bread with the cornstarch glaze and slash the top with a razor blade. About six 4-inch diagonal slashes spaced 2 inches apart should fit this loaf.

12. Pour a cup of warm water into the pan in the oven. Using the peel or baking sheet, immediately slide the loaf of bread onto the baking stone in the oven. Turn the heat down to 425°F.

13. Bake the loaf for 3 to 4 minutes, then create steam by pouring another cup of water in the pan in the bottom of the oven. Bake 5 minutes, then steam the oven again. Bake the loaf for 25 minutes, then reduce the heat to 400°F and continue baking for another 15 to 20 minutes, until the crust is rich, dark brown. Insert an instant-read thermometer into the bread, and if the internal temperature is 205°F to 210°F, it is done.

14. Remove the bread from the oven and immediately place the loaf on a wire rack to cool.

Stored at room temperature covered with a kitchen towel, this bread will stay fresh for two days. For longer storage, wrap it in plastic and freeze for up to three weeks.

Swedish Wheat Berry Loaf

One 12-inch
loaf

Fermentation:

45 minutes to 1
hour at room
temperature,
70°F to 72°F

Proofing:

45 minutes to 1
hour at room
temperature

The Scandinavians are known for their long-keeping, dense rye breads. Limpa loaf, with its slightly tangy flavor is the best known. Top thin buttered slices with smoked fish and cold meats for a typical smorgasbord.

The food processor kneads this dense dough with ease. If you don't have stone-ground rye flour, any rye flour may be used. Expect to add a bit more water to the dough if you use a finer rye flour, because fine ground rye absorbs more moisture than coarse rye flour. Regular rye flours make for a slightly stickier dough.

Like many pumpernickel and dark rye breads, the color in this loaf comes from the addition of cocoa powder and dark molasses. Coffee substitutes like Postum, readily available in grocery and health food stores, give a deep color and rich grain taste to this dough. You may substitute instant coffee powder dissolved in a tablespoon of the water or more molasses.

Each slice of this loaf is generously studded with cooked wheat berries, the unhulled grain from which flour is made. The whole wheat berries require lengthy cooking, until most of them have popped open, or they will be too firm to chew. Wheat berries are sold in health food stores.

Do not overbake this bread. When stored in a plastic bag, its crust remains moist and pliable.

European Rye Starter (page 178)	about 180 grams	about 6 ounces	3/4 cup
Unbleached bread flour	200 grams	6 ounces	about 1 1/2 cups
Stone-ground rye flour	300 grams	10 ounces	2 to 2 1/2 cups
Wheat bran	10 grams	1/2 ounce	1/4 cup
Instant grain beverage like Postum	1 tablespoon	1 tablespoon	1 tablespoon
Sesame seeds	1 tablespoon	1 tablespoon	1 tablespoon
Cocoa powder	2 teaspoons	2 teaspoons	2 teaspoons
Fine sea salt	15 grams	2 3/4 teaspoons	2 3/4 teaspoons
Instant yeast	1 teaspoon	1 teaspoon	1 teaspoon
Dark molasses	1 tablespoon	1 tablespoon	1 tablespoon
Water	250 grams	8 ounces	1 cup
Cooked wheat berries, well drained	280 grams	10 ounces	2 cups

1. Two to four hours before you plan to mix the dough, feed the European Rye starter as described on page 173. Allow the starter to sit at room temperature until it is frothy, bubbly, and visibly active.

2. Place the flours, wheat bran, instant grain beverage, sesame seeds, cocoa powder, salt, yeast, and molasses in a food processor fitted with the metal blade. Measure ¾ cup of the active starter and pour it into the processor. (Cover the remaining starter with plastic wrap and place it in the refrigerator for future use.)

3. Using an instant-read thermometer, adjust the water temperature so that the combined temperatures of the flour and the water give a base temperature of 130°F if using a Cuisinart or KitchenAid or 150°F if using a Braun. (See page 33 for other models.) With the machine running, pour all but 2 tablespoons of the water through the feed tube. Process for 35 seconds. Process 10 seconds longer, adding the remaining water if the dough does not appear to be coming together, for a total of 45 seconds.

4. If the dough seems too dry, stop the machine, turn the dough over, and add a few more tablespoons of water. Pulse a few times, then continue to process. If fine ground rye flour was used and the dough seems too sticky, stop the machine, turn the dough over, and sprinkle it with more flour. Pulse until it comes together, then finish the mixing. If the dough feels hard, lumpy, and uneven, divide it in half, and process each piece for an additional 5 seconds. This additional mixing will not significantly affect the temperature.

5. Stop the machine and take the temperature of the dough with an instant-read thermometer, which should read between 75°F to 80°F. If the temperature is lower than 75°F, process for an additional 5 seconds, up to twice more, until it reaches the desired temperature. If the temperature is higher than 80°F, remove the thermometer, scrape the dough from the food processor into an ungreased bowl, and refrigerate for 5 to 10 minutes. Check the temperature after 5 minutes; it should be 80°F or cooler by that time.

6. Remove the dough from the processor and place it on a generously floured work surface. It will be firm, with a moist claylike texture. With floured hands, press it out into approximately 12 inches square. Sprinkle the surface with half of the wheat berries and roll the dough into a log shape. Fold it in half and knead for about 2 to 3 minutes to incorporate the wheat berries throughout. Flatten the dough again and fold and knead in the remaining wheat berries.

7. Place the dough in a large ungreased bowl and cover with plastic wrap. Allow to ferment for about 45 minutes to 1 hour at room temperature,

Once it has cooled completely, slice it thinly, then place the bread in a plastic bag. Store this bread in the freezer or refrigerator.

70°F to 72°F. The dough will have increased somewhat but don't be concerned by how much.

8. Brush a narrow 12-inch loaf pan or standard 8-inch loaf pan with vegetable oil or coat with vegetable cooking spray. Set aside.

9. Turn the dough onto a lightly floured work surface. Press it into a rectangle about 2 inches high and slightly longer than the loaf pan in which it will be baked. Fold in the right and left edges about 1 inch. Roll the dough into a log and place it in the prepared pan, seam side down. Press the dough into the corners of the pan.

10. Cover the loaf pan with plastic wrap or a sheet of plastic. Allow to proof for about 45 minutes to 1 hour at room temperature until the dough increases by half its size and approaches the rim of the pan.

11. One hour before baking, put the oven rack on the second shelf from the bottom of the oven and place the baking stone on the rack. Preheat the oven to 450°F.

12. Place the pan in the oven on the baking stone and reduce the heat in the oven to 425°F. Bake the loaf for 30 minutes. Remove the bread from the oven, carefully take it out of the pan, and set it directly on the baking stone. Bake for about 20 more minutes, until the crust is a uniform dark brown. Do not overbake. Insert an instant-read thermometer into the bread, and if the internal temperature is 205°F to 210°F, it is done.

13. Remove the bread from the oven and place it on a wire rack to cool.

To cook wheat berries:

2 cups cooked wheat berries

Water	1,000 grams	32 ounces	4 cups
Winter wheat berries	140 grams	8 ounces	1 cup

Bring the water to boil in a 2-quart saucepan set over high heat. Add the wheat berries. Cover and reduce the heat to a low simmer. Cook the wheat berries from 1½ to 2 hours until tender. Check them from time to time to see that there is enough water left in the pan, adding more as needed. The berries are cooked when about half of them have popped open.

Seeded Deli Rye Bread

This is the kind of chewy rye bread that the best delis pile high with hot pastrami and succulent corned beef. Good, commercial rye bread is difficult to find these days, so I was determined to develop one that could be made by the food processor method.

American deli rye is made with high-gluten wheat flours blended with just enough rye and whole wheat flours to flavor the bread. The gluten in the wheat flours gives this loaf its bouncy texture. Unlike many bread doughs with a larger percentage of sticky rye, this dough mixes easily in the food processor. Use regular, medium, or fine ground rye flour to give this bread a light texture. Stone-ground rye flour will make a loaf with a denser crumb.

If you don't have a rye starter on hand, you can easily make one by feeding some wheat starter with rye flour. Since rye ferments quickly, a fresh rye starter can easily be made overnight. Make a small batch and plan to bake a couple of the memorable rye breads in this chapter.

This loaf is steamed three times to give it a shiny, thin crust.

One 14-inch loaf

Fermentation: 2½ to 3 hours at room temperature, 70°F to 72°F

Proofing: 1 to 1½ hours at room temperature

FOR THE CORNSTARCH GLAZE:

Cornstarch	1 tablespoon	1 tablespoon	1 tablespoon
Cold water	250 grams	8 ounces	1 cup

FOR THE DOUGH:

European Rye Starter (page 178)	about 180 grams	about 6 ounces	¾ cup
Whole wheat flour	200 grams	6 ounces	about 1½ cups
Unbleached bread flour	250 grams	10 ounces	2 to 2½ cups
Rye flour	60 grams	2 ounces	about 2 tablespoons
Fine sea salt	15 grams	2¾ teaspoons	2¾ teaspoons
Instant yeast	¾ teaspoon	¾ teaspoon	¾ teaspoon
Caraway seeds	5 tablespoons	5 tablespoons	5 tablespoons
Water	250 grams	8 ounces	1 cup
Cornmeal for the baking sheet			

1. Two to four hours before you plan to mix the dough, feed your starter as described on page 173. Allow the starter to sit at room temperature until it is frothy, bubbly, and visibly active, and has increased in volume by half.

2. Dissolve the cornstarch in 2 tablespoons of the cold water. Bring the remaining water to a boil in a small saucepan and stir in the cornstarch mixture. Whisk the glaze to cook the cornstarch for about 2 minutes. Remove from heat and set aside for later use.

3. Place the flours, salt, and yeast in a food processor fitted with the metal blade. Measure ¾ cup of the active starter and pour it into the processor. (Cover the remaining starter with plastic wrap and place it in the refrigerator for future use.) Add 1 tablespoon of the caraway seeds to the processor.

4. Using an instant-read thermometer, adjust the water temperature so that the combined temperatures of the flour and the water give a base temperature of 130°F if using a Cuisinart or KitchenAid or 150°F if using a Braun. (See page 33 for other models.) With the machine running, pour all but 2 tablespoons of the water through the feed tube of the processor. Mix for 20 seconds. With the machine running, check the moistness of the dough. If it seems too dry and crumbly add the remaining water. Process 25 seconds longer, for a total of 45 seconds.

5. Stop the machine and take the temperature of the dough with an instant-read thermometer, which should read 75°F and 80°F. If the temperature is lower than 75°F, process for an additional 5 seconds, up to twice more, until it reaches the desired temperature. If the temperature is higher than 80°F, remove the thermometer, scrape the dough from the food processor into an ungreased bowl, and refrigerate for 5 to 10 minutes. Check the temperature after 5 minutes; it should be 80°F or cooler by that time.

6. Scrape the dough from the processor onto a lightly floured work surface. It will be elastic and slightly sticky. Press the dough out into a rectangle and sprinkle it with another 2 tablespoons of the caraway seeds. Fold the dough over onto itself and knead for 1 or 2 minutes until the seeds are incorporated. Use a dough scraper to lift the dough from the work surface should it seem sticky and difficult to handle. If it seems difficult to knead, cover it with plastic wrap and allow it to rest for 10 minutes before continuing.

7. Form the dough into a loose ball, place it in a bowl about twice its size, and cover with plastic wrap. Allow the dough to ferment for 2½ to 3 hours at room temperature, 70°F to 72°F.

8. Turn the dough onto a lightly floured work surface and press it gently to deflate some of the air bubbles that may have formed during rising. Form the dough into a football shape (page 38). Sprinkle a baking sheet with cornmeal. Place the loaf diagonally on the pan so that it fits comfortably without touching the edges. Dust the loaf lightly with flour.

9. Cover the baking sheet loosely with plastic wrap and let the loaf proof for 1 to 1½ hours at room temperature.

10. One hour before baking, put the oven rack on the second shelf from the bottom of the oven and place the baking stone on the rack. Place a small pan for water on the floor of the oven. Preheat the oven to 450°F.

11. Uncover the loaf, brush it with cornstarch glaze, and sprinkle on the remaining caraway seeds. Make diagonal 4-inch slashes across the top of the loaf, spacing them 2 inches apart.

12. Pour about 1 cup of warm water into the pan in the oven. Immediately place the bread in the oven and reduce the temperature to 425°F. Bake 3 to 4 minutes, then create steam in the oven by pouring another cup of water into the pan. Bake the bread for another 3 or 4 minutes, then steam again. After another 3 to 4 minutes, steam a third time. Bake the bread about 25 to 30 minutes longer, until the crust is a shiny, dark brown. Insert an instant-read thermometer into the bread and if the internal temperature is 205°F to 210°F, it is done.

13. Remove the bread from the oven and place the loaf directly on a wire rack to cool completely before serving or slicing.

This bread is best stored covered at room temperature for one day. After that, it keeps its moistness best when stored tightly wrapped in plastic.

Pumpernickel Bread

Two 10-inch
loaves

Fermentation:

3 to 3½ hours
at room
temperature,
70°F to 72°F

Proofing:

1½ to 2 hours
at room
temperature

This dark, dense bread is similar to the classic one made by Orwasher's Bakery in New York. This dough is relatively wet and may require mixing in two batches in a smaller food processor. Instead of being scored before baking, this bread is "docked," which means that a wooden skewer or the end of a wooden spoon is pushed about ¼ inch into the top of the formed loaf in a few places. These small holes give low-gluten doughs some room for expansion but not so much as to actually deflate the loaf.

Caramel coloring, available at specialty food stores and through mail-order baking sources, gives this loaf its dark color. Two tablespoons of instant coffee powder dissolved in 1 teaspoon of water will give the same effect.

Barley malt, another staple in the commercial bakery, feeds the yeast and adds a very mild sweetness to dough. Honey is an ideal substitute.

FOR THE CORNSTARCH GLAZE:

Cornstarch	1 tablespoon	1 tablespoon	1 tablespoon
Cold water	250 grams	8 ounces	1 cup

FOR THE DOUGH:

European Rye Starter (page 178)	about 250 grams	about 8 ounces	1 cup
Unbleached bread flour	375 grams	14 ounces	about 3½ cups
Vital wheat gluten	60 grams	2 ounces	2 tablespoons
Water	275 grams	10 ounces	1¼ cups
Instant yeast	½ teaspoon	½ teaspoon	½ teaspoon
Rye flakes	60 grams	2 ounces	about ½ cup
Rye flour	140 grams	5 ounces	about 1¼ cups
Cocoa powder	3 tablespoons	3 tablespoons	3 tablespoons
Fine sea salt	15 grams	2¾ teaspoons	2¾ teaspoons
Barley malt or honey	1 tablespoon	1 tablespoon	1 tablespoon
Vegetable oil	1 tablespoon	1 tablespoon	1 tablespoon
Caramel coloring	2 tablespoons	2 tablespoons	2 tablespoons
Poppy seeds or black sesame seeds for garnish			
Cornmeal for the baking sheet			

1. Two to four hours before you plan to mix the dough, feed your starter as described on page 173. Allow the starter to sit at room temperature until it is frothy, bubbly, and visibly active.

2. Dissolve the cornstarch in 2 tablespoons of the cold water. Bring the remaining water to a boil in a small saucepan and stir in the cornstarch mixture. Whisk the glaze to cook the cornstarch for about 2 minutes. Set aside.

3. Sift the bread flour with the vital wheat gluten to distribute the gluten evenly throughout the flour. Set aside. Take ½ cup of the cool tap water and sprinkle the yeast over it to dissolve. Set aside.

4. Place the rye flakes in the bowl of a food processor fitted with a metal blade. Process for 10 seconds to coarsely grind them. Add the rye flour, bread flour, cocoa powder, salt, barley malt or honey, vegetable oil, caramel coloring, and dissolved yeast mixture to the bowl of the food processor.

5. Measure 1 cup of the active starter and pour it into the processor. (Cover the remaining starter with plastic wrap and place it in the refrigerator for future use.) Process the ingredients for 10 seconds to moisten the flour. Using an instant-read thermometer, adjust the temperature of the remaining water so that the combined temperatures of the flour mixture and the water give a base temperature of 130°F if using a Cuisinart or KitchenAid or 150°F if using a Braun. (See page 33 for other models.)

6. With the machine running, add all but 3 tablespoons of the water to the machine. Process for 20 seconds. With the machine running, check the dough. If it appears to be too dry and crumbly, add the remaining water. If it is too wet and is not forming a ball in the bowl of the food processor, sprinkle a few spoonfuls of bread flour through the feed tube with the machine running. Process 25 seconds longer, for a total of 45 seconds.

7. Stop the machine and take the temperature of the dough with an instant-read thermometer, which should read between 75°F and 80°F. If the temperature is lower than 75°F, process for an additional 5 seconds, up to twice more, until it reaches the desired temperature. If the temperature is higher than 80°F, remove the thermometer, scrape the dough from the food processor into an ungreased bowl, and refrigerate for 5 to 10 minutes. Check the temperature after 5 minutes; it should be 80°F or cooler by that time.

This bread will keep for two days covered with a kitchen towel at room temperature.

8. Remove the dough from the processor, place it in a large ungreased bowl, and cover with plastic wrap. Allow the dough to ferment for 3 to 3½ hours.

9. Scrape the dough from the bowl onto a lightly floured work surface and divide it into 2 equal pieces. Form them into 2 small round loaves (page 35). Dust a baking sheet with cornmeal and place the loaves, spaced 4 inches apart, on the sheet. Cover loosely with plastic wrap and let proof for 1½ to 2 hours, until roughly doubled in bulk.

10. One hour before baking, put the oven rack on the second shelf from the bottom of the oven and place the baking stone on the rack. Place a small pan for water on the floor of the oven. Preheat the oven to 450°F.

11. Uncover the loaves, brush the tops with the cornstarch glaze, and sprinkle heavily with poppy seeds or black sesame seeds. Use the handle of a wooden spoon to dock the top of the bread once in the center; press the end of the spoon about ¼ inch into the center of the bread to form a small indentation in the dough.

12. Pour about 1 cup warm water into the pan in the oven. Immediately place the bread in the oven and reduce the temperature to 425°F. Bake 3 to 4 minutes, then create steam in the oven by pouring 1 cup of water into the pan in the oven. Bake 3 to 4 minutes longer, then steam the oven again. Bake for another 25 to 30 minutes, until the crust is a shiny, deep brown. Insert an instant-read thermometer into the loaves and if the internal temperature is 205°F to 210°F, the bread is done.

13. Remove the baking sheet from the oven and place the loaves directly on a wire rack to cool completely.

The Second Time Around: Using Leftover Bread

It's almost impossible to imagine that you will ever have leftover bread, but if you do, here are some of my favorite recipes for using extra bread or bread that's past its prime. The quality of the bread translates into the quality of the crouton, toast, or crumb it becomes. I don't think of these as leftovers but enhancements.

Bread Crumbs

The uses for bread crumbs are endless. Top a potato gratin with a dusting of bread crumbs. Dip chicken cutlets in beaten egg, then dredge them in bread crumbs before sautéing. Fresh bread crumbs are the base for aioli, the garlic mayonnaise spread known as the butter of Provence. When sautéed with melted or browned butter, dry bread crumbs become a nutty condiment on a Sicilian-style cauliflower, caper, and anchovy sauce for pasta. Then there are the baker's secret pastry fillings (pages 166, 168) in which butter, flavorings, and sugar are extended with crumbled stale bread or day-old Danish pastries.

There are three different types of bread crumbs I use regularly—fresh, dry, and fine dry.

Fresh Bread Crumbs

About 1½ cups

Bread crumbs made from fresh country-style bread are coarser than granular dry crumbs, and because of their size, each crumb retains the identity of the bread from which it was made.

When you dredge a fillet of flounder, sole, or cod in fresh bread crumbs before sautéing or broiling, the bread crumbs form a shaggy crust that contrasts with the soft, flaky fish. Sprinkled on creamed vegetables, slightly coarse fresh crumbs form a crunchy topping that contrasts with the velvety sauce. Fresh bread crumbs act like Lilliputian sponges capturing the juices when sprinkled over a cut tomato before broiling. Fresh bread crumbs sautéed with olive oil, garlic, and dried oregano make a nutty condiment for sprinkling on salads or pasta dishes.

2 thick slices fresh The Best Bread Ever
   (page 50) or Semolina Bread
   (page 60)

Trim the crusts from the bread. Tear the bread into 1-inch pieces and place them in the bowl of a food processor fitted with the metal blade. Process for about 1 minute until all of the bread is uniformly crumbled and resembles fluffy, cooked rice. Stop the machine and pulse 3 or 4 times before using.

Dry Bread Crumbs

About 1 cup

*It's no wonder supermarkets stock varieties of dry bread crumbs; there are so
many ways to use this economical ingredient.*

*Unlike fresh bread crumbs, which remain coarse and crumbly, dry crumbs
are finely ground like toasted meal and are more delicate than their robust
cousins. Dry bread crumbs cling to battered foods and are used to coat thick slices
of mozzarella or shrimp before deep frying. Dredge pounded veal or pork cutlets
in beaten egg and dry bread crumbs before sautéing for schnitzel.*

*The Best Bread Ever (page 50) or the Classic Pullman Loaf (page 127)
make delicate dry crumbs. Dried brioche crumbs make a good dessert topping for
fried bananas or sliced apples.*

> 2 thick slices The Best Bread Ever
>   (page 50), or Classic Pullman Loaf
>   (page 127)

Preheat the oven to 250°F. Trim the crusts from the bread. Break the
bread up into 1-inch pieces, place on a baking sheet, and bake for 8 to 10
minutes, until the pieces have dried but are not brown. Place the dry bread
in the bowl of a food processor fitted with the metal blade and process for 1
to 2 minutes until finely ground. (For truly fine dry bread crumbs, process
the bread for up to 3 minutes, then sift the crumbs through a fine mesh
strainer.)

Croutons

About 1 cup

The French word for crust is la croûte *and a crouton is a big piece of crust and crunch. A classic crouton, the kind of crouton that makes a Caesar salad memorable, is made by gently pan-frying a slice of bread in oil. I often slice a ficelle or baguette and make these fried croutons for a frisée and bacon salad.*

Country Bread Croutons

1 tablespoon extra virgin olive oil

2 whole garlic cloves, peeled

2 thick slices (about 3 ounces) Peasant Wheat Loaf (page 191) or The Best Bread Ever round loaf (page 50), crusts removed

1/4 teaspoon kosher salt

1/2 teaspoon dry herb mixture such as herbes de Provence

1. In a nonstick frying pan over medium heat, warm the olive oil. Flatten the garlic cloves with the flat side of a knife and add them to the oil. Cook the garlic about 5 minutes, until golden brown, and discard. Cut the bread into 1-inch cubes. While the oil is still hot, immediately add the cubed bread. Toss to coat evenly with the oil.

2. Cook the croutons 7 or 8 minutes, until golden brown, turning frequently so that they brown evenly on all sides. Add an additional teaspoon of oil if they seem to be too dry.

3. Just before serving, while they are still hot, toss the croutons with a sprinkling of salt and herbs.

Dry Croutons

When a crunchy crouton is called for in soup, I make these dry croutons, simply a slice of baguette, round loaf, or other bread baked at 250°F until it is dry, but not browned. For a provençal fish soup, I place the dry crouton in the bottom of the bowl, top it with rouille (a hot pepper–garlic mayonnaise), and ladle the soup on top. Bread that has dried out because it is a few days old often still has a bit of moisture in it. It can be tough like taffy and difficult to chew. Bread dried out in the oven at a low temperature is crunchy like a brittle cracker.

Panzanella

Throughout Italy, cooks transform stale bread into a zesty salad called panzanella. Best made a day ahead, this bread salad works only if you have the finest quality ingredients—vine-ripened tomatoes, hearty country bread, and extra virgin olive oil. Don't be shy with the seasonings. Like pasta salad, the mild bread absorbs the juices of the fresh vegetables, briny capers, and a garlicky dressing. Garnish this salad with crisply cooked pancetta bacon just before serving.

8 servings

2 cloves garlic, minced

1/2 teaspoon fine sea salt

1/2 teaspoon freshly ground black pepper

1/4 teaspoon cayenne

1/4 cup red wine vinegar

1/2 cup extra virgin olive oil

About 8 cups Country Baguettes with Starter (page 180) or The Best Bread Ever (page 50), baked in a round loaf, thickly sliced, and crust removed

1 small red onion, cut into 1/4-inch-thick slices

6 scallions, cut into 1/4-inch pieces

3 medium tomatoes, diced (about 3 cups)

1/2 cup parsley leaves, stems removed (about 1 small bunch)

1 cup torn basil leaves

1/3 cup drained capers

1/2 cup pitted, halved black olives

6 anchovy fillets, cut into 1/4-inch pieces (optional)

Salt and freshly ground black pepper

1. Combine the minced garlic, the 1/2 teaspoon sea salt, the 1/2 teaspoon freshly ground pepper, cayenne, and vinegar in a small bowl. Whisk to blend and dissolve the salt. Whisk in the olive oil. Let the dressing sit while the salad is being prepared.

2. Tear the bread into irregular 1-inch pieces. You should have about 8 cups of bread cubes. Preheat the oven to 350°F and dry out the bread on a baking sheet in the oven for 5 to 8 minutes. Place the bread in a large salad bowl.

3. Combine the bread with the remaining salad ingredients. Use a slotted spoon to stir the salad so that all ingredients are evenly distributed. Whisk the dressing and pour over the salad. Stir until all the bread has been coated with the dressing.

4. Cover the salad with plastic wrap and refrigerate it for at least 4 hours before serving, or prepare one day ahead to allow the flavors to come together. Just before serving, adjust the seasonings with more salt and freshly ground pepper.

Leblebia—Tunisian Bread Soup

4 servings

A common street food in Tunisia, leblebia is a soothing, restorative soup made with bread crumbs, capers, olives, and tuna fish moistened with hot broth. On a cold, soggy day, the kick of hot pepper, pungent garlic, and cumin rising from a steaming bowl of this soup will chase away a chill and bring in the sunny flavors of the Mediterranean.

Throughout North Africa, harissa is the name for both a fiery hot pepper and a seasoning made from it. In Morocco, it is added to the broth in couscous just before serving. The moment you sit down in any café in Tunisia, this condiment is offered, along with an assortment of olives and a chopped tomato and cucumber salad. Harissa may be purchased in ethnic stores and through the Source Guide (page 259). If unavailable, use hot red pepper flakes in its place.

1¹/₂ cups chicken broth	1 teaspoon harissa or red pepper flakes
About 4 cups fresh bread crumbs made from white or whole wheat bread	1 teaspoon ground cumin
	1 teaspoon minced garlic
One 16-ounce can chick-peas, drained	Juice of 1 lemon
One 6-ounce can tuna, drained	Freshly ground black pepper
4 tablespoons capers	
¹/₄ cup flat leaf parsley leaves	

1. Heat the chicken broth over medium heat. Set out 4 large soup bowls.

2. Divide the bread crumbs evenly among the soup bowls. Put in each bowl some of the chick-peas, tuna, capers, parsley, harissa or red pepper flakes, cumin, and garlic. Ladle some of the broth into each bowl, just enough broth into each bowl to moisten the contents. Squeeze lemon juice over the hot broth and season with freshly ground pepper before serving.

Leek and Parsnip Gratin

In everyday French, the word gratin means high society, or "upper crust." In the culinary world, a gratin is a humble baked dish of vegetables, béchamel, and a dusting of bread crumbs. Serve this parsnip and leek combination as a vegetarian main course or as a side dish with roasted game or poultry. To get the most out of each leek, careful trimming of the dark, outer leaves preserves as much of the tender pale leaves as possible.

4 servings

4 whole leeks	¹/₄ cup chicken stock
4 large parsnips, peeled	2 tablespoons heavy cream
2 teaspoons unsalted butter	Grating of fresh nutmeg
2 teaspoons flour	¹/₂ cup fresh bread crumbs
²/₃ cup milk	Salt and freshly ground pepper

1. Butter a 2- or 3-quart casserole. Preheat the oven to 400°F.

2. Cut off the roots of each leek leaving the bulb intact. Place a leek on a cutting board with the root end closest to you. Holding a knife at a 45 degree angle toward the center of the leek, cut away only one layer of the dark green leaves at a time. Work your way up the length of the leek, removing only the upper parts of the tough outer leaves. Leave as much of the tender leaves hidden inside as possible. Trim the root ends of the leeks to a total length of about 6 inches. Cut each leek in half lengthwise to within 1 inch of the root. Wash the leeks carefully in cold running water. Quarter the parsnips and cut them into 2-inch pieces.

3. Cook the leeks and parsnips in salted boiling water for about 10 minutes until tender. Drain well, then cut the root ends of the leeks into 2-inch pieces. Arrange the vegetables in the casserole.

4. Melt the butter in a small saucepan over medium heat. Whisk in the flour and cook for 2 minutes. Pour in the milk, stock, cream, and nutmeg. Raise the heat to high and bring the sauce to a boil. Cook, stirring constantly, for 5 minutes until the sauce thickens.

5. Pour the sauce over the vegetables. Sprinkle with the salt and pepper and bread crumbs. The gratin may be prepared ahead to this point. Bake it for 10 minutes, until the sauce is bubbling and the surface is evenly browned. (If the gratin has been refrigerated, it may take up to 25 minutes to heat and bubble.)

Vanilla-Almond Butter Spread

About 1 cup

Frugal bakers recycle day-old croissants into a delight called croissants aux amandes. Soaked with simple syrup and iced with a butter and almond blend, these pastries are often more popular than their fresh cousins. I make a rich almond butter, spread it on dry brioche, and then pass the whole thing under the broiler until the topping bubbles for a breakfast pastry or teatime snack.

$1/2$ cup almond paste

2 tablespoons sugar

1 vanilla bean, split in half lengthwise

$1/2$ teaspoon orange flower water

$1/4$ cup unsalted butter

4 or 5 slices leftover Brioche à Tête (page 135), Coarse Oatmeal Bread (page 71), or Challah (page 130)

1. Place the almond paste and sugar in the bowl of a food processor fitted with the metal blade. Blend for about 20 seconds to combine. Using the tip of a paring knife, scrape the seeds from the vanilla bean into the mixture. (Save the vanilla bean pod to flavor a custard.) Add the orange flower water and butter. Blend another 20 seconds until smooth.

2. Spread this mixture evenly over one side of each slice of bread. Toast the slices under the broiler for 3 to 4 minutes or until the topping has melted and is brown and bubbling.

Raspberry Brioche French Toast with Ricotta Lemon Cream

There is a debate in our house whether this dish should be served at breakfast or for dessert. I prefer to serve these tangy brioche slices after a light supper. This French toast can be made ahead and refrigerated for use the next day. Reheat any leftovers in the toaster.

6 servings

6 thick slices Brioche Mousseline (page 137), Challah (page 130), or Classic Pullman Loaf (page 127)	¹/₂ cup milk
	¹/₂ cup yogurt or heavy cream
	1 teaspoon grated lemon zest
4 cups fresh or frozen raspberries	¹/₂ teaspoon vanilla extract
¹/₂ cup sugar	2 tablespoons unsalted butter
3 eggs	

RICOTTA CREAM:

1 cup ricotta cheese	1 teaspoon grated lemon zest
2 tablespoons sugar	Confectioners' sugar for garnish
2 tablespoons lemon juice	

1. Slice the bread into ³/₄-inch-thick slices. Lay them in a shallow pan. Set aside.

2. Reserve 1 cup of the raspberries for garnish. Place the remaining raspberries in a small saucepan with the sugar and ¹/₂ cup of water. Bring the mixture to a boil, reduce the heat to medium, and simmer the berries for 8 to 10 minutes until they are completely cooked and the pan is full of their juice. Pour the berries into a strainer set over a bowl. Using the back of a spoon, press all of the juices from the berries. Discard the pulp and reserve the syrup. Let it cool for 5 minutes before using.

3. Beat the eggs with the milk and yogurt or cream in a small bowl. Add the lemon zest, vanilla, and ¹/₄ cup of the reserved raspberry syrup. Pour the egg mixture over the sliced bread. Let it sit for 5 minutes, then turn the bread in the egg mixture so that each slice is well coated. Cover the pan with plastic wrap and let the bread sit for 30 to 45 minutes to absorb the batter.

The cooked brioche slices may be refrigerated or frozen, then reheated in the oven or toaster for 3 to 4 minutes before saucing, garnishing, and serving.

4. While the bread is soaking, make the ricotta cream: Blend the ricotta cheese with the granulated sugar, lemon juice, and lemon zest. Set aside.

5. Melt 1 tablespoon of the butter in a medium nonstick pan over medium heat. When the butter stops sizzling, put in as many slices of brioche as will fit without crowding. Fry the bread for 5 to 7 minutes until golden. Flip the bread. Increase the heat to medium-high and brown on the other side. Remove the bread slices from the pan. (Keep them warm on a plate or baking sheet placed in a 250°F oven.) Wipe the frying pan of any browned butter. Add the remaining 1 tablespoon of butter and cook the rest of the bread slices.

6. To serve, place one slice of brioche French toast on each serving plate. Spoon 1 tablespoon of the ricotta cream on each piece of bread. Drizzle with the reserved raspberry syrup and sprinkle each plate with a few of the reserved raspberries. Dust with confectioners' sugar.

Chocolate Brioche Bread Pudding with Caramel Sauce

One 9 × 12-inch pudding

For those bewitched by chocolate, this pudding is the ultimate potion. Use a rich bread like brioche to complement the chocolate custard. Even leftover stollen works, the bits of dried fruit enhanced by cinnamon. If left to soak overnight before baking, the bread will completely disintegrate, making a creamier pudding with a uniform texture.

2 tablespoons unsalted butter, melted	5 large eggs
1³/₄ cups milk	¹/₂ cup sugar
1 cup heavy cream	7 to 8 cups stale Brioche à Tête, (page
³/₄ cup chopped bittersweet chocolate	135), Holiday Stollen (page 152), or
¹/₂ teaspoon ground cinnamon	Alsatian Kugelhopf (page 143), torn
1 tablespoon dark rum	into coarse pieces

1. Preheat the oven to 375°F.

2. Brush a shallow 2-quart casserole or 12 muffin tins with some of the melted butter.

3. Combine the milk and cream in a large sauce pan and bring to a boil over medium heat. While the milk is heating, chop the chocolate into several smaller chunks. Add the chopped chocolate to the milk. Turn off the heat and cover the pan. Let the chocolate sit for 10 minutes to melt in the milk. Remove the cover after 10 minutes and stir the mixture with a wire whisk to blend. Add the cinnamon and the rum.

4. Break the eggs in a large bowl and beat them with a wire whisk to combine thoroughly. Add the sugar and beat to blend. Pour in about a cup of the chocolate and beat, then pour in the remaining chocolate. Beat to combine, then pour the chocolate mixture over the crumbled bread. Let the bread sit to soak up the chocolate cream for at least 1 hour. (The mixture may be covered and left to soak overnight in the refrigerator.)

5. Pour the bread pudding mixture into the prepared casserole or muffin tins. Brush a sheet of aluminum foil with the remaining melted butter and place it, buttered side down, over the pudding. Place the casserole in the oven on the center shelf and bake for 25 minutes. Uncover the pudding and bake it for another 10 minutes, until the top is well browned and the pudding is set.

6. Remove the pudding from the oven and cool it on a wire rack for 10 minutes before serving. Cut the pudding into 3-inch squares and serve with caramel sauce and whipped cream. Or, use a knife to loosen the individual puddings from the muffin tins and invert them onto individual serving plates.

Caramel Sauce   2 cups

1 cup brown sugar	1 cup heavy cream
1/2 stick unsalted butter	

Combine all the ingredients in a small saucepan over medium high heat. Bring to a boil and cook for about 5 to 6 minutes, until the sauce comes together. Serve immediately.

Summer Pudding

8 servings

British in origin, this dish is a combination of fragile fresh berries layered in a bowl lined with a plain bread.

Make this pudding at least one day ahead so that the bread soaks up all of the juices from the berries. During months when fresh berries are unavailable, unsweetened frozen berries may be substituted.

About 1 pound Brioche à Tête (page 135), The Best Bread Ever (page 50), or Classic Pullman Loaf (page 127), thinly sliced and crusts removed

3 cups fresh blueberries or currants
1/2 cup sugar
3 cups fresh raspberries or blackberries

1. Select a deep glass bowl with about a 2-quart capacity. Line the bottom and sides of the bowl with half of the bread slices, cutting them to fit so that the bowl is completely covered. Keep the slices as large as possible but don't be concerned about small gaps.

2. Place the blueberries or currants in a small saucepan with 1 tablespoon of water and 1/4 cup of the sugar. Bring to a boil over high heat. Stir once, taking care not to crush the berries too much. Reduce the heat and simmer for 8 minutes, until the juices begin to flow. Strain the juice from the berries into a bowl. Reserve the juice and set the berries aside until ready to assemble the pudding.

3. In a separate saucepan, combine the raspberries or blackberries with 1 tablespoon of water and the remaining 1/4 cup sugar. Bring the mixture to a boil over high, reduce the heat to low, and simmer about 5 minutes, until the juices begin to flow. Stir the berries as little as possible so as not to crush the fruit. Strain the juices from the berries into a bowl and set juice and berries aside.

4. To assemble the pudding, layer half of the blueberries or currants in the bottom of the bread-lined bowl. Top with a few slices of bread. Moisten the bread with some of the reserved berry juice. Spoon all of the cooked raspberries over the bread slices, then top with a few more slices of bread moistened with some of the fruit juice. Cover with the remaining blueberries or currants. Cover the pudding with enough sliced bread to seal the top completely. As this will form the bottom of the finished pudding, be generous with the last layer of bread. Cover the pudding with plastic wrap, weight with a heavy dinner plate, and place in the refrigerator overnight. Reserve any unused juice.

5. The next day, just before serving, uncover the pudding. Place a large plate on top, invert the pudding onto the plate, and remove the bowl. If any sections of bread have not been saturated with berry juices, moisten them with some of the reserved juice.

6. Cut the pudding into wedges and serve it with unsweetened crème fraîche or whipped cream and more of the reserved juices.

Harvest Bread Pudding

8 servings

This is an old-fashioned pudding made with bread immersed in a silken custard studded with tart apples and dried cranberries and blueberries. Pears or fresh quince may be used in place of the apples in this recipe. Bake it in a shallow casserole to create a brittle top crust over creamy slices of bread.

1 tablespoon vegetable oil	2 cups milk
About 12 small apples, peeled and cut into ¼-inch slices (8 cups)	2 cups heavy cream
	5 large eggs
1⅓ cups sugar	4 teaspoons grated orange zest (from about 1 medium orange)
6 cups (about 1½ pounds) cubed Challah (page 130), Normandy Cider Bread (page 203), or Classic Pullman Loaf (page 127)	½ cup dried blueberries
	½ cup dried cranberries
	Confectioners' sugar for garnish

1. Preheat the oven to 350°F. Brush a shallow 8-cup casserole with the vegetable oil. Set aside.

2. Place the sliced apples and ⅓ cup of the sugar in a heavy saucepan set over medium heat. Stir to evenly coat the apples with the sugar. Cover the pan and cook the apples for 20 minutes until they soften.

3. While the apples are cooking, combine the bread with the milk and cream in a large bowl. Let the bread sit to absorb the liquid for 15 minutes.

4. When the apples are softened, stir them into the bread mixture. In a separate bowl, beat the eggs with the remaining 1 cup sugar and the orange zest. Add the egg mixture to the bread and apples. Stir in the dried fruit.

5. Pour the pudding into the prepared pan and place it in the oven. Bake for 45 minutes or until it is set and lightly browned on top.

6. Dust the pudding with the confectioners' sugar before serving. Serve at room temperature.

Bread Makes the Meal: Good Things to Eat with Bread

What could be better than a crust of bread and a few shreds of good cheese? Or a lunch of leftover salads and cooked vegetables with a chunk of nutty bread? The answer—a perfect roast beef sandwich made with buttered, homemade, white bread, rare roast beef, and salt. From the simplicity of grilled bread rubbed with garlic to a sophisticated salad with blue cheese toast, these recipes are some of my favorite ways to enjoy bread.

Warm Rosemary, Basil, and Garlic Oil

About 3/4 cup

Dip toasted slices of Altamura Loaf (page 197), Ciabatta (page 116), or The Best Bread Ever baguettes (page 50) in this. Bits of herbs and drops of oil cling to the crusty holes in the bread.

1 whole head garlic
1/2 cup extra virgin olive oil
3 sprigs fresh rosemary or 2 teaspoons
    dried rosemary leaves

1/2 teaspoon fine sea salt
1/4 cup tightly packed basil leaves

1. Preheat the oven to 400°F. Cut the head of garlic in half horizontally and place it in a small covered casserole in the oven. Bake for 15 to 20 minutes, until softened.

2. Heat the olive oil, rosemary, and salt over medium heat in a small saucepan for 5 minutes. Squeeze the roasted garlic into the olive oil mixture. (The soft paste will slip right out, leaving the peel behind.)

3. Tear the basil leaves and add them to the olive oil mixture. Let the mixture stand for a few minutes before serving.

Whole Roasted Garlic

4 servings

In Lorna Sass's book on cookery in the Middle Ages, To the King's Taste, *she writes that garlic was boiled and served like a potato. When I tried this at home, I was surprised by the mild, almost bland taste of this normally assertive vegetable. Baking garlic, however, is a much better way to preserve and concentrate its sweet flavors while removing the harshness that makes a raw head of garlic inedible.*

You need no special equipment to bake garlic. To make it easier to serve, you may want to slice the garlic heads in half horizontally before baking. Simply place the two halves back together, bake, then serve.

Use the pulp from baked garlic as a spread on bread or stir the paste into a combination of chopped tomatoes, onions, and parsley for a bruschetta topping.

4 large heads of fresh garlic   1 tablespoon olive oil or vegetable oil

1. Preheat the oven to 400°F.

2. In a small bowl, toss the garlic heads in the oil to coat thoroughly.

3. Bake the garlic for 20 to 25 minutes, until a fork can be easily inserted.

4. To serve, slice the garlic heads in half horizontally and squeeze some of the paste onto fresh bread or toasts.

Syrian Toasts with Zahtar, Garlic, and Pepper Oil

36 crisps

A combination of wild thyme, sesame seeds, and sumac, zahtar is an eastern Mediterranean herb blend used throughout Lebanon, Turkey, and Syria. Sumac gives a citric sparkle to foods and is a terrific seasoning for anyone looking to reduce salt in their diet. These toasts are good for dipping into Chick-pea, Coriander, and Roasted Red Pepper Spread (page 248) or served alongside a pungent curry.

While zahtar and sumac may only be available through ethnic markets or mail-order suppliers (see the Source Guide, page 259), a combination of equal parts dried thyme, sesame seeds, paprika, and lemon zest will create a similar flavor profile in this dish.

3 loaves Whole Wheat Pita Pockets (page 123)
2 tablespoons zahtar
2 cloves garlic, chopped

1/2 teaspoon red pepper flakes
1/4 cup extra virgin olive oil

1. Preheat the oven to 450°F.

2. Cut the pita bread into triangles measuring about 3 inches in length. Arrange the cut bread in one layer on a baking sheet, place the baking sheet in the oven, and bake for 5 minutes to dry slightly.

3. Combine the zahtar, garlic, red pepper flakes, and olive oil in a small bowl. Brush the pita triangles with some of the oil, then return the baking sheet to the oven. Bake the toasts for another 5 to 8 minutes, until they brown lightly. Remove them from the oven and let the toasts cool for a few minutes before serving.

Note: The Middle Eastern sumac plant is related to the sumac and squaw-bush shrubs found throughout North America. Native American tribes have used this plant for centuries for its sour taste and medicinal value. (A word of caution: Edible sumac has a red hairy blossom. Related varieties such as swamp sumac, poison ivy, and poison oak have white blossoms and are very toxic. Do not consume wild sumac.)

Bruschetta

Throughout Italy, simple toasted bread, rubbed with garlic and brushed with olive oil, is known as bruschetta or fettunta. There are two secrets to making good bruschetta—flavorful bread with a well-developed structure, and a glowing wood fire. When the bread is sliced and toasted, its holes act like a grater grabbing the raw garlic as it is swiped across the surface. If you've mastered making the bread, a broiler will do for the toasting. Three recipes for toppings follow.

4 slices bread such as Country Baguettes with Starter (page 180), Peasant Wheat Loaf (page 191), or Ciabatta (page 116)

1 clove garlic, cut in half
2 tablespoons extra virgin olive oil

Toast the bread over a wood fire that is glowing but not flaming. Or, use a toaster. While the bread is still warm, rub it on each side with the cut clove of garlic. Use a pastry brush to spread each slice lightly with olive oil. Serve immediately.

Tomato, Basil, and Olive Topping

2 medium tomatoes, peeled
2 teaspoons extra virgin olive oil
2 cloves garlic, sliced
8 leaves of basil, torn

16 pitted brine-cured olives such as niçoise or kalamata, coarsely chopped
Salt and freshly ground black pepper

Cut the tomatoes in half. Squeeze out all the seeds and chop the tomatoes into 1/4-inch pieces. Combine with the olive oil, garlic, basil, and olives. Season with salt and freshly ground pepper. Let sit for an hour or more before serving as a topping for warm bruschetta.

Mushrooms, Caramelized Shallots, and Balsamic Vinegar Topping

1 cup

1/2 cup olive oil

4 shallots, peeled

2 cups thinly sliced assorted
  mushrooms such as cremini, white
  button, and small portobello
  varieties

Salt and freshly ground black pepper

1 tablespoon balsamic vinegar

1. Heat the olive oil in a shallow skillet over medium heat. Quarter the shallots and add them to the hot oil. Cover and cook the shallots for about 6 to 8 minutes, shaking the pan from time to time to keep them from sticking.

2. Remove the cover and add the mushrooms. Cover the pan, raise the heat to high, and cook for 3 or 4 minutes, until the mushrooms begin to soften and release some of their liquid. Uncover and continue to cook another 4 to 5 minutes, until the mushrooms are lightly browned and most of their moisture has evaporated. Season them with salt and pepper and stir in the balsamic vinegar just before serving as a topping for warm bruschetta.

White Bean, Herb, and Tomato Topping

White bean purée is a classic topping for bruschetta. Here I have added chopped tomatoes and coarse sea salt to give flavor and texture to this dish.

2 cups

2 tablespoons extra virgin olive oil

2 cloves garlic, chopped

1 teaspoon each of at least 3 fresh herbs such as parsley, rosemary, thyme, oregano, and sage

1/2 teaspoon red pepper flakes

2 cups cooked and drained white beans such as cannellini, or 1 (15-ounce) can white beans, drained

Coarse sea salt and freshly ground black pepper

1 medium tomato, peeled, seeded, and chopped

1. Heat the olive oil in a medium saucepan over medium heat. Add the garlic, chopped herbs, and pepper flakes. Cook for 2 or 3 minutes. Add the beans and season with salt and pepper to taste.

2. Cook the bean mixture for 5 minutes, stirring frequently with a wooden spoon to crush them. Scrape the mixture into the bowl of a food processor fitted with the metal blade. Process for about 45 seconds until smooth.

3. Spoon the warm bean mixture onto bruschetta. Top each piece with some of the chopped tomatoes and more salt and pepper.

Chick-pea, Coriander, and Roasted Red Pepper Spread

1½ cups

Serve this spread with Anise-Scented Moroccan Bread (page 62) or Focaccia (page 107) for a palate-pleasing appetizer or light luncheon.

1 (12-ounce) can chick-peas
2 tablespoons extra virgin olive oil
1 teaspoon chopped garlic (about 2 cloves)
1 small white onion, finely chopped
1 red bell pepper, roasted, seeded, and finely diced

1 teaspoon ground cumin
Fine sea salt
Freshly ground black pepper
2 tablespoons chopped fresh coriander
Juice of half a lemon

1. Drain the chick-peas and reserve the canning liquid. Heat the olive oil in a small saucepan over medium heat. Add the garlic, onion, and diced pepper. Cook, stirring frequently, for about 7 or 8 minutes, until the onion is soft but not brown. Add the chick-peas and cumin. Cook for 5 more minutes to heat the chick-peas thoroughly. Season with salt and pepper.

2. Scrape the mixture into the bowl of a food processor fitted with the metal blade, add a few tablespoons of the canning liquid from the chick-peas, and process for 30 to 40 seconds, until the mixture is smooth and creamy. Add a few more tablespoons of canning liquid if the mixture seems too dry and is not forming a smooth paste in the food processor. Stir in the chopped coriander. Squeeze with lemon juice just before serving.

Tapenade

Black like caviar and nearly as prized in southern France, tapenade is a pungent
spread made with black olives, garlic, and herbs. Serve tapenade as a spread with
pieces of fougasse or as a dip for vegetables. Add a teaspoon or two to vinaigrette
dressing, spread it on leg of lamb before roasting, or use it in a sauce made from
the pan juices of a roasted chicken.

1 cup

When making tapenade, taste one of the olives, and if they are too salty,
rinse them under cold running water, drain, and pat dry before using. Keep a jar
of tapenade on hand for unexpected guests. Pack it in a small container, then top
with a thin layer of olive oil. When covered tightly and stored this way in the
refrigerator, it will keep for three weeks.

1 cup pitted brine-cured black olives
such as niçoise or kalamata
2 anchovy fillets
1 large garlic clove, roughly chopped
2 tablespoons fresh lemon juice

1/4 teaspoon herbes de Provence
3 tablespoons extra virgin olive oil
1/4 teaspoon cayenne
Freshly ground black pepper

Place the olives, anchovy fillets, and garlic in the bowl of a food processor fitted with the metal blade. Process for 30 to 40 seconds, until the olives
are completely pulverized. Add the lemon juice, herbs, olive oil, and
cayenne. Process for 20 seconds to blend well. Season with pepper and add
more lemon juice if the mixture seems too firm.

Garlic Mayonnaise

2 cups

Serve this spread with a platter of just-picked radishes, cherry tomatoes, and wedges of Fougasse (page 120), Focaccia (page 107), or Olive Rosemary Bread (page 188).

¼ cup fresh bread crumbs	¼ teaspoon salt
1 whole egg	⅛ teaspoon hot Hungarian paprika
1 egg yolk	¼ teaspoon Dijon mustard
2 whole cloves of garlic, peeled	1¼ cups extra virgin olive oil
1 tablespoon fresh lemon juice	Freshly ground black pepper

1. Moisten the bread crumbs with 3 tablespoons water. Squeeze out all of the water and set aside. Place the egg, yolk, and garlic in the bowl of a food processor fitted with the metal blade. Blend until the egg is light and frothy and the garlic is minced. Add the lemon juice, salt, paprika, mustard, and bread crumbs. Blend until the mixture is smooth.

2. With the processor running, add all of the olive oil in a slow steady stream through the feed tube. Stop the machine, scrape down the sides of the bowl, then blend again. Adjust the seasoning with more salt or pepper.

Store, covered, in the refrigerator for up to one week.

Variation:

For instant garlic mayonnaise, combine 2 cups of store-bought mayonnaise with 2 teaspoons chopped garlic, ⅛ teaspoon hot Hungarian paprika, and ¼ teaspoon Dijon mustard.

Sesame Bagel with Smoked Salmon and Crème Fraîche

A bagel becomes brunch when paired with silky smoked salmon. Crème fraîche is a European-style slightly sour cream. Its velvety thickness makes it an ideal spread, though sour cream may be used in its place.

4 sandwiches

2 sesame-coated New York Bagels (page 88)

4 slices (about 4 ounces) smoked salmon

1/3 cup crème fraîche or cream cheese

Freshly ground black pepper

Slice the bagels in half. Place one slice of salmon on each bagel. Spread with crème fraîche and season with freshly ground pepper.

Turkey Pastrami Hero on Sour Raisin Rye

Here is a light version of a classic pastrami and cheese sandwich that has all the taste of the original and far less fat.

4 generous sandwiches

8 slices Sour Raisin Rye (page 215)

1/4 cup Dijon mustard

1/4 cup mayonnaise

1/2 pound turkey pastrami (about 24 thin slices)

4 ounces sliced Swiss cheese

4 scallions, trimmed to 4-inch pieces

1. Preheat the oven to 350°F. Spread 4 slices of the bread with mustard and the other 4 slices with mayonnaise. Layer slices of turkey pastrami on 4 slices of the bread and top with the Swiss cheese. Place a few pieces of scallion on each and close the sandwiches.

2. Place the sandwiches on a baking sheet and put them in the oven for 5 minutes to melt the cheese.

Panini Stazione Termini

2 large
sandwiches

The main railway station in Milan, the Stazione Termini, is a nineteenth-century wonder with carved marble and skylights of iron scrollwork. The joy of visiting the station is not its architectural splendor nor timely trains, however, but the array of sandwiches sold in cafés and by street vendors around the terminal.

Generous square sandwiches with artichokes and egg salad, a few slices of mortadella, or a wedge of fresh roasted pork are stacked behind glass cases. My favorite is a combination of olive-oil-packed tuna, hard-boiled eggs, arugula, and bacon. At home I make it on ½-inch-thick slices of Classic Pullman Loaf (page 127) or The Best Bread Ever baked in a loaf pan (page 50).

4 slices bread, crusts trimmed
1 (6-ounce) can oil-packed tuna,
   drained
½ teaspoon dry mustard
½ cup mayonnaise
2 hard-boiled eggs, peeled

Fine sea salt and freshly ground white
   pepper
A handful of arugula leaves
2 thin slices of tomato
4 slices crisp-cooked bacon

1. Toast the bread, then set it on a rack to cool. Blend the tuna with the mustard and 2 tablespoons of the mayonnaise. Set aside. Chop the eggs and blend them with 2 tablespoons of the mayonnaise, the salt, and pepper. Set aside.

2. Spread the remaining mayonnaise on one side of each piece of toast. Place pieces of arugula on two of the slices, then layer with the tuna salad, a slice of tomato, the egg salad, and the bacon. Cover with the remaining slices of bread. Cut each sandwich in half.

Black Pepper Burger on Semolina Toast

Slices of toasted semolina bread soak up the meat juices in this very grown-up hamburger. Serve it with a fresh tomato and onion salad.

4 open-faced sandwiches

1 pound ground chuck or sirloin
1 tablespoon whole black peppercorns, crushed
2 tablespoons vegetable oil
1 tablespoon chopped shallots
1 ounce scotch whiskey
1 teaspoon chopped fresh tarragon
1 tablespoon chopped fresh parsley
1/3 cup beef stock or Worcestershire sauce
Fine sea salt
4 thick slices toasted Semolina Bread (page 60) or Stout Bread (page 200)

1. Divide ground chuck or sirloin into four 4-ounce portions and shape into patties. Place the crushed peppercorns on a plate and dip each patty into the pepper so that some of it adheres to each side of the burger. Set aside.

2. Heat 1 tablespoon of the oil in a saucepan set over medium heat. Add the shallots and cook until they are translucent. Add the whiskey, tarragon, and parsley and cook for a few minutes to loosen any juices that may have stuck to the pan. Add the stock or Worcestershire sauce and cook for 3 minutes over medium heat to combine the flavors. Taste and correct the seasoning. Set sauce aside, then reheat before serving.

3. Heat the remaining 1 tablespoon of oil in a nonstick skillet over medium-high heat. Sprinkle the burgers with salt and cook them about 3 to 4 minutes on each side for medium-rare.

4. Place a slice of toasted bread on each plate. Top with a pepper burger and drizzle with some of the sauce.

Pan Bagnat

4 sandwiches

Pan bagnat is always something we eat by the shore after a day in the sun (sometimes we do more eating than swimming). A popular sandwich in the south of France, pan bagnat means bathed bread, for it swims in a mixture of garlic and olive oil and the juices of ripe summer vegetables. This recipe is adapted from a recipe in Patricia Wells's book Bistro Cooking. *Make these sandwiches on large rolls; the plump rolls soak up the juices and the crisp crust holds them in.*

4 sandwich rolls made from The Best
  Bread Ever (page 50) or Country
  Baguettes with Starter (page 180)
1 garlic clove, minced
1/2 teaspoon fine sea salt
1/4 cup extra virgin olive oil
2 (6-ounce) cans water-packed tuna,
  undrained
2 tablespoons capers

2 green onions, minced
1 ripe medium tomato, cut into 4 slices
1 roasted red pepper, peeled, seeded,
  and cut into 4 pieces
1 roasted green pepper, peeled,
  seeded, and cut into 4 pieces
1 small Bermuda onion, peeled and cut
  into thin slices
4 anchovy fillets

1. Preheat the oven to 350°F. Cut each roll almost in half, keeping the top and bottom attached. Combine the minced garlic, salt, and olive oil in a small dish and brush the insides of each roll with this mixture. Place the rolls on a baking sheet and bake for 5 to 6 minutes to crisp the crust.

2. Combine the tuna, capers, and green onions. Divide this mixture evenly among the rolls. Add a slice of tomato to each roll. Layer a slice of red pepper, green pepper, and Bermuda onion on each sandwich and top each with an anchovy fillet. Close each roll, cover with plastic wrap, and place a dinner plate on top of them. Let the rolls sit at least 1 hour before serving.

Grilled Vegetable Sandwich

The combination of vegetables brushed with herbs, garlic, and olive oil and grilled until slightly charred, with a creamy herb-flavored cheese spread on a homemade roll, is delightful. If you don't have an outdoor grill, a cast-iron grill pan is a good substitute, but the vegetables won't have that smoky flavor.

6 generous
sandwiches

1 small eggplant, cut into ¼-inch-thick
  slices
1 teaspoon fine sea salt
1 small zucchini, cut lengthwise into
  ¼-inch-thick slices
1 small yellow squash, cut lengthwise
  into ¼-inch-thick slices
2 red peppers, halved, seeded, and cut
  into 1-inch strips
1 small red onion, cut into ¼-inch-thick
  slices

⅓ to ½ cup olive oil
3 cloves garlic, minced
¾ teaspoon herbes de Provence
½ cup herb-garlic cheese, such as
  Boursin or Alouette
6 sandwich rolls made from The Best
  Bread Ever (page 50) or Country
  Baguettes with Starter (page 180)
6 thin slices prosciutto or smoked ham
  (optional)
Freshly ground black pepper

1. Preheat the grill. If using a cast-iron grill pan on top of the stove, preheat over medium heat about 15 minutes before cooking.

2. Sprinkle the eggplant slices with salt and set aside in a colander to drain for 10 minutes.

3. Dry the zucchini, yellow squash, and eggplant with paper towels and place them on a baking sheet with the pepper strips and onion slices. Brush the vegetables with some of the olive oil and sprinkle them with the garlic and herbes de Provence.

4. Brush the grill lightly with oil and place the vegetables on the grill without crowding them. Grill until lightly charred on one side; turn them after 4 to 5 minutes. Cook for an additional 4 to 5 minutes. As each vegetable slice finishes cooking, remove it. (The vegetables may be prepared a day ahead of serving. Refrigerate until needed.)

5. Spread the herb-garlic cheese generously on the top half of each roll. Place a slice of prosciutto or ham, if using, on the bottom half of each roll, and layer on the vegetables. Season with pepper, close the rolls, and serve.

Curly Endive, Pear, and Walnut Salad with Gorgonzola Toasts

4 servings

A perfect balance of bitter, sweet, creamy, and crunchy, serve this salad in fall or winter when bitter greens are at their peak. Any combination of firm and assertive greens works well. Arugula, radicchio, and romaine lettuce would be good additions to the salad bowl.

The gorgonzola toasts are a great appetizer on their own. You may want to make extra in case you find yourself nibbling them while preparing the salad.

3 ounces Gorgonzola, crumbled

2 tablespoons unsalted butter, softened

6 thin slices Altamura Loaf (page 197), Walnut Bread (page 185), or The Best Bread Ever (page 50)

$1/4$ cup red wine vinegar

1 clove garlic, minced

Salt and pepper to taste

$1/4$ cup vegetable oil

$1/4$ cup heavy cream

2 small heads curly endive, washed and broken into 3-inch pieces

2 heads Belgian endive, cut into 2-inch pieces

3 large ripe pears, halved, cored, and thinly sliced

$1/2$ cup toasted walnuts

1. Preheat the oven to 400°F.

2. In a small bowl, mash the Gorgonzola and butter into a smooth paste. Spread a few tablespoons of the mixture on one side of each slice of bread. Bake the toasts on a baking sheet for 5 to 6 minutes, until lightly browned. Cut each toast in half diagonally. Set aside.

3. Combine the vinegar, garlic, and salt and pepper. Stir in the vegetable oil and cream. Set aside.

4. Toss the curly endive and Belgian endive with the pear slices and walnuts. Coat with the dressing and toss again. Divide the salad among 4 plates and serve with the Gorgonzola toasts.

Spicy Sausage, Mussel, and Clam Stew

6 servings

A chunk of crusty bread, a glass of dry white wine, and this zesty stew make the perfect end to a great day. A chunk of bread sops up the juices of the briny mussels and clams and more bread on the table is welcome for dunking in the garlic mayonnaise.

Our local Italian butcher makes a hot fennel and garlic sausage that works perfectly in this dish, but a Portuguese-style chorizo would also be delicious.

Use a fresh hot pepper to spice the broth, such as a cherry pepper or a long hot Hungarian green pepper. If you cannot purchase fresh hot peppers, substitute 1/2 cup diced red bell pepper combined with 1/2 teaspoon cayenne.

1 baguette sliced into 1/2-inch-thick slices	2 cups canned crushed tomatoes, drained
1 tablespoon olive oil	1 teaspoon paprika
1 pound hot pork sausage, cut into 1-inch pieces	1 cup white wine
2 large white onions, peeled and sliced into 1/4-inch strips	2 pounds (about 20) mussels, cleaned
3 large cloves garlic, minced	20 scrubbed littleneck clams in their shells
1 hot cherry pepper, seeded and minced	1/2 cup Garlic Mayonnaise (page 250)

1. Preheat the oven to 400°F. Spread the slices of bread on a baking sheet and place them in the oven for 6 to 8 minutes to dry out and brown lightly. Remove them from the oven, turn them over, and bake them another 4 to 5 minutes on the other side. Set aside.

2. In a heavy skillet, heat the olive oil over medium-high heat. Add the sausage and cook until it is lightly browned and some of the fat is rendered, about 8 minutes. Drain all but 2 tablespoons of the fat in the pan. Add the chopped onions, garlic, cherry pepper, tomatoes, paprika, and wine. Bring the sauce to a boil; reduce the heat and simmer it, covered, for 15 minutes.

3. Add the cleaned shellfish, cover, and cook 8 to 10 minutes longer, just until the mussels and clams open.

4. To serve, place 2 or 3 slices of bread in the bottom of each of 6 shallow soup plates or bowls. Divide the shellfish evenly among them and spoon some of the sausage sauce over each portion. Top each serving with another slice of bread and a spoonful of garlic mayonnaise.

Santa Fe Welsh Rarebit

4 servings

An old-fashioned dish, Welsh rarebit is traditionally made with a sauce of melted Cheddar cheese and beer poured over toasted bread. Here, the dish is given a contemporary twist by using Jack cheese and hot pepper sauce.

2 tomatoes, cut in half

Fine sea salt and freshly ground black pepper to taste

A few drops of hot pepper sauce or jalapeño sauce

1 tablespoon extra virgin olive oil

1 teaspoon dried herb blend such as Beau Monde seasoning or herbes de Provence

2 tablespoons unsalted butter

$1/2$ cup dark beer

8 ounces jalapeño Jack cheese, grated

$1/2$ teaspoon dry mustard powder

$1/2$ teaspoon steak sauce

$1/4$ teaspoon cayenne

6 slices Classic Pullman Loaf (page 127) or Stout Bread (page 200), crusts trimmed

2 tablespoons chopped fresh chives

1. Preheat the oven to 400°F. Place the tomatoes on a baking sheet, cut sides up. Season each tomato with salt, pepper, and hot pepper sauce, drizzle with the olive oil, and sprinkle with the herbs. Bake the tomatoes for 10 to 12 minutes, until they soften and lightly brown.

2. While the tomatoes are baking, melt the butter in a double boiler over simmering water. Add the beer. Warm the mixture for about 3 to 4 minutes, then add the grated cheese, mustard powder, steak sauce, and cayenne. Stir with a wire whisk until the cheese melts, keeping the heat below boiling at all times.

3. Toast the bread. Cut each slice of toasted bread in half diagonally.

4. To serve, place half a baked tomato on each plate. Layer 3 toasted bread triangles in a row alongside. Spoon on some of the cheese sauce and garnish with chopped chives.

Source Guide

Equipment

Braun
Food Preparation Division
400 Union Park Drive
Woburn, MA 01801
617-939-8912
Manufacturer of food processors,
electric slicers, and other small
kitchen appliances.

Cuisinart
1 Cummings Point Road
Stamford, CT 06904
800-726-0190
Manufacturer of food processors,
electronic scales, and other kitchen
appliances.

European Kitchen Bazaar
PO Box 4099
Waterbury, CT 06704
800-225-0760
Distributor of Cuisinart, KitchenAid,
and Robot Coupe food processors
and replacement parts. Catalog
available.

KitchenAid Portable Appliances
701 Main Street
St. Joseph, MI 49085
800-541-6390
Manufacturer of food processors,
mixers, and kitchen appliances.

Polder
8 Slater Street
Port Chester, NY 10573
914-937-8200
polder@aol.com
Manufacturer of instant-read timer-
thermometers.

Taylor
PO Box 1349
Fletcher, NC 28732
704-684-5178
Manufacturer of instant-read
thermometers.

Baking Equipment

Bridge Kitchenware
214 East 52nd Street
New York, NY 10022
212-688-4220
Complete source for all tools and
supplies for the professional chef
with mail-order catalog and
showroom open to the public.
Good source for brioche molds and
specialty utensils.

The Chef's Catalog
3215 Commercial Avenue
Northbrook, IL 60062-1900
800-338-3232
Mail-order source for food processors,
scales, instant-read thermometers,
oven stones, and baking supplies.

Lamalle Kitchenware
36 West 25th Street
New York, NY 10010
212-242-0750
lamalle@aol.com

Mail-order and retail supplier of all
kitchenware, baking pans, and hard-
to-find items for the professional
kitchen.

*New York Cake and Baking
Distributors*
56 West 22nd Street
New York, NY 10010
212-675-CAKE
Retail store and mail-order sales of
baking supplies, parchment paper,
pastry brushes, and special baking
pans.

Williams Sonoma
PO Box 7456
San Francisco, CA 94120-7546
800-541-2233
Mail-order and retail source for food
processors, SAF Instant yeast, baking
stones, baking pans, bannetons, and
many other supplies for the home
baker.

Ingredients

American Almond Products Co.
103 Walworth Street
Brooklyn, NY 11205
800-8 ALMOND
Manufacturer of almond paste and
nut products for the baking industry.
Call for distributor information.

Kalustiyan's
123 Lexington Avenue
New York, NY 10016
212-685-3451
Quality purveyor of Mediterranean,
Indian, Asian, and Middle Eastern

ingredients such as harissa, poppy seeds, sesame seeds, and zahtar. They will ship mail orders.

Hodgson Mill
1901 South Fourth Street
Effingham, IL 62401
800-525-0177
Millers of whole wheat, rye, and specialty flours available nationwide.

King Arthur Flour Baker's Catalogue
PO Box 876
Norwich, VT 05055-0876
800-827-6838
Complete mail-order source for everything a home baker might need from flour and nuts to instant yeast, baking peels, and baking stones. Because of its leadership role in promoting home baking, its catalog is the most up-to-the-minute source for ingredients and supplies.

Mozzarella Company
2944 Elm Street
Dallas, Texas 75226
800-798-2954
MozzCo@aol.com
Makers of fiore di latte, fresh mozzarella cheese, feta, mascarpone, and other fresh Italian-style cheeses available by mail order.

Orsini's Italian Sausages
254 Main Street
Old Saybrook, CT 06475
860-388-5937
www.dhinet.com/orsini
Mail-order source for hot fennel garlic sausage and other Italian specialties.

SAF Products
400 South Fourth Street
Suite 310
P.O. Box 15066
Minneapolis, MN 55415
800-641-4615
Manufacturer of high-quality instant yeast. Call for distributor information.

Bibliography

Assire, Jérome. *The Book of Bread*. Paris: Flammarion, 1996.

Bilheux, Roland and Alain Escoffier, Daniel Hervé, Jean-Marie Pouradier. *Special and Decorative Bread*. New York: Van Nostrand Reinhold, 1989.

Burher, Em and W. Zehr. *Le pain à Travers les Ages*. Paris: Editions Herme, 1985.

Castagna, Patrick and Eric Kayser, *Pain, Evolution et Tradition*. St. Maur des Fossés, France: Paris Victor S.A.R.L., 1994.

Clayton, Bernard Jr. *The Breads of France*. Indianapolis and New York: Bobbs-Merrill, 1978.

Dannenberg, Linda. *Paris Boulangerie Patisserie*. New York: Clarkson Potter Publishers, 1994.

David, Elizabeth. *English Bread and Yeast Cookery*. New York: Viking Press, 1980.

Field, Carol. *The Italian Baker*. New York: Harper & Row, 1985.

Greenspan, Dorie. *Baking with Julia*. New York: William Morrow and Company, 1996.

Greenstein, George. *Secrets of a Jewish Baker*. Freedon, California: The Crossing Press, 1993.

Leader, Daniel and Judith Blahnick. *Bread Alone*. New York: William Morrow and Company, 1993.

McGee, Harold. *On Food and Cooking*. New York: Charles Scribner's Sons, 1984.

Ortiz, Joseph. *The Village Baker*. Berkeley, CA: Ten Speed Press, 1993.

Poilane, Lionel. *Guide de l'Amateur de Pain*. Paris: Editions Robert Laffront, 1981.

Robertson, Laurel. *Laurel's Kitchen Bread Book*. New York: Random House, 1984.

Silverton, Nancy. *Breads from the La Brea Bakery*. New York: Villard, 1996.

Index

....

breads; fruit and nut
breads
sweeteners, 11
Swiss Twist Ham and
Gruyère Loaves, 85
Syrian Toasts with Zahtar,
Garlic, and Pepper
Oil, 244

T

Tapenade, 249
techniques. *See* bread-
making techniques
temperature
base temperature of
ingredients, 32–33
for fermentation, 33–34
of fully baked bread, 45
of oven, 10, 45–46
for proofing, 43
and retardation, 34
thermometers, 22–23
timers, 25–26
toast. *See also* French Toast
Curly Endive, Pear, and
Walnut Salad with
Gorgonzola Toasts,
256
Syrian Toasts with Zahtar,
Garlic, and Pepper
Oil, 244
Vanilla-Almond Butter
Spread on, 234
tomatoes
Bright Tomato Sauce, 100
Cheddar Pepper Brioche
with Sun-Dried
Tomatoes, 140
in Pan Bagnat, 254
in Panzanella, 231
Sun-dried Tomato and
Basil Bread, 55
Tomato, Basil, and Olive
Topping for
Bruschetta, 245
White Bean, Herb, and
Tomato Topping for
Bruschetta, 247

To the King's Taste (Sass), 243
truffle oil, 103
tuna
in Pan Bagnat, 254
in Panini Stazione Termini,
252
Tunisian Bread Soup
(Leblebia), 232
Turkey Pastrami Hero on
Sour Raisin Rye, 251

U

unbleached flour, 2–3

V

Vanilla-Almond Butter
Spread, 234
vegetable breads
Olive Rosemary Bread,
188
Savory Carrot and Leek
Bread, 83
Simple Olive Bread, 55
Summer Vegetable Bread,
55
vegetables. *See also specific
vegetables*
Grilled Vegetable
Sandwich, 255
in Pan Bagnat, 254
vital wheat gluten, 11

W

walnuts
in Autumn Harvest Loaf,
55
Curly Endive, Pear, and
Walnut Salad with
Gorgonzola Toasts,
256
Walnut Bread, 185
water, 8–9
and flour absorbency, 6
measuring by weight, 28,
58

and mixing technique, 20
ratio to flour weight, 58
water pan, 26
weighing ingredients, 25,
28–30, 58
Wells, Patricia, 254
Welsh Rarebit, Santa Fe, 258
wheat, cream of, as
substitute in Porridge
Bread, 74
wheat, hard vs. soft, 2
wheat berries
to cook, 220
Swedish Wheat Berry Loaf,
218
wheat bran, 2
wheat flours, 1–5
wheat germ, 2
Wheat Rolls, Crunchy, 77
wheat shafts (*epis*), forming,
42
wheat starters
Natural Sour Wheat
Starter, 176
Simple Wheat Starter, 175
White Bean, Herb, and
Tomato Topping for
Bruschetta, 247
whole-grain flours, 2, 3–4, 5.
*See also specific type of
flour*
breads made with (*see also*
cereal breads):
Brittany Rye Bread, 213
Country Wheat Crown,
183
King of Bread (Peasant
Wheat Loaf), 191
Multigrain Sandwich
Loaf, 206
Normandy Cider Bread,
203
Olive Rosemary Bread,
188
Pumpernickel Bread,
224
Seeded Deli Rye Bread,
221